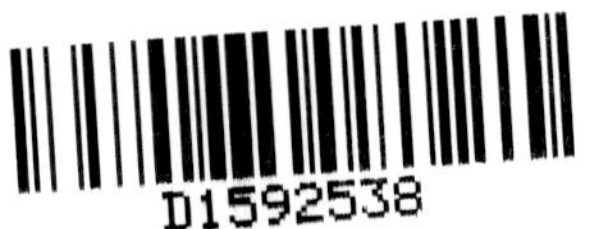

The Stranger in Medieval Society

MEDIEVAL CULTURES

SERIES EDITORS
Rita Copeland
Barbara A. Hanawalt
David Wallace

Sponsored by the Center for Medieval Studies at the University of Minnesota

Volumes in the series study the diversity of medieval cultural histories and practices including such interrelated issues as gender, class, and social hierarchies; race and ethnicity; geographical relations; definitions of political space; discourses of authority and dissent; educational institutions; canonical and non-canonical literatures; and technologies of textual and visual literacies.

VOLUME 12
Edited by F. R. P. Akehurst and Stephanie Cain Van D'Elden
The Stranger in Medieval Society

VOLUME 11
Edited by Karma Lochrie, Peggy McCracken, and James A. Schultz
Constructing Medieval Sexuality

VOLUME 10
Claire Sponsler
Drama and Resistance: Bodies, Goods, and Theatricality in Late Medieval England

VOLUME 9
Edited by Barbara A. Hanawalt and David Wallace
Bodies and Disciplines: Intersections of Literature and History in Fifteenth-Century England

VOLUME 8
Marilynn Desmond
Reading Dido: Gender, Textuality, and the Medieval Aeneid

VOLUME 7
Edited by Clare A. Lees
Medieval Masculinities: Regarding Men in the Middle Ages

VOLUME 6
Edited by Barbara A. Hanawalt and Kathryn L. Reyerson
City and Spectacle in Medieval Europe

VOLUME 5
Edited by Calvin B. Kendall and Peter S. Wells
Voyage to the Other World: The Legacy of Sutton Hoo

For other books in the series, see p. 150

The Stranger in Medieval Society

✣

F. R. P. Akehurst and Stephanie Cain Van D'Elden, editors

Medieval Cultures
Volume 12

University of Minnesota Press
Minneapolis
London

Published by the University of Minnesota Press
111 Third Avenue South, Suite 290, Minneapolis, MN 55401-2520
http://www.upress.umn.edu

Printed in the United States of America on acid-free paper

Library of Congress Cataloging-in-Publication Data
The Stranger in medieval society / F. R. P. Akehurst and Stephanie Cain Van D'Elden, editors.
p. cm. — (Medieval cultures ; v. 12)
Selection of papers from a conference, held Feb. 1994, and sponsored by the Center for Medieval Studies at the University of Minnesota.
Includes index.
Contents: The merchants of the Mediterranean / Kathryn L. Reyerson — Voluntary strangers, European merchants and missionaries in Asia during the later Middle Ages / William D. Phillips — Home again, the Jews in the kingdom of France, 1315–1322 / William Chester Jordan — Strangers in the late fourteenth century London / Derek Pearsall — Knights in disguise, identity and incognito in fourteenth-century chivalry / Susan Crane — The sexual stranger, the sexual quest in Wolfram's Parzival / Edward R. Haymes — Creating credibility and truth through performance, Kelin's Encomium / Maria Dobozy — The stranger and the problematics of the epic of revolt, Renaut de Montauban / William Calin — Who was that masked man? / Janet L. Solberg.
ISBN 0-8166-3031-3 (alk. paper). — ISBN 0-8166-3032-1 (pbk. : alk. paper)
1. Literature, Medieval—History and criticism. 2. Strangers in literature. I. Akehurst, F. R. P. II. Van D'Elden, Stephanie Cain. III. Series.
PN682.S75S77 1998
809'.93352—dc21 97-21249

Contents

Preface

In February 1994, the Center for Medieval Studies at the University of Minnesota organized a conference titled "Strangers in Medieval Society." During the two-day conference, sixteen papers were presented by scholars in different fields; this volume offers a selection of those papers.

The stranger is a central issue in medieval studies. The subject can be found in the research of almost all medievalists: we all deal with cultures that include strangers in their midst, or with persons who go out into strange cultures. Although one traditional view of the Middle Ages as static and agrarian has some justification, the period between the twelfth and fifteenth centuries saw enormous changes, and these were often sparked by or carried out by people who came from elsewhere: strangers.

The term *stranger* may need some elucidation (a notion further examined in Pearsall's chapter in this volume). In English, it shares a semantic field with the word *foreigner,* which has some but not all of the same connotations. The French word *étranger,* the Spanish word *estranjero,* and the German word *Fremde* all mean both "stranger" and "foreigner." On the other hand, the meaning of *stranger* that we wish to explore is not that of "alien" or "marginal." A recent conference at Binghamton dealt with these last meanings: the alien(ated), the prostitute, the insane. Our conception of stranger includes those persons who have their own community and culture, and who come into a new environment. They are within the law, they tend not to be parasites, and they may be very beneficial in their new milieu.

It was in fact common for medieval persons to view themselves as strangers: in the Christian tradition as exiles from the earthly paradise, in the Muslim tradition as colonizers and (to a lesser extent) converters to Islam of African and European countries.

Medieval explorers, conquerors, and traders frequently left the known for the unknown; in literature, the hero is often a stranger, sometimes a stranger even to himself. In England the Normans were strangers, in Spain the Arabs were strangers, and almost everywhere the Jews were strangers. The histories of these kinds of strangers followed very different courses. Armies of crusaders went to strange lands on the pretext that some other strangers had conquered them. United by faith and the Latin language, monks and other clerics could pass from one country to another to become bishops or reformers. Foreign missionaries founded the monasteries in Luxueil, Canterbury, Iona, Bobbio, Fulda, and St. Gall, among many others. The conversion of European countries was almost always carried out by foreigners; examples include St. Augustine (Britain), St. Boniface (Germany), and the brothers Cyril and Methodius, known as "the Apostles of the Slavs." Teachers took their learning to other countries: Alcuin to Aachen, Aquinas and Brunetto Latini to Paris, Placentinus to Montpellier, Ockham to Munich. Strangers were not always seen as alien or threatening: the Germanic tribes that entered the declining Roman Empire were frequently treated as friends.

In literature, also, the stranger was to be found in many genres: epics tell of fiefs attacked, defended, and won; romances tell of wandering knight-heroes seeking adventure or the Grail; many genres tell of fairyland, reached in a boat without sails or rudder, or through a deep forest that is like the ocean. In literature, voyagers could go to the other world, beyond death, and return (the Voyage of St. Brendan), or they could go to St. Patrick's Purgatory (Marie de France); they could even go to heaven and return after having spoken to God (the Monk of Montaudon).

Those presenting papers at the conference spoke about strangers in treating topics that are on the cutting edge of research in their own fields. Historians, art historians, and literary scholars have been discussing strangers for decades, if not for a century or more. Historians do not necessarily include the word *stranger* or *foreigner* in the titles of their books and articles. Nevertheless, publications on outlaws, merchants, pilgrims, or crusaders do deal with the specifics of being a "stranger" without necessarily using the word. Paintings, sculptures, and illuminated manuscripts (such as the recently published *Pilgrim's Guide to Santiago*) also contain illustrations of strangers, either individuals or groups. Literary scholars often deal with strangers: the person coming into a new society and learning about it and the young person completing his or her education are traditional devices used by poets to introduce audiences to new ideas as their heroes experience them. Each discipline thus deals with strangers separately, and experts from each field bring a certain amount of baggage with them to a discussion with representatives of other areas of inquiry, forming a sophisticated matrix that can enrich each of the disciplines.

The Middle Ages were not the only time when strangers (and xenophobia) were common. The refugee problem is still immediate and acute, even in today's Europe. Many strangers are present in almost all societies, and our own in the United States of America could perhaps be said to consist almost entirely of strangers. It is our hope that the publication of a selection of the conference papers will allow these essays to reach a wider public and will encourage interdisciplinary studies in this area. It is clear that the conference did not say all that could be said on the topic of strangers in medieval society; what we hoped to do was to point out this unifying theme or motif and show how it can be used in various scholarly disciplines to organize a mode of perception and conceptualization common in the Middle Ages and still valid today. The selected essays are drawn from the historical and literary fields.

At the conference, presentations were to some extent organized by common areas, such as history and English, French, and German literature. Some themes recurred in different areas: for example, cross-dressing in English literature (Crane) and in French literature (Solberg), problems of language (Reyerson, Phillips, and Solberg), and Jewish issues in fourteenth-century France (Jordan) and in Spain (papers not published here by Moshe Lazar and Dwayne Carpenter). This crosscurrent of area and theme created a problem for our ordering of the essays in this volume. The reader may not agree with the ordering of the essays as they are presented here, but nothing prevents a reader from choosing a new order of reading according to his or her own interests. The brief summaries given below are intended to indicate the contents of the essays, and so to help the reader make his or her selections.

Kathryn Reyerson's essay provides a paradigm for the consideration of strangers in the Middle Ages: the difficulties and rewards of merchants, especially those trading around the Mediterranean. Reyerson shows that whereas Muslims tended to travel only to other Islamic countries in Asia and Africa, Europeans resorted to a variety of techniques for trading in the eastern Mediterranean and even in North Africa. Some merchants learned foreign languages, but it was possible for many to do business by using local interpreters and notaries, and to found veritable outposts or colonies of Europeans in Muslim and Byzantine areas, where they sometimes stayed as strangers for many years. The experiences of bold merchants in the Middle Ages helped prepare Europeans for the age of exploration that was to follow.

William Phillips discusses the journeys of Europeans to China during the Mongol Empire (mid-thirteenth to mid-fourteenth centuries). This includes the period of Marco Polo's famous sojourn in China, but also the journeys of other travelers. Some of the earliest travelers were sent to seek a Mongol alliance against the Muslims, who barred the other routes to the Far East. All of the travelers depended on the protection and goodwill of the local rulers, as "voluntary strangers in alien environments" who needed to "assimilate somewhat into their host country." Phillips ends with an account of Westerners' struggles with the Mongol language or languages.

In his chapter, William Chester Jordan deals with a group of persons who were doubly strangers: some thirty thousand Jews who, expelled from France in 1306, came back under an experimental agreement a few years later. For various reasons, including the change in weather patterns in the early fourteenth century and lingering animosities toward those expelled a decade earlier, the experiment was not a success. Jordan's essay explores the binding nature of medieval agreements between Christians and non-Christians and the power of the last Capetians to accomplish popular and unpopular acts of state. For him, these Jews were "sojourners," remaining only for a short time and maintaining contacts with their place of origin (in this case, paradoxically, also their place of exile).

In his essay, Derek Pearsall looks at the occurrence of the word *straunge* in a number of literary texts from the fourteenth century and then examines the events that were taking place in England with reference to strangers. He finds that *straunge* refers to foreigners, to those of a different social group, and to those not a member of one's family. There was a concerted effort to control these people, because often they were perceived to be an economic threat. Paradoxically, at the same time that the city of London was attempting to limit the activities of foreign merchants, the crown was attempting to extract revenue from them. "The poisonous mix of economic jealousy and xenophobic hatred" produced tensions that occasionally led to disastrous results (the murder of Janus Imperial and the peasants' revolt, for example). Unlike Langland, who expresses distaste for peddlers and beggars while sympathetically describing foreigners performing menial tasks as porters, water carriers, hucksters, and the like, Chaucer seems to reduce the shouts of the London rioters pursuing the stranger Flemings to the inhuman sounds of barnyard beasts, thus seemingly echoing the Londoners' delight in the removal of a public nuisance and hence the dehumanization of a whole group of strangers.

Susan Crane's knights, historical and fictitious, appear incognito in a peculiar kind of self-presentation, a self-dramatization that forces the chivalric community to recognize them. The tension between the knight's private desires and his social commitments—the struggle between "individual" and "society," as we would put it today—is a recurring theme in the Middle Ages, as noted in several of these essays (see Haymes's chapter, for example). Crane looks at historical and literary instances of chivalric disguise in which the disguise works to concentrate attention on the knight's chivalric skill and courage independent of his established status as sovereign, or military leader, or hero of a romance. Ironically, instead of concealing, it draws attention. Thus Edward III is known to have participated in tournaments disguised as a simple knight bachelor, a gesture that, although it focused attention on his present actions without regard for his true identity, also forced others to reevaluate him in a new light. Similarly, the actions of the fictional Gawain of *Sir Gawain and the Green Knight* force the court to reassess their expectations of his public reputation, the discrepancy between the knight's self-assessment and the assessment of his peers.

Edward Haymes discusses the "quest romance," in which a stranger searches for sexual knowledge. Although Haymes considers this desire for sexual knowledge to be a universal one, for present purposes he focuses on the romances of Chrétien de Troyes and their reception in Germany by Hartmann von Aue and Wolfram von Eschenbach. The knights in these romances consummate their relationships with their wives, but remain strangers until a new relationship is established, one built on mutual respect, including a balance of love and chivalry. Haymes concentrates on Wolfram's adaptation and completion of Chrétien's *Perceval.* Parzival and Condwiramurs, strangers to each other and ignorant of sex, consummate their love on their third night together. Immediately thereafter, Parzival embarks on a long journey that, four years later, culminates in his reaching the Grail and recovering his sexual Other. In a parallel fashion, Gawan, Parzival's surrogate, embarks upon his own quest for a sexual partner. One of Wolfram's contributions to the romance is to make sexually explicit scenes in which Chrétien leaves the audience to fill in the blanks. Gawan is allowed to engage in sexual adventures denied Parzival, whose quest was of a spiritual nature. At the end of the romance, Gawan has gained the knowledge that is necessary for his existence. Parzival, while remaining true to Condwiramurs, is no longer a stranger; indeed, he has become king of the Grail.

Itinerant poet-minstrels, or *Spruchdichter,* were familiar strangers in medieval Germany. They performed an important function, disseminating information across wide geographic areas and creating reputations for their wealthy patrons. However, they were defined by law as strangers, outside the law. Since they had no permanent place of abode, they lacked legal rights that would entitle them to serve as judge, doomsman, witness, or advocate in a court of law, and especially they were ineligible to clear themselves with a cleansing oath if accused of a crime. Maria Dobozy demonstrates how one poet, known as Kelin, from the mid-thirteenth century was able to turn the handicap of being an outsider to his advantage. Acting as the equivalent of the modern speechwriter or ghostwriter, Kelin traveled from Swabia to Bavaria, creating a positive image of his patron and flattering his audience while auditioning for new commissions. His stranger status allowed him the independence to view society from a distance, and yet he was a familiar figure in many courts.

William Calin treats the issues of "strangerness" in the late French epic *Renaut de Montauban.* These issues are defined as the binary opposites of outside versus inside, other versus self, and margin versus center, as seen in the conflict of the feudal and the monarchical, and mirrored in the spatial configuration of the epic. Calin sees this story as an example of the point of development of the French epic where Charles, the emperor, has become an evil figure, working against the claims of the feudal aristocracy. Written in the reign of Philippe Auguste, *Renaut de Montauban* mirrors the politics of that age. As a new, "Gothic" and marginal or "stranger" genre, it came to displace the old "central," "Romanesque" epic such as the *Chanson de Roland,* only to be marginalized in its turn by a new "central" form, the Italian romance epic.

Last but not least, Janet Solberg leads the reader on a romp through three French short stories concerning deception and cross-dressing, where a male stranger disguises himself as a woman and thereby gains access to some social group that would normally exclude him: the bourgeois marriage and a nunnery. The situations in the three stories are all treated humorously and permit their writers (and Solberg) a good deal of verbal gymnastics in the form of metaphor and double entendre. The ambiguity of the protagonist is reflected in the problem of knowing which pronoun to use to refer to him/her. The three males who maintain for a while the fiction that they are women do so by maintaining that they are "strangers," or "unanchored, floating signifiers that are invested with meaning by their interpreters." The motif of language, which is mentioned many times in the various essays in this volume, here finds its most extensive treatment as Solberg invokes modern linguistic and literary theory in her discussion of late-medieval and Renaissance tales.

We wish to express our thanks to the Center for Medieval Studies and its director, Professor Barbara Hanawalt, for support in the preparation and holding of the conference, and for the preparation and editing of the present volume. Our thanks also go to Professor David Wallace, holder of the Frenzel Chair at the University of Minnesota, for his support for the conference. The editors of this volume also wish to express their thanks to the following students at the University of Minnesota for their help in the preparation of the index for this book: Sarah Grace Heller, Michelle Reichert, Jean-Luc Roche, and Anne Zerby. Finally, we offer our thanks to all those who attended the conference and enriched the event by their comments and contributions.

CHAPTER 1

The Merchants of the Mediterranean: Merchants as Strangers

Kathryn L. Reyerson

The movement of medieval merchants in search of profits and markets was a driving force in the expansion of European frontiers and in the creation of world-systems.[1] Medieval merchants traveled beyond the boundaries of their cultural spheres and encountered peoples and ecosystems very different from those they knew at home. They experienced the status of stranger in European and non-European cultures of the Mediterranean world. The documents of trade rarely address the topic of merchants as strangers in straightforward fashion, but how merchants coped abroad was a harbinger of their business success or failure. In the following pages, I examine the merchant-as-stranger experience in the Mediterranean from a western European perspective, occasionally interspersed with non-European viewpoints.[2]

The significance of the topic of merchant-as-stranger rests in the effects that this status as "other" had on the nature and operation of trade; on its success or failure; on its skewing of direction or product emphasis in areas where only some avenues of commerce were available to foreigners; on the emergence of local arrangements to accommodate foreign merchants; on the development of new professional tracks to service foreigners as translators and as intermediaries to penetrate the rules and regulations, protocol, and methods relating to the local, regional, and international levels of trade. The expanding corporations of our day need mediators to make their penetration into some parts of the globe possible. We see advertisements on television by businesses offering to assist other businesses in the process of "going global" or entering some difficult market area. The medieval western European merchant in the Mediterranean world faced some of the same types of problems and challenges that modern counterparts do, with a host of differences related to the medieval world. By the same token, the merchant's status as "stranger" affected the nature of the mercantile career—its shape, restrictions, and possibilities—and the contour of mercantile careers in turn had consequences for the politics and economy of the home communities. This topic is thus multifaceted and immense. What follows can do no more than begin an exploration of its richness.

The merchant to whom travel was second nature coped constantly with the challenge of learning new business practices and mastering new languages, whether in the role of temporary visitor or permanent expatriate. Given the extreme localism of the Middle Ages, once beyond the confines of his native home, the merchant was perceived as an outsider. He was driven by the profit motive and the love of risk and adventure.[3] He made and lost fortunes. He returned home to retire to the life of sedentary investment and politics, or he died in foreign parts, leaving his will and goods in the care of colleagues.

The topic of the merchant-as-stranger has another side, the nature of the merchant's reception in foreign parts. Attitudes toward strangers differed widely among towns of the Mediterranean world. Residency requirements for citizenship, restrictions on contacts and trade, and constraints on freedom of movement varied, as did official efforts to promote and protect merchant travel or to prohibit and limit interaction among locals and foreigners, particularly those of another religion, to assimilate outsiders or to hold them at bay. Experiences might differ for the merchant in passage—the temporary resident—and the permanent transplant, for the isolated traveler-merchant or the merchant traveling with colleagues or joining a colony of compatriots whose existence was organized by *fundaco* (colony) treaties.

In a general sense, the medieval merchant was a stranger even at home, standing as he did outside the archtypical tripartite vision of medieval society: those who fought, those who prayed, and those who worked.[4] From a sociological perspective, the medieval merchant was a marginal, even deviant figure, whose disposition toward change and adaptation might lead to innovation.[5] We might say that he was a deviant in a traditional, conformist society, a risk taker in a conservative culture. Moreover, the merchant's loci, the city and the town, were at first anomalies and always the lifestyle choice of a minority of inhabitants in an otherwise overwhelmingly rural society.[6] Indeed, the growth of cities has been used as an explanation for the decline of rurally based feudal institutions.[7] The concerns of urban law and commercial law were not those of agricultural or feudal law.[8] The "piepowder" court was the antithesis of the manor court. The position of the merchant at home in western Europe would, if anything, have prepared him well to face the challenges of "stranger" status abroad.

Deeply embedded in medieval mentality was a xenophobic streak. The *droit des hôtes* had echoes up and down the hierarchy of medieval society and in rural and urban contexts. For the merchant, it might entail a limited residency permit in a particular town. Jean Favier notes that foreigners often entered the sphere of international trade and banking and the wholesale trade more easily than they did the local business and retail trade.[9] The *hansa*, admittedly non-Mediterranean, restricted foreigners to the import-export trade. It was often necessary for the foreigner to join a local guild to do business, as did Jacques Coeur in the case of the Arte della Lana in Florence. Towns feared the departure of capital to foreign parts, and sometimes prohibited the export of funds. The protectionism of medieval industry and business is legend. By the same token, hanging over the foreigner's head was the possibility of expulsion and confiscation of goods, not an uncommon experience for the Italians in France.[10]

Local traditions of expatriation differed greatly in western Europe. Many Italians, merchants and artisans, voluntarily (the Genoese) or through exile (in the case of Florentines and Lucchese), set down roots outside their natal environment.[11] In the course of his career, the great merchant and naval entrepreneur Benedetto Zaccharia acted as Philip the Fair's admiral in France and inserted himself as a significant player in Andalusian society, all the while controlling the eastern Mediterranean island of Phoecia and a significant proportion of the Mediterranean production of alum, a vital fixative in the dyeing of cloth.[12]

The means of assimilation of foreigners into local society varied. Marriage with a local woman might assist in the process of integration and help to create business contacts.[13] Restrictions on admission to urban citizenship differed greatly from town to town, but such naturalization was frequently denied the foreigner, or access to local acceptance was severely limited. In Venice, one had to fulfill a twenty-five-year residency requirement. Genoa was the exception in requiring only an oath to the commune.[14] There is, moreover, no reason to assume that a merchant desired to become a permanent resident or naturalized citizen of a foreign place.

A common technique of coping with foreign residence was the colony, which I will examine in greater detail in due course. Colonies were an example of what Philip Curtin has termed "merchant diasporas" in cross-cultural trade.[15] In his broad geographic and chronological study, Curtin found many variables at work among trade diasporas.[16] At one extreme was the pariah whose toleration was based on usefulness—the Jew in western Europe was an example. At the other was the independent community of merchants neutral in political conflict in the host country. Curtin points to the asymmetrical relationship between merchants and the host country, which was whole and complete in terms of the range of occupations, while merchants were specialized in trade. In preindustrial societies, merchants were necessarily a minority, because most hands were needed for subsistence. Merchants, moreover, were easy targets of suspicion and viewed as nonproductive.

The Mediterranean world presented to the medieval western European merchant an overlay of many cultures. Common Roman inheritance was lost only slowly, and the persistence of Christian communities in regions such as northern Africa continued even into the fifteenth century.[17] The multicultural environment of Al-Andalus was synonymous with Mediterranean cosmopolitanism. The Muslim world was indifferent to the presence of other religious groups. There were cantons of foreigners in major

North African towns. Voyagers and itinerants traversed the Mediterranean from early times. Georges Jehel argues for the considerable mobility of labor in the Middle Ages and in the Mediterranean, a theme that Fernand Braudel previously announced for the early modern period.[18] Significant migration of peoples and individual in-migration occurred. For Jehel, the Mediterranean represented a combination of universality and particularism of outlook, where Muslim and Christian powers alternated and the concept of national community was of little importance. He sees this process illustrated in the political experience of Spain, Egypt, the Maghreb, Sicily, and the Balkans.[19]

A serious challenge to international trade and to merchants as strangers lay in religious differences. How foreigners fared throughout the Mediterranean world depended on the religious tolerance or indifference in their ports of call. Initially, Muslim areas were certainly more open to trade by individuals of other religious beliefs than were Christian regions. Christian Europe was generally hostile to all non-Christians. The Crusades introduced greater contacts after the eleventh century; they represent a kind of watershed in relations between Muslims and non-Muslims, with a hardening of Muslim attitudes toward foreigners.[20] Nonetheless, when the Muslims reconquered lands, they allowed European merchants to continue to trade in former Crusader areas and in Egypt and other areas the Europeans had not controlled. Christian minorities, speaking Arabic but with knowledge of European languages, were important in bridging the gap between Muslims and Christians. Yet contacts remained limited primarily to commerce.

For merchants, however, Islam continued to show considerable receptivity. It is worth noting the high position occupied by merchants within Islamic society. Muhammad himself was a merchant. He came from a trading town, from trader origins. His people were nomadic originally and in the seventh century had relatively recently settled down in towns. On the surface of things, Western merchants could expect a level of acceptance as traders in Islamic and eastern Mediterranean society that they may not have enjoyed at home in Europe.

In general, one can contrast Islam's receptivity to merchants with a long-ingrained suspicion and basic disdain among Westerners in western Roman and later medieval societies for the merchant's occupation. Roman senators would not sully their hands with trade, preferring to participate in profit through their freedmen, while medieval merchants and urban culture, as noted above, were left out of the traditional tripartite medieval conception of society. Towns and merchants were a long time in gaining respect and acceptance by the ruling classes within Europe. One might argue that it was only the economic woes of the nobility that ultimately led to the admission of intermarriage with the urban bourgeoisie in western Europe. The eastern Mediterranean in Roman and later

Byzantine times seems to have escaped this negative perspective on trade and merchants, albeit with greater state regulation of commerce.

The southern, eastern, and—until the successes of the Spanish *reconquista*—the western shores of the Mediterranean were dominated by Islam. Moreover, the Islamic world beyond the Mediterranean offered, among other things, an enormous religiocultural sphere under Islamic domination that extended across the Sahara into sub-Saharan Africa, throughout the Near East and into Central Asia, into northern India and into Southeast Asia. The Muslim world was very different from that of Europe in that Arabic served as a unifying link among Muslim lands, joined later by Persian and Turkish, whereas Europeans were fractured into many language groups.[21]

The underlying question of Mediterranean trade is how merchants acquired sufficient cultural baggage and language skills to gain the subtlety of approach necessary to do business on a high level. In this Europeans had an advantage, as they had fewer foreign languages to learn. There were interpreters at major commercial sites, and dictionaries were constructed: Arabic-Latin and, in one case, a three-language Latin, Turkish, Persian dictionary.[22] In addition to the clerical language of Latin, within Europe French acted as a kind of international language, perhaps because of the Champagne fairs. Italian succeeded to this role among Europeans in the Mediterranean world. Accounts were kept in the vernacular, offering an impetus for the growth of vernacular languages.[23]

Among merchants from the south of France, Catalonia, and the north of Italy, it is reasonable to assume some general ability to function in the languages of these regions. Spaniards and Italians claim to be able to understand each other in general terms today when speaking their own languages. Foreign merchants of diverse origin appeared before the notaries in towns of these regions and transacted business with the same ease, it would seem, as did native merchants. The local notaries were able to grasp the gist of the business at hand and translate it into Latin notarial jargon and legal formulas.[24] The forms of notarial acts recorded for these merchants' groups did not differ markedly according to city. The notary was generally precise in noting the geographic origin of his clients, but that was the end of distinctions he felt it necessary to make for strangers. Foreign merchants also functioned at the Champagne fairs, where there was a special setup to facilitate exchanges.[25] In the Levant and in the Black Sea region in the Genoese notaries' surviving registers, the same generalizations about homogenization of records can be made.[26] However, the way in which merchants functioned in eastern Mediterranean areas outside western colonies is more difficult to ascertain. In the Greek world of Constantinople, most European merchants would have been ill equipped. They gravitated to Pera, the Genoese colony.[27] By the same token, few if any spoke Arabic for trading in Alexandria, though trade they did. The same problems would have presented themselves in Tunisia and Morocco, but there existed a significant current of Western trade out of Marseille with Bougie and Ceuta in the mid-thirteenth century.[28]

Beyond dictionaries, merchant manuals provided some assistance to Europeans in coping with the unfamiliar. Pegolotti's *La pratica della mercatura* (1310–40), the best known, included all manner of useful information for the foreigner. Weights and measures, currency, local practices, detailed information on merchandise, and hints on quality of specialties were duly noted by Pegolotti and his fellow authors.[29] If such manuals were widely consulted, and this remains to be proved, then the merchant foreigner would have been relatively well informed upon entering unknown territory. In contrast, although the superb Arab geographers left detailed descriptions of foreign lands, Muslims had little interest in foreign languages, even in Spain. Bernard Lewis notes that it was generally the Europeans who learned the Muslim languages.[30] The art of translation flourished in Spain, however. Muslims were not encouraged to travel to Christian lands, although prisoners ended up in Europe at times.[31] Muslims traveled more readily to Africa and Asia than to Europe. The attractions were greater in gold and slaves from Africa and in Asian products, including spices and silks. Weapons, slaves, and English wool were the only important imports from Europe before the end of the Middle Ages. European intolerance was a further deterrent to travel. But there would seem to have been a certain allergy among Muslims for Christian places. Ibn Jubayr from Valencia, visiting the great Crusader port of Acre on the Syrian coast, remarked:

> The city of Acre, may God destroy it and return it to Islam. This is the chief city of the Franks in Syria . . . the assembly point of ships and caravans, the meeting place of Muslim and Christian merchants from all parts. Its streets and roads are thronged with such crowds of people, that one can hardly walk. But it is a land of unbelief and impiety, swarming with pigs and crosses, full of filth and ordure, all of it filled with uncleanliness and excrement.[32]

Other elements also affected trading relations. The Western Christian church forbade trade with the infidel, but, as William D. Phillips has commented, Christian-Muslim trade retained its vigor in spite of papal prohibitions of exports of weapons and slaves.[33] Repeated trading contacts of European merchants with Muslim areas of the Mediterranean can be traced from the Early Middle Ages, documented in the early trade of the Italo-Byzantine town of Amalfi at the beginning of the Commercial Revolution, and continuing through the heyday of medieval Mediterranean commerce and beyond.[34]

If papal threats were not a deterrent, nonetheless European merchants faced challenges in international commerce that led them to develop coping techniques. On the highways and seaways, bandits, robbers, pirates, corsaires were everywhere. European partnerships such as *commendae* (limited partnerships) for maritime travel make this point better than any other documented contracts, with their clauses regarding responsibility for loss due to fire or evil men.[35] Long legal proceedings, with the application in some cases of the law of marque (reprisals), were necessary to recover goods taken through piracy.[36] Not only could goods be taken, but the merchant risked loss of life or capture and enslavement. The traditional support networks were not present, and new ones had to be developed for protection as well as for ease of trade: *hansas* for traveling merchants, *fondachi,* colonies, special privileges, and safe conducts.[37] In light of the dangers, it is understandable that merchants traveled in groups in the Mediterranean world and elsewhere.[38]

Variations on this behavior have been identified by David Abulafia, who points to the "phenomenon of substitution, by which merchants of one city passed themselves off as merchants of a different, and privileged, community."[39] Thus the Sangimignanesi posed as Pisans, and the merchants of Montpellier were subsumed under the label of merchants of Marseille in the eastern Mediterranean at Cyprus and Acre. Marseille was itself for a while under the tutelage of Pisa.[40] The grouping of merchants of western Europe is well illustrated at the Champagne fairs, where southern French merchants were represented by a consul, often from Montpellier, and where northern European merchants trafficked as the *hansa* of seventeen towns.[41] Collaborative efforts among merchants of different towns were very common, as merchants sailed under various flags.[42]

The actual assumption of foreign identity is a further extension of this tactic. David Jacoby traces the experience of merchants of the Crusader principalities after the fall of Acre in 1291.[43] The fate of refugees from the Crusader principalities differed. The grant of Pisan nationality to Tuscans in the Levant existed before the fall of the principalities and continued afterward. Genoa's colonies in lands taken by the Muslims in the late thirteenth century included among their population inhabitants from the Ligurian Riviera and other Latins and Syrians who had obtained Genoese nationality in the Levant. These grants apparently did not include Genoese citizenship at home.[44]

Perhaps the most intriguing detail about refugees' experience in Cyprus concerns their ability to insert themselves into the Cypriot commercial arena. In the case of artisans, they carried with them skills of which they could avail themselves in a city such as Famagousta. For the commercial classes the situation was more difficult, but merchants had expertise in the Levant trade and in Levantine languages, which proved useful. Arabic language abilities of Latin refugees from Syria gave them an advantage in Cyprus. They could function as intermediaries and middlemen, sometimes acting as interpreters in transactions involving other Latin merchants and Arabic-speaking Syrians.[45]

Other tactics eased the shock of foreigner status for the merchant. Diplomacy was the handmaiden of trade, leading to treaties granting certain protections to merchants and to the establishment of colonies for foreigners.[46] The colonies established by western European cities in the Crusader principalities, by the Venetians and Genoese in Byzantium and the Black Sea, and by Catalans and Italians in the Maghreb suggest the need perceived by European merchants for a support structure in their commerce abroad. As strangers, they benefited from extraterritorial rights within the colony, which became a kind of home away from home. Their quarters or *fondachi* contained warehouses for safe storage of goods, churches for the practice of their cult, mills for the provision of their specific food needs. They were provided with assistance in currency transactions and weights and measures. Foreign merchants were generally defended by a consul and policed by their fellows through a court system. The Near East provides the most numerous examples of the colony structure.[47] Colonies aided merchants in dealing with a foreign environment, but the merchants remained strangers. Some areas foreign to Europeans retained a more restrictive posture than others. Byzantium provides an example of trade restrictions on foreigners and occasional backlash against foreign merchants, as in the expulsion of the Venetians from Constantinople in 1171.[48]

The Catalan and Italian colonies in northern Africa also had an infrastructure supportive of foreign trade. As Charles Dufourcq notes, the customs agency was the institution responsible for the official welcome, protecting merchants and maintaining the honesty of trade. Representing the merchant communities were "consuls d'outre mer."[49] At the market there were porters and interpreters, secretaries, and accountants associated with the customs service, of which certain were natives. Probably also a notary was present. Frequent auctions took place. Extraterritorial rights prevailed. There was thus a significant support system that went some distance toward simplifying the merchant-as-stranger's experience.

In medieval European trade a lot has been written about Western colonies in non-Western lands. But western European towns also had *fondachi.*[50] Venice had a German house where all German merchants were supposed to do business. They were, in fact, prevented from doing business elsewhere in Venetian territory. The staples of the north were a counterpoint to these southern European *fondachi.* By the same token, as R. S. Lopez and Irving Raymond have noted, in many towns in Mediterranean France and Catalonia there were no constraints on the residence and trading of foreigners.[51]

My own work in the commercial history of Montpellier echoes what I have just traced generally. Merchants of Montpellier developed a *consul de mer* tradition that allowed them representation in the Levant. They signed treaties throughout the Mediterranean and established some colonies in the western and eastern basins.[52] The notarial evidence of Marseille in 1248 reflects the benefits of these negotiations: an active export trade by Montpelliérains out of Marseille to Acre and to northern Africa.[53] With the loss of the Crusader principalities on the Syrian coast, Montpellier's diplomacy in treaties followed the fallback trading positions to Cyprus, Lesser Armenia, and the Byzantine Empire.

The receptive posture of the town of Montpellier regarding newcomers offers the other side of the coin. The 1204 charter of *consuetudines* invited in-migration, for foreigners marrying in Montpellier and intending to become residents were exempted for a year and a day from urban military service. Only the textile and dyeing trades, prestigious medieval occupations, had restrictions. Retail cloth transactions were restricted to residents, with the exception of peddlers. Cloth dyeing, of which scarlet dyeing was Montpellier's specialty, was closed to foreigners by the 1204 regulations, but in the course of the thirteenth century, from 1226 to 1251, residency and property requirements were introduced and then diminished, permitting the participation of newcomers. The presence of Jews was noted among Montpellier dyers at the end of the thirteenth century. Overall, in the course of the thirteenth and fourteenth centuries, Montpellier enjoyed the influx of many in-migrants.[54]

The local trading environment of Montpellier seems to reflect, in overall effect if not in specifics, the infrastructure that characterized the well-organized Champagne fairs, with their stalls, their notaries, their sergeants, their courts, and so on, and for the Mediterranean world the colonies of any commercial site of significance. International market organization was supportive of commerce overall and of merchants local and foreign. The significance of brokers and auctioneers in the economic transactions in Montpellier has not been emphasized to date, although these players were responsible for the smooth running of local and international markets. The widespread representation of these types of support professions has been noted in the Mediterranean world by Aaron Greif, an economist using the Geniza documents for a study of eleventh-century Jewish Mediterranean trading communities in the Maghreb: "The trade within each center was free and competitive, with many buyers and sellers interacting in bazaars and storehouses, where they negotiated and competed over prices, using brokers, open-bid auctions, and direct negotiation."[55] The foreign merchants' experience was greatly enhanced by the preparations in place to facilitate business transactions.

European merchants of the Mediterranean underwent long apprenticeships in the techniques of trade as traveling partners in foreign markets and colonies before returning—if they did—to settle in their home communities. International commerce involved lengthy travel, long stays abroad, and a repetition of the process year in and year out.[56] It is hardly surprising that Claude Carrère in Barcelona and David Herlihy in Florence have detected late marriage patterns for members of the international mercantile elite of those cities.[57] Urban politics on a year-round basis was run by older sedentary merchants whose presence could be assumed. The urban economy was regulated by this same group, with the result that even within the novel environment of the medieval town, tradition and conservatism were the rule among the elite.

New occupational niches were another offshoot of the merchant-as-stranger experience. International trade was underpinned by support professions of the commercial infrastructure in foreign ports. Overall, given the cultural diversity of the Mediterranean world, the openness of trade is striking. Aided by their infrastructure, European merchants functioned with great facility in foreign environments and succeeded in building huge personal fortunes, and, in the case of the mercantile giants of Genoa, Pisa, and Venice or Barcelona and, for a time, Marseille and Montpellier, in furthering the fame and fortune of a whole urban community. Stranger/foreigner status added an extra challenge and additional risk to international trade. Rewards could be phenomenal. During the commercial boom of the Middle Ages in a Romano Mairano or a Benedetto Zaccaria, the excitement of the unknown and the challenge of making a profit combined to forge the medieval merchant par excellence.[58] The exploits of medieval merchants framed the preconditions for the age of exploration and the closing of the ecumene.

Notes

1. On world-systems, see Immanuel Wallerstein, *The Modern World-System I: Capitalist Agriculture and the Origins of the European World-Economy in the Sixteenth Century* (New York: Academic Press, 1974); Immanuel Wallerstein, *The Modern World-System II: Mercantilism and the Consolidation of the European World-Economy, 1600–1750* (New York: Academic Press, 1980); Eric Wolf, *Europe and the People without History* (Berkeley: University of California Press, 1982); Janet Abu-Lughod, *Before European Hegemony: The World System A.D.* 1250–1350 (Oxford: Oxford University Press, 1989).

2. There are other dimensions of the merchant-as-stranger experience that I will not trace in this essay; these relate to cross-cultural contacts. The merchant-as-stranger became the mediator between cultures: he transmitted ideas; cultural, aesthetic, and moral values; and religious beliefs in the course of his contacts with indigenous inhabitants. The merchant brought a cultural mind-set but was also transformed by experiences in foreign lands, returning home with new ideas and widened horizons. On cross-cultural contacts, see the volume of Medieval Studies at Minnesota conference papers that I coedited with Marilyn J. Chiat, *The Medieval Mediterranean: Cross-Cultural Contacts* (St. Cloud, Minn.: North Star Press of St. Cloud, 1989).

3. On merchants and their mentality, see Erich Mäschke, "La mentalité des marchands européens au moyen âge," *Revue d'histoire économique et sociale* 42 (1962): 457–84; Jacques Le Goff, *Marchands et banquiers du moyen âge* ("Que sais-je?" no. 699) (Paris: Presses Universitaires de France, 1962 [1956]). On the financial aspects of "otherness," see Benjamin N. Nelson, *The Idea of Usury: From Tribal Brotherhood to Universal Otherhood* (Princeton, N.J.: Princeton University Press, 1949).

4. On the tripartite vision of society, see Georges Duby, *The Three Orders: Feudal Society Imagined,* trans. Arthur Goldhammer (Chicago: University of Chicago Press, 1980).

5. Gerald A. J. Hodgett evokes the sociological perspective in *A Social and Economic History of Medieval Europe* (New York: Harper & Row, 1974), 93.

6. Europe was about 10 percent urban in the High and Late Middle Ages. Rural society and values thus remained exceedingly important.

7. For general background, see Marc Bloch, *Feudal Society*, trans. L. A. Manyon, 2 vols. (Chicago: University of Chicago Press, 1961; Phoenix, 1964).

8. On urban law, see Harold J. Berman, *Law and Revolution: The Formation of the Western Legal Tradition* (Cambridge: Harvard University Press, 1983), chap. 12.

9. Jean Favier, *De l'or et des épices. Naissance de l'homme d'affaires au moyen âge* (Paris: Fayard, 1987), chap. 6, especially 137–44.

10. For one perspective on the actions of the French king toward Italians, see my article "Les opérations de crédit dans la coutume et dans la vie des affaires à Montpellier au moyen âge: le problème de l'usure," in *Diritto comune e diritti locali nella storia dell'Europa* (Milan: Giuffrè, 1980), 189–208.

11. Favier, *De l'or et des épices*, 145–54. See also Armando Sapori, *The Italian Merchant in the Middle Ages*, trans. Patricia Ann Kennen (New York: Norton, 1970), chap. 3. On Lucchese emigration, see Florence Edler (de Roover), "The Silk Trade of Lucca during the Thirteenth and Fourteenth Centuries" (Ph.D. diss., University of Chicago, 1930).

12. Favier, *De l'or et des épices*, 152–53; R. S. Lopez, *Genova marinara nel Duecento: Benedetto Zaccaria ammiraglio e mercante* (Messina-Milan: Principato, 1933).

13. Favier, *De l'or et des épices*, 153–54.

14. For a contrast of the experiences of Venice and Genoa, see R. S. Lopez, "Venise et Gênes: deux styles, une réussite," *Diogène* 71 (1970): 43–51; trans. *Diogenes* 71 (1970): 39–47. See also Benjamin Z. Kedar, *Merchants in Crisis: Genoese and Venetian Men of Affairs and the Fourteenth Century Depression* (New Haven, Conn.: Yale University Press, 1976).

15. Philip D. Curtin, *Cross-Cultural Trade in World History* (Cambridge: Cambridge University Press, 1984). J. R. S. Phillips, *The Medieval Expansion of Europe* (Oxford: Oxford University Press, 1988), provides an interesting perspective for the Middle Ages.

16. See Curtin, *Cross-Cultural Trade*, 5–6, for comments here.

17. Georges Jehel, *La Méditerranée médiévale de 350 à 1450* (Paris: Armand Colin, 1992), 100ff.

18. Jehel, *La Méditerranée*, 165; Fernand Braudel, *The Mediterranean and the Mediterranean World in the Age of Philip II*, 2 vols. (New York: Harper & Row, 1972, 1975 [Paris: Armand Colin, 1949]), see, for example, 1:334, regarding the "indispensable immigrant."

19. Jehel, *La Méditerranée*, 172.

20. Bernard Lewis, *The Muslim Discovery of Europe* (New York: Norton, 1982), 25.

21. Ibid., 71–72.

22. Le Goff, *Marchands et banquiers*, 102.

23. Ibid., 101–2.

24. For a treatment of medieval notaries, see Kathryn L. Reyerson, "Reflections on the Infrastructure of Medieval Trade" (paper presented at the Shelby Cullom Davis Center for Historical Studies Conference of Medieval and Early Modern Business, Princeton University, January 1996), to be published in *Business, Enterprise, and Culture* (Brepols, forthcoming).

25. Robert-Henri Bautier, "Les foires de Champagne. Recherches sur une évolution historique," in *Recueils de la Société Jean Bodin*, vol. 5, V: *La Foire* (Brussels: Editions de la Librairie Encyclopédique, 1953), 97–147.

26. For examples of *oltremare* notarial editions, see my article "Montpellier and Genoa: The Dilemma of Dominance," in "The Genoese and Their Rivals in Medieval Mediterranean Commerce: Studies in Honour of Hilmar C. Krueger on his Ninetieth Birthday" (special issue), ed. George S. Robbert, Louise Buenger Robbert, and John E. Dotson, *Journal of Medieval History* 20 (1994): 357–72.

27. See my article "Montpellier and the Byzantine Empire: Commercial Interaction in the Mediterranean World before 1350," *Byzantion* 48 (1978): 456–76.

28. On the details of the trade of Montpelliérains in these areas, see my dissertation, "Commerce and Society in Montpellier: 1250–1350," 2 vols. (Ph.D. diss., Yale University, 1974).

29. Francesco di Balduccio Pegolotti, *La pratica della mercatura*, ed. Allan Evans (Cambridge: Harvard University Press, 1970[1936]). See also Mäschke, "La mentalité des marchands européens," 481–82; Le Goff, *Marchands et banquiers*, 103.

30. Lewis, *Muslim Discovery of Europe*, 73, 77–78.

31. Ibid., 89–91.

32. Quoted in ibid., 98.

33. William D. Phillips Jr., *Slavery from Roman Times to the Early Transatlantic Trade* (Minneapolis: University of Minnesota Press, 1985), 103. For more on the importance of European trade with the East, see the comments of J. R. S. Phillips, *Medieval Expansion of Europe*, 102–4.

34. On Amalfi, see Armand O. Citarella, "Patterns in Medieval Trade: The Commerce of Amalfi before the Crusades," *Journal of Economic History* 28 (1968): 531–55. On such trade by the Languedocian town of Montellier, see my "Commerce and Society in Montpellier."

35. See my monograph *Business, Banking and Finance in Medieval Montpellier*, Studies and Texts 75 (Toronto: Pontifical Institute of Mediaeval Studies, 1985), app. I, pp. 135–36, for a transcription of such a *commenda* partnership.

36. For an interesting study of such legal embroglios, see Fredric L. Cheyette, "The Sovereign and the Pirates, 1332," *Speculum* 45 (1970): 40–68.

37. On *fondachi* of the Pisans and the Genoese in Montpellier, see my article "Patterns of Population Attraction and Mobility: The Case of Montpellier, 1293–1348," *Viator* 10 (1979): 278.

38. Archibald R. Lewis, *Nomads and Crusaders* A.D. 1000–1368 (Bloomington: Indiana University Press, 1988), 186.

39. David Abulafia, *Italy, Sicily and the Mediterranean, 1100–1400* (London: Variorum Reprints, 1987), x.

40. Ibid., "Crocuses and Crusaders: San Gimignano, Pisa and the Kingdom of Jerusalem," 231; "Marseille, Acre and the Mediterranean, 1220–1291," 27.

41. Bautier, "Les foires de Champagne."

42. See my "Montpellier and Genoa." The common denominator in trade and business throughout the Middle Ages was family, but this is a topic that falls outside my consideration in this chapter.

43. David Jacoby, "The Rise of a New Emporium in the Eastern Mediterranean: Famagusta in the Late Thirteenth Century," in *Meletai kai hypomnemata* (Nicosia: Hidryma archiepiskopou Makariou III, 1984), 157–58.

44. Ibid., 160. The property of foreigners in the Levant was often in jeopardy. A Venetian report of 1242–43 discussed expropriation by the king, the Hospitaliers, and the Templars on Cyprus. In response to Venetian complaints, the king of Cyprus seems to have offered compensation rather than restitution. Venetians constituted the largest group of refugees from the Syrian coastal states in Famagousta. Some returned to Venice, some stayed on. See ibid., 165–66. Southern French merchants were less prevalent in Cyprus, but by 1302 Marseille could count a consul and *fondaco* in Famagousta. Ships of the Hospitaliers and Templars conveyed merchants from Marseille to Cyprus. Although the king of Cyprus, Henry I, in 1236 had lowered customs dues for merchants of Marseille, Montpellier and cities of Provence were not well represented in Cyprus in the thirteenth century and even in 1300, according to Jacoby. One finds exceptions to this generalization, however; see ibid., 172.

45. Ibid., 173–78.

46. See my article "Montpellier and the Byzantine Empire." Recent work by Olivia Remie Constable on the trade between Genoa and Spain again underlines this fact. See her "Genoa and Spain in the Twelfth and Thirteenth Centuries: Notarial Evidence for a Shift in Patterns of Trade," *Journal of European Economic History* 19 (1990): 637: "The

diplomatic, narrative, and notarial records often complement and confirm each other, although they were written with different intentions and present different information." See also her recent monograph *Trade and Traders in Muslim Spain: The Commercial Realignment of the Iberian Peninsula 900–1500* (Cambridge: Cambridge University Press, 1994).

47. For insights into colonies in the Near East, see David Jacoby's articles collected in *Studies on the Crusader States and on Venetian Expansion* (London: Variorum Reprints, 1989). On colonies in the Maghreb, see Charles-Emmanuel Dufourcq, *L'Espagne catalane et le Maghrib aux XIIIe et XIVe siècles* (Paris: Presses Universitaires de France, 1966), 68ff.

48. Frederic C. Lane, *Venice: A Maritime Republic* (Baltimore: Johns Hopkins University Press, 1973), 52.

49. Dufourcq, *L'Espagne catalane,* 69–70.

50. On *fondachi,* see note 37, above.

51. R. S. Lopez and Irving Raymond, *Medieval Trade in the Mediterranean World* (New York: Columbia University Press, 1961[1955]), 84–86.

52. See my "Commerce and Society in Medieval Montpellier."

53. See Louis Blancard, ed., *Documents inédits sur le commerce de Marseille au moyen-âge,* 2 vols. (Marseille, 1885); John H. Pryor, *Business Contracts of Medieval Provence: Selected "Notulae" from the Cartulary of Giraud Amalric of Marseilles, 1248,* Studies and Texts 54 (Toronto: Pontifical Institute of Mediaeval Studies, 1981).

54. See my "Patterns of Population," 265; and my article "Le rôle de Montpellier dans le commerce des draps de laine avant 1350," *Annales du Midi* 94 (1982): 17–40.

55. Aaron Greif, "Maghribi Traders," *Journal of Economic History* 49 (1989): 860.

56. On apprenticeship in Montpellier, see my article "The Adolescent Apprentice/Worker in Medieval Montpellier," in "The Evolution of Adolescence in Europe" (special issue), ed. Barbara A. Hanawalt, *Journal of Family History* 17 (1992): 353–70.

57. Claude Carrère, *Barcelone centre économique, 1380–1462,* 2 vols. (Paris: Mouton, 1967); David Herlihy, "The Tuscan Town in the Quattrocento: A Demographic Profile," *Medievalia et Humanistica,* new series 1 (1970): 81–109. See also David Herlihy and Christiane Klapisch-Zuber, *Tuscans and Their Families: A Study of the Florentine Catasto of 1427* (New Haven, Conn.: Yale University Press, 1985). It should be noted that there was a high proportion of single men in Florence, perhaps another reflection of the merchant career profile.

58. See Lopez, "Venise et Gênes."

CHAPTER 2

Voluntary Strangers: European Merchants and Missionaries in Asia during the Late Middle Ages

William D. Phillips Jr.

In the Middle Ages, no Europeans penetrated farther into alien societies than the merchants, missionaries, and envoys who traveled to Asia during the thirteenth and fourteenth centuries. Isolated by distance, culture, race, language, and attitude, they were truly strangers in the Mongol lands, China, and India. To be sure, they were voluntary strangers, having consciously chosen the paths that led them to unknown, distant lands. Each group of medieval travelers had its own purpose in the enterprise: merchants sought wealth through trade, missionaries sought souls through conversion, and the envoys of popes and kings sought military allies. Their status as strangers hampered them in pursuing their goals, and to some degree they all sought to lessen the differences between themselves and the members of their host societies. Complete assimilation was impossible, even for someone as fortunate and talented as Marco Polo, and the missionaries entertained the grand hope of effecting the assimilation of their hosts into the Christian religion. Nevertheless, the Westerners all used similar strategies to approach the alien societies of Asia, adapting to circumstances. Their strategies serve as the focal point of this essay, but first I must set the framework and sketch in the background.

From ancient times, there had been a trickle of trade from Asia to western Europe. At the height of the Roman Empire, that trade temporarily became regular. After the fall of Rome, Asian goods reached Europe only occasionally, though Asia retained its allure as a source of riches. From the time of the First Crusade in the last decade of the eleventh century, western Europeans living in the Crusader states developed a taste for the spices and silks of Asia, but they could obtain them only through Muslim intermediaries. In order for the silks and spices to reach Europe, Westerners had to purchase them—at high prices—from Muslim merchants in the markets of the eastern Mediterranean, particularly in Alexandria.

Before long, some Westerners conceived the idea of seeking direct access to the source of the silks and spices, by establishing a route to the Asian markets. The Muslims blocked the most obvious trajectories, which led from the Red Sea or the Persian Gulf into and across the Indian Ocean to India. Theoretically, an all-water route through the Atlantic around

Africa and through the Indian Ocean to India was also possible. In 1291, just as the last Crusader states were falling to the Muslim reconquest, two brothers from Genoa named Vivaldi took a fleet of galleys through the Strait of Gibraltar on the first leg of a proposed voyage to India. They vanished with hardly a trace.

If the sea route was not feasible, there was still another way to Asia, over the caravan routes through Central Asia. For a period from the mid-thirteenth to the mid-fourteenth century, Europeans could travel the overland routes through Central Asia to China and India. That awesome journey was possible only because for that period the *Pax Mongolica* (Mongol Peace) reigned throughout northern Asia, a consequence of the vast Mongol conquests and their policy of toleration—or perhaps indifference—toward peoples of differing religions and ethnicity.

The conquests began early in the thirteenth century, when a young nobleman called Temujin gained control of the Mongols and a number of related tribes. Taking as his new name Genghis Khan, "ruler of the universe," he led his followers on a career of conquest that spanned the breadth of Asia. Superb horsemen who had mastered the techniques of mounted warfare, the Mongols traveled light—even with women and children in tow—normally living off the land; they could reputedly subsist on mare's milk and the blood of their horses, if need be.

The Mongols invaded northern China, took Beijing by 1215, and entered Russia and Persia in 1223. By the time of the death of Genghis Khan in 1227, Mongol power stretched across Asia to the eastern fringes of Europe. One contingent of Mongols traveled nearly to Vienna, and Kublai Khan, the grandson of Genghis, conquered all of China by 1276. By then, however, the Mongols had already begun to encounter resistance they could not overcome. In 1260, the Mamluks of Egypt defeated them in Palestine. They failed to take Burma and Vietnam, mainly because of their unfamiliarity with jungle warfare. They failed to take Java with a naval expeditionary force and they failed in attempts to invade Japan in 1274 and again in 1281.[1]

The Mongol empire eventually broke apart in the fourteenth century, but while it lasted the *Pax Mongolica* guaranteed the safety of travelers along the overland routes spanning the Mongol empire. Asian goods, and Asia itself, came within the reach of Europeans, and Mediterranean merchants explored the possibilities for direct trade with the markets of Asia. Missionaries dreamed of converting the huge Asian populations to Christianity. Popes and princes became aware that beyond the Islamic world lived other peoples who might be willing to form alliances against the Muslims of the Middle East. The more Europeans learned about the world east of Jerusalem, the more they searched for ways to travel there.

The *Pax Mongolica* allowed contacts between Europe and Asia that were impossible beforehand, including a series of visits to Asia by remarkable European missionaries and merchants, men who returned to tell their stories to Europeans fascinated by tales of faraway lands and untold riches. Their accounts, produced between the 1240s and the 1350s, gave Europe a view of Asia and opened the overland path to reach it, but continued access was dependent upon the Mongols.

In fact, with the decline of the Mongols, those contacts were severed so thoroughly that the best-informed European geographers a century later would not even know that Mongol khans no longer sat on their thrones in Khanbalik (Beijing). Forgotten also were the hard-won victories of the missionaries, who had established bishoprics and secured a small handful of Asian converts to Christianity. The Jesuit missionaries to China in the sixteenth century thought they were the first Western Christians to arrive. Merchants, on the other hand, kept alive the dream of travel to Asia. Christopher Columbus, among many others, read Marco Polo and tried to calculate the distance necessary to sail across the western ocean to Asia.[2] Ironically, Europe's seaborne expansion of the late fifteenth century seems to have owed much to the reports of those who followed overland caravan roads during the *Pax Mongolica.*

In this essay, I will analyze certain features of the cross-cultural trade and long-distance missionary activity that Europeans carried out in the period of the *Pax Mongolica.* Except for Marco Polo and his relatives, the merchants left far fewer traces than the missionaries, but there are a few tantalizing glimpses of the social world of the European merchants in Asia. One reveals the Vilioni family, which first surfaced in Venice in the twelfth century. In 1264, Pietro Vilioni wrote his will in Tabriz, near the Black Sea on the famous Silk Road. The tombstones of two other members of the family, Catarina Vilioni (who died in 1342) and her father, Domenico Vilioni, were uncovered in 1951 when the city walls of Yangchow in China were being torn down. As J. R. S. Phillips notes, this shows a family's involvement "in the commerce of Asia for the better part of a century, as well as evidence for the existence of a European community in China that was well enough established and sufficiently secure to have unmarried women in its midst."[3] Phillips even suggests that Marco Polo had a connection with the Vilionis, for it was in Yangchow that Polo is supposed to have served in the Chinese bureaucracy. If that is true, it illustrates a pattern that historians of trade have often found: merchants in faraway places relied on networks of fellow countrymen and relatives in order to conduct their business. Although the ruling political power in an area controlled initial access, merchants had to create their own opportunities for trade once they arrived.

The most detailed sources for the story of Europeans in Asia during the *Pax Mongolica* come from a handful of missionaries and merchants who made the trek and later wrote about it (or dictated their impressions), and from a Florentine banker who distilled a century of mercantile experience in Asia into a remarkable guidebook. Their motivations may have varied, but as a group the travelers can still impress modern readers with their willingness to risk the uncertainties of travel over the breadth of Eurasia. The accounts of their travels are necessarily one-sided. They are the strangers, although their recorded experiences include the reactions of the indigenous people to them.

The first account comes from the papal envoy John of Piano Carpini, whose embassy to the Mongols came at the behest of Pope Innocent IV. Europeans had secured an early impression of the Mongols as they conquered parts of eastern Europe, and that impression was decidedly negative. In 1240, Matthew Paris, writing from the comparative safety of England, called them "inhuman and of the nature of beasts, rather to be called monsters than men."[4] Despite this image, several popes saw important reasons to seek contacts with the Mongol empire. However blood chilling the stories about them, the Mongols were a distant threat. They might prove useful against a much closer threat—the Muslims—an especially appealing idea in the mid-thirteenth century, when the Crusader states were falling to Islamic forces.

As knowledge of the Mongols filtered through to the West, Pope Innocent IV (1243–54) came to look upon them as potential allies. He was especially concerned because the fall of Jerusalem to the Muslims in 1244 demanded a bold response by the leader of Western Christianity. Consequently, the pope assembled an embassy to send to the court of the Mongol khan, led by the Franciscan friars John of Piano Carpini and Lawrence of Portugal, and later joined by a Polish Franciscan named Benedict. Their main assignments were to ask the khan to recognize the pope's religious supremacy and to suggest the possibility of a military alliance against the Muslims.[5]

Piano Carpini had worked as a Franciscan missionary in northern and eastern Europe and knew part of the route well. He led his companions by land from Kiev to the Mongol court near Karakorum, where they witnessed the coronation of Guyuk Khan. Far from recognizing papal supremacy, however, the khan called on Piano Carpini to lead the kings of the West to the khan's court to render *him* homage!

Nothing came of papal plans for a military alliance with the Mongols, but Europeans at least gained more knowledge about Asia from the expedition, and hope remained that the Mongols could one day be brought into an alliance. Piano Carpini returned with a written account, which he developed into his *Historia Mongolorum,* including the first Western description of China. His account was copied into a history of the world by Vincent of Beauvais, court historian of King Louis IX of France (1226–70).

Innocent IV in 1247 sent a second mission to the Mongols, led by a Dominican, Brother Ascelin, and four companions. They reached the headquarters of the Mongol chieftain in the west, Baiju, west of the Caspian Sea, but unfortunately succeeded in angering their host. Fortuitously, Aljigiday, a lieutenant of the Great Khan, arrived and sent the Latin embassy back with two Mongol envoys to the pope and to the leader of the Western Crusaders, Louis IX of France, who was then residing on Cyprus.[6]

Louis, who eagerly sought allies against the Muslims, sent two embassies to the Mongol court. The first, led by Andrew of Longjumeau in 1248, failed to obtain an alliance and received instead a Mongol demand that Louis and his fellow Western kings render homage to the Mongols. The second embassy, headed by William of Rubruck, also reached the Mongol court, but with no greater success. Rubruck, however, produced one of the best and most appealing accounts of travel through the Mongol lands.[7]

In direct contacts with China, Italian merchants were at least as active as missionaries, willing to try new ventures in their search for economic gain. Marco Polo is, of course, the best known of all the merchant travelers to Asia during the late Middle Ages. Nonetheless, his trip, like the earlier one by his brother and father, was not simply a commercial effort, but had diplomatic overtones as well.

In 1260, the Venetian merchants Niccolo and Maffeo Polo departed from Constantinople for the Crimean peninsula on the Black Sea, where Italian (especially Genoese) merchants had been established for some time. From there they traveled through Mongol lands on a trading expedition and reached the camp of Barka Khan, Mongol leader in the west, on the Volga River. Military campaigns in the area prevented them from going back along the same route. Instead, they penetrated deep into Mongol territory, and at Bukhara joined a party on its way to Kublai Khan's court in China. The Great Khan designated them as his envoys to the pope, and he requested through them that the pope send "up to a hundred men learned in the Christian religion, well versed in the seven arts.... Furthermore the Great Khan directed the brothers to bring oil from the lamp that burns above the sepulchre of God in Jerusalem."[8]

The Polo brothers returned to Acre in the Crusader states in 1269, and found that the pontifical office was vacant following the death of Clement IV the previous year. They reported to the papal envoy in the Crusader states, Teodoldo Visconti, and, when the papal vacancy stretched into years, resolved to return on their own, taking Niccolo's son Marco with them. Shortly after they departed, Visconti was elected pope, taking the papal name Gregory X. He assigned them two friars, who soon deserted the expeditions. With the pope's gifts and greetings for Kublai Khan, the Polos returned to China.

Marco Polo lived for eighteen years in China, serving as a bureaucrat in the court of Kublai Khan. He traveled throughout China and visited India as well before returning to Europe. His return journey brought him back by sea from India, which gave him a view of the vast trade around the Indian Ocean that linked India with the Red Sea and the Persian Gulf.[9]

After Marco Polo returned to Venice in 1292, he fell victim to the seemingly endless wars among the Italian city-states. Captured by the Genoese, he spent 1298–99 as a prisoner of war, an unfortunate occurrence for him but an extraordinarily fortunate one for history. In jail he met another prisoner, Rustichello of Pisa, who was a writer. Presumably to occupy his idle hours, Polo told Rustichello about his travels in China and the East. Rustichello wrote it all down, embellishing in places and not completely understanding all of it, but nonetheless preserving a tale that might otherwise have been lost forever. The resulting book is not a merchant's manual, and Polo's personal history seldom intrudes. Rather, it is about the wonders of Asia that Polo witnessed or heard described, filtered through Rustichello's prose.[10]

A younger contemporary of Marco Polo, John of Monte Corvino, a Franciscan, left Rome in 1289, commissioned as a papal envoy to the Mongol court. He reached China after a detour through India. The rest of his life was spent in successful missionary activity, first in the region of Öngut (or Tenduc), then in Khanbalik (Beijing), and finally at the great port called in the Middle Ages Zayton (or Zaitun, Ch'uan-chou, or Quanzhou). He was designated as the first bishop of Beijing, and bishoprics soon developed elsewhere along major Chinese trade routes, staffed by Western friars. Monte Corvino's accounts are valuable for the details they show of his missionary work. He reported baptizing thousands of new Christians, and proudly reported on the churches he built, including two in Beijing. His letters helped build the European impression of the significance of the Mongol empire and, not incidentally, Monte Corvino's place in it. "Concerning the lands of the Orientals and especially the empire of the Lord Chaan, I declare that there is none greater in the world. And I have a place in his court and the right of access to it as the legate of the Lord Pope, and he honours me above the other prelates, whatever their titles."[11]

Another Franciscan, Odoric of Pordenone, wrote a spirited account of his journey to Asia. Designated a missionary to China in 1320, Odoric traveled through Persia, then sailed to India and Ceylon (on Muslim vessels), and visited Sumatra, Borneo, and Java before reaching China in 1325. After several years, he returned to the West, traveling along the overland caravan routes through northern Asia.[12]

Still another Franciscan, John of Marignolli, left Avignon in 1338, as a member of a missionary team to China. He reached Beijing in 1342 after traversing the caravan routes. After visiting the Franciscan establishment in Zayton, he left China in 1347 and returned by way of India, reaching Avignon in 1353. His disjointed account offers a description and location of the terrestrial paradise (in or near Ceylon, he says), but it also shows his rational views and dismissal of some of the stock tales about "wonders of the East." After listing all the supposed monstrous races that were said to exist, including dog-headed people, people with one eye in the middle of their forehead, and those who lie on their backs shading themselves with their single huge foot, Marignolli was emphatic about his views:

> I have travelled in all the chief countries of the earth, and in particular to places where merchants from all parts of the world do come together..., and yet I never could ascertain that such races of men really do exist.... The truth is that no such people *do* exist as nations, though there may be an individual monster here and there.[13]

By the early fourteenth century, the Italian merchant community knew much about the products of Asia and the routes toward their points of origin, thanks to a century or more of trade through ports in the eastern Mediterranean and the Black Sea. One of the most important written works dealing with the European view of Asia came from a person who never got farther east than Cyprus. In 1340, Francesco di Balduccio Pegolotti wrote a commercial guide listing the goods sold and the prices they fetched in the markets around the Mediterranean and the Black Sea, especially the high-priced spices that had made the fortunes of many Italian city-states. He prefaced his book, now known as *La pratica della mercatura,* with a brief but detailed guide for travel between Italy and China, based on information he collected from merchants and other travelers who had made the journey and had returned to describe it. Pegolotti, from the commercial connections he gained as a trusted employee of the Bardi trading company of Florence, learned much about the routes to Asia, for which he listed itineraries and offered practical advice regarding mounts and pack animals, provisions, and safety precautions.[14]

These works were known to a lesser or greater degree during the Late Middle Ages, and modern scholarship has certainly not neglected them. For two centuries, geographers and historians have mined their riches straightforwardly for what they reveal about the travelers and the places they traveled.[15] Recently, scholars have used these materials for the relevance they may have for a series of diverse fields of scholarship. The anthropologist Mary Helms has put the travel stories into a category of the enhancements that knowledge provides to power. In her view, the acquisition of knowledge of distant places, peoples, and customs further distinguishes those in power from those over whom they wield that power.[16]

Mary Campbell, a professor of English literature, has analyzed more than a thousand years of European travel writing to show how the features of descriptions of visits to distant lands and exotic people evolved into a variety of genres: the novel and the autobiography, ethnology, and anthropology. The accomplishment of travel writers seemingly as different as Marco Polo and William of Rubruck was to harmonize "the two chief tones of travel writing—the journey and the journey's setting—more effectively than anyone had before them." With these travelers, Campbell sees the beginning of the emergence of travel writing as a distinct genre.[17]

The European—particularly Italian—merchants in China and other parts of Asia during the *Pax Mongolica* probably made up what Philip Curtin describes as a "merchant diaspora" or trade settlement:

> Commercial specialists would remove themselves physically from their home community and go to live as aliens in another town... important in the life of the host community. There, the stranger merchants could settle down and learn the language, the customs and the commercial ways of their hosts. They could then serve as cross-cultural brokers, helping and encouraging trade between the host society and the people of their own origin who moved along the trade routes.[18]

This seems to be exactly what the Western merchants did in Zayton and other Chinese cities, aided by the Mongol's distrust of their Chinese subjects and their need for foreigners as administrators and intermediaries. Unfortunately, the sources available do not permit a full examination of the activities of the European merchants.

On the other hand, the sources are sufficiently detailed to allow us to examine the personal reactions and social responses of merchants and missionaries as they ventured into the farthest reaches of Asia. Their reactions to the peoples they encountered were on a different plane from the reactions of Europe's oceanic explorers of the fifteenth and sixteenth centuries. Unlike Columbus in the Western Hemisphere or Albuquerque in South Asia, they had no technological advantage in China—quite the contrary. They traveled in small groups, mostly unarmed, and were dependent on the goodwill and protection of the Mongol authorities. Consequently, both missionaries and merchants had to act circumspectly merely to be allowed to remain in China. They were voluntary strangers in alien environments under someone else's control. To pursue their goals, they needed to lose their status as complete strangers and assimilate to some degree into their host country. To succeed, they could not rely exclusively on the intermediation of their hosts, but sought to establish direct communication, and that required the acquisition of the local language. Surprisingly, not all the travelers' accounts mention language, and those that do often mention it very briefly. Equally surprisingly, modern scholars seem to have neglected this most basic component of the challenges that faced the travelers. The Europeans in Mongol lands faced far greater linguistic hurdles than their fellow merchants who traded with the Muslims in the Mediterranean ports.[19] Europeans in Asia confronted problems unknown to the famous Muslim traveler Ibn Battuta, who made his way from Morocco to Asia and back in the same period. He covered more ground than Marco Polo, but many of the lands he traversed shared Islamic culture and Arabic as a common language. When he left the lands under direct Muslim control, he could still find Arabic speakers to aid him.[20]

Pegolotti's guidebook, which distilled a century's experience by Italian merchants, approached the question of language forthrightly. After telling prospective travelers to China to let their beards grow long, his first piece of practical advice, he counsels: "At Tana [in the Crimea] you should furnish yourself with a dragoman [interpreter]. And you must not try to save money in the matter of dragomen by taking a bad one instead of a good one. For the additional wages of the good one will not cost you so much as you will save by having him."[21] A long history of bitter experience can be inferred from this laconic admonition.

William of Rubruck would certainly have agreed with Pegolotti. Rubruck rued his inability to speak the language of the Mongols almost as much as he regretted hiring his particular interpreter, named Abdullah:

> I was especially vexed by the fact that whenever I wanted to do some preaching to them my interpreter would say, "Do not make me preach, since I do not know how to express these things." He was right. Later, when I acquired some little knowledge of the language, I noticed that when I said one thing he would say something totally different, depending on what came into his head. After that I realized the danger of speaking through him, and chose rather to say nothing.[22]

As his journey progressed, Rubruck and his companions had greater access to high-ranking Mongols who traveled in the same caravan. The ecumenical Mongols asked the Westerners to pray for them, and Rubruck obliged. "Had I been possessed of a good interpreter, this would have given me an opportunity of sowing much good seed."[23]

Rubruck made efforts to learn Mongol languages, but he continued to need interpreters. His final interpreter in the court of the khan Möngke (or Mangu) in Karakorum was the son of a French goldsmith. The smith's name was William Buchier, members of whose family were jewelers in Paris and who himself had been captured and enslaved in Hungary. In Karakorum, although he was the khan's slave, he lived well. He had married a Hungarian woman, also a slave. They entertained William of Rubruck while he was in Karakorum, and their son acted as Rubruck's interpreter in his final meetings with the khan.[24] Buchier was an involuntary resident of Karakorum, but his skills made him a valued artisan at the khan's court. His family, particularly his son, were learning the ways of the Mongols and gaining a command of their language, enabling them to serve as intermediaries for Rubruck in his dealings with the khan and his entourage.

John of Monte Corvino, the missionary who became the first Christian bishop of Beijing, had greater skills in languages. For his missionary work, he used the local languages and also used other stratagems:

> Also I have gradually bought one hundred and fifty boys, the children of pagan parents, and of ages varying from seven to eleven, who had never learned any religion. These boys I have baptized, and I have taught them Greek and Latin after our manner. Also I have written out Psalters for them, with thirty Hymnaries and two Breviaries. By help of these, eleven of the boys already know our service, and form a choir and take their weekly turn of duty as they do in convents, whether I am there or not.[25]

He learned one of the Mongol languages, which, according to Christopher Dawson, could have been Uighur or Jagatay or Mongol.[26] As Monte Corvino explained his life's work:

> I have myself grown old and grey, more with toil and trouble than with years; for I am not more than fifty-eight. I have got a competent knowledge of the language and character which is most generally used by the Tartars. And I have already translated into that language and character the New Testament and the Psalter, and have caused them to be written out in the finest penmanship they have. . . . And I had been in treaty with the late King George, if he had lived, to translate the whole Latin ritual, that it might be sung throughout the whole extent of his territory; and whilst he was alive I used to celebrate mass in his church, according to the Latin ritual, reading in the before-mentioned language and character the words of both the preface and the Canon.[27]

Monte Corvino thus gained a command of the language necessary for him to preach among the Mongol elite. It should be noted that he did not learn a Chinese language, nor was his preaching directed toward the Chinese, but only toward the Mongols and other non-Chinese. That is characteristic of the other Western missionaries as well. It is therefore easily understandable why the Western Christian presence would not outlast the collapse of the Mongol empire and its replacement by a native Chinese dynasty.

The other merchants and missionaries do not mention problems with language or translators. Like Marco Polo's book, their accounts are travel literature, designed to present the places they visited and the wonders they beheld. They are not intended to display the difficulties their authors may have experienced in understanding their hosts or making themselves understood. In Marco Polo's account, the main mention of languages comes in Rustichello's introductory chapter, not in the body of the book. Rustichello reports that Polo "acquired a remarkable knowledge of the customs of the Tartars and of their languages and letters. I assure you for a fact that before he had been very long at the Great Khan's court he had mastered four languages with their modes of writing."[28] He was a stranger who made a successful effort to adjust.

Polo was remarkable in his abilities, as perhaps was Monte Corvino. Their contemporaries had, to be fair, lesser advantages than Polo, who began his Chinese sojourn as a favorite of Kublai Khan. Their struggles to understand and to be understood were only part of a larger process. In addition to language, they had to learn the customs of dress, grooming, personal hygiene, and diet of their hosts.

Their mixed successes are apparent from the experience of William of Rubruck, whom we saw as frustrated in his efforts to overcome linguistic differences. Although he quickly developed a taste for *qumiz* (or *qimiz, kemis* in Marco Polo), the fermented mare's milk that was a popular alcoholic drink among the Mongols, he stepped into difficulties when he tried to maintain his Franciscan order's custom of going barefoot. This became increasingly clear as the year progressed and colder weather arrived. Rubruck first entered Mongol territory in June, and by September the Mongol commander in the west, Batu, decided to send the friar eastward to meet the khan Möngke. The guide provided by Batu told Rubruck, "It is a four month journey, and the cold there is so intense that rocks and trees split apart with the frost,"[29] then inspected his wardrobe and provided him with warm clothes and boots. When he reached the khan's encampment, in late December, he reverted to his custom of going barefoot, to the amazement of onlookers. He had to abandon it quickly, however. On the morning of the second day without shoes, he reports with classic understatement, "the tips of my toes froze, with the result that I could no longer go around barefoot."[30]

The efforts to assimilate, even though they were no doubt always imperfect and whether they were made easily or painfully, were necessary for the voluntary strangers. Only after they had tried to learn the languages and customs of their hosts—or, in Rubruck's case, bowed to the imperatives of climate—could they begin to bridge the distance between the societies. Only then could they begin to conduct business or proselytize. Only then could they begin to lose their status as strangers.

Notes

1. Regarding the Mongols, see J. J. Saunders, *The History of the Mongol Conquests* (London: Routledge & Kegan Paul, 1971); D. Morgan, *The Mongols* (Oxford: Basil Blackwell, 1986); René Grousset, *The Empire of the Steppes: A History of Central Asia,* trans. Naomi Walford (New Brunswick, N.J.: Rutgers University Press, 1970).

2. For a discussion of the background of Columbus's geographic ideas, see William D. Phillips Jr. and Carla Rahn Phillips, *The Worlds of Christopher Columbus* (Cambridge: Cambridge University Press, 1992); William D. Phillips Jr., "Columbus and European Views of the World," *American Neptune* 53 (1993): 260–67.

3. J. R. S. Phillips, *The Medieval Expansion of Europe* (Oxford: Oxford University Press, 1988), 111–12.

4. *Matthew Paris's English History from the Year 1235 to 1273,* trans. J. A. Giles, 3 vols. (New York: AMS Press, 1968[1852]), 1:312–13.

5. The most easily available edition of Plano Carpini's *Historia Mongolorum,* translated by a nun of Stanbrook Abbey, is in Christopher Dawson, ed., *Mission to Asia: Narratives and Letters of the Franciscan Missionaries in Mongolia and China in the Thirteenth and Fourteenth Centuries* (New York: Harper & Row, 1966).

6. On Louis's Crusading career, see William C. Jordan, *Louis IX and the Challenge of the Crusade: A Study in Rulership* (Princeton, N.J.: Princeton University Press, 1979).

7. *The Mission of Friar William of Rubruck: His Journey to the Court of the Great Khan Möngke, 1253–1255,* trans. Peter Jackson; introduction, notes, and appendices by Peter Jackson and David Morgan (London: Hakluyt Society, 1990).

8. *The Travels of Marco Polo,* trans. R. E. Latham (Harmondsworth: Penguin, 1982 [1958]), 36.

9. K. N. Chaudhuri, *Trade and Civilisation in the Indian Ocean: An Economic History from the Rise of Islam to 1750* (Cambridge: Cambridge University Press, 1985).

10. Jacques Heers, *Marco Polo* (Paris: Penguin, 1983); Leonardo Olschki, *Marco Polo's Asia: An Introduction to His "Description of the World" called "Il Milione,"* trans. John A. Scott (Berkeley/London: University of California Press/Cambridge University Press, 1960); *Travels of Marco Polo.* For a challenge to the traditional story, see Frances Wood, *Did Marco Polo Go to China?* (London: Secker and Warburg, 1995).

11. John of Monte Corvino's letters, together with letters of his fellow missionaries, are in Henry Yule, ed., *Cathay and the Way Thither, Being a Collection of Medieval Notices of China,* trans. Henry Yule, rev. ed. Henri Cordier (London: Hakluyt Society, 1914), vol. 3. Excerpts, better translated, appear in Dawson, *Mission to Asia.* This quotation comes from *Mission to Asia,* 230.

12. *The Travels of Friar Odoric* are found in Yule, *Cathay and the Way Thither,* vol. 2.

13. From Marignolli's account as it is found in Yule, *Cathay and the Way Thither,* 3:256.

14. Francesco di Balduccio Pegolotti, *La pratica della mercatura,* ed. Allen Evans (Cambridge: Harvard University Press, 1970[1936]). Evans's edition contains the Italian text of the book. A partial English translation is available in Yule, *Cathay and the Way Thither,* 3:143–71. A better translation is in Robert S. Lopez and Irving Raymond, eds., *Medieval Trade in the Mediterranean World* (New York: Columbia University Press, 1961), 355–58.

15. For an early-nineteenth-century account, see Hugh Murray, *Historical Account of Discoveries and Travels in Asia, from the Earliest Ages to the Present Time,* 3 vols. (Edinburgh: A. Constable, 1820), 1:69–197. Other more recent studies include C. Raymond Beazley, *The Dawn of Modern Geography,* 3 vols. (New York: Peter Smith, 1949[1897–1906]); A. P. Newton, ed., *Travel and Travellers of the Middle Ages* (London/New York: K. Paul, Trench, Trubner/Alfred A. Knopf, 1926); J. K. Wright, *Geographical Lore in the Time of the Crusades* (New York: Dover, 1965[1925]); Pierre Chaunu, *L'expansion européenne du XIIIe au XVe siècle* (Paris: Presses Universitaires de France, 1969); James Muldoon, *Popes, Lawyers, and Infidels: The Church and the Non-Christian World 1250–1550* (Philadelphia: University of Pennsylvania Press, 1979); James Muldoon, ed., *The Expansion of Europe: The First Phase* (Philadelphia: University of Pennsylvania Press, 1977); Michel Mollat, *Les explorateurs du XIIIe au XVIe siècle: Premiers regards sur des mondes nouveaux* (Paris: J. C. Lattes, 1984); Phillips, *Medieval Expansion of Europe.*

16. Mary W. Helms, *Ulysses' Sail: An Ethnographic Odyssey of Power, Knowledge, and Geographical Distance* (Princeton, N.J.: Princeton University Press, 1988).

17. Mary W. Campbell, *The Witness and the Other World: Exotic European Travel Writing, 400–1600* (Ithaca, N.Y.: Cornell University Press, 1988), 121.

18. Philip D. Curtin, *Cross-Cultural Trade in World History* (Cambridge: Cambridge University Press, 1984), 2.

19. Kathryn L. Reyerson has mentioned the ways Mediterranean merchants overcame linguistic barriers; see her chapter, "The Merchants of the Mediterranean: Merchants as Strangers," in this volume.

20. Ross E. Dunn, *The Adventures of Ibn Battuta: A Muslim Traveler of the 14th Century* (Berkeley: University of California Press, 1986).

21. From Yule, *Cathay and the Way Thither,* 3:151.

22. *Mission of Friar William of Rubruck,* 108.

23. Ibid., 141–42.

24. Ibid., passim. The editors cite a modern biography of the goldsmith: Leo Olschki, *Guillaume Boucher: A French Artist at the Court of the Khans* (Baltimore: Johns Hopkins University Press, 1946).

25. In Yule, *Cathay and the Way Thither,* 3:46–47.

26. Dawson, *Mission to Asia,* xxxiii.

27. In Yule, *Cathay and the Way Thither,* 3:50.

28. *Travels of Marco Polo,* 40. The translator comments: "Marco probably knew both Mongol and Turkish, which are related (Altaic) languages, and it is not always clear which form he was trying to reproduce. He also seems to have had some knowledge of Persian; but it is doubtful which was the fourth language he claimed to have mastered. It can scarcely have been Chinese" (28). Leonardo Olschki offers a series of conjectures about how, when, and to what extent the Polos acquired their Asian languages. *Marco Polo's Asia,* 81, 86, 89, 100.

29. *Mission of Friar William of Rubruck,* 136.

30. Ibid., 175.

CHAPTER 3

Home Again: The Jews in the Kingdom of France, 1315–1322

William Chester Jordan

In November 1314, the king of France, Philip IV the Fair, lay dying. He was hard-pressed to make a "good death" by medieval standards. With the provincial aristocracies in rebellion against his government, he expressed reasonable doubts about the quality of his rule.[1] He must also have been uncertain that his son, the future Louis X, would be up to the task of containing the rebellion, let alone of preserving the powerful monarchy that had been built up with painstaking determination by him and his most eminent predecessors, Saint Louis and Philip Augustus.[2] In fact, Philip the Fair underestimated his son's abilities, but he might still have been disappointed if he had foreseen some of Louis's plans, for after his father's death in late November, the new king, in order to reduce turmoil and assuage the more important nobles, felt obliged to renounce certain taxes and similar levies. This in turn compelled him to find other ways of raising money. As part of that effort, on 28 July 1315 he authorized readmitting Jews to the kingdom.[3] His agents had been in contact and negotiating with Jewish leaders in borderland principalities since spring.[4] The act of readmission is remarkable in that Louis annulled a decree of expulsion that his father had issued almost ten years before, in the summer of 1306.[5]

To purchase the privilege of resettlement, the leaders of the Jewish community were to raise 22,500 pounds, which they had difficulty doing.[6] From the government's point of view, this was not a large sum, no more than about a 5 percent supplement to royal income in an ordinary year, and the amount was dwarfed by what Philip the Fair and his barons had made by seizing all the lands, goods, and debts of the Jews during the expulsion of 1306.[7] Nonetheless, in the crisis facing Louis X everything mattered. The promise the Jewish leadership made in an elaborate agreement covering the charge of readmission, to contribute 10,000 pounds per year to the treasury, was small change, but in the circumstances every little bit helped.[8]

Who were the Jews who took advantage of the agreement their leaders had made? Presumably most of them, except for children under age ten, were men and women who had been living in France before the expulsion of 1306. An agreement between the king and the Burgundian nobility on 17 May 1315 that confirmed the rights of the latter and was part of a series of conventions meant to encourage the provincial nobilities to end their rebellion had launched a trial balloon about admitting Jews to the kingdom. There it was clearly expressed that the offer, if it should come about, was meant to target Jews who had lived in the kingdom before 1306. It was also indicated that suitable arrangements would be made to respect Burgundian nobles' rights over returning Jews who had lived under their lordship before that date.[9] As to the number of returnees after the charter of settlement was issued in July, various factors (several of which will be indicated in the pages to come) lead me to believe that it was relatively low, perhaps about thirty thousand, probably 30 percent of those expelled in 1306.[10]

For most of the Jews who took advantage of the king's charter of 28 July, therefore, the settlement was a homecoming of sorts, but in three ways their status was marked as that of aliens, sojourners, and enemies—in a word, as strangers—in a strange land. They were aliens in law. They were sojourners, in the vocabulary of sociologists and cultural and economic anthropologists, owing to the impermanence of their expected residence. They were enemies because of their economic role in the years 1315–22.[11]

Aliens

The Jews who began to settle in France in the summer of 1315 were aliens in the sense that they were arbitrarily denied the legal benefits that inhered in being Christian and law-abiding (for a Christian could be stripped of property, liberty, or life for felony).[12] What constituted these benefits—the irreducible rights of a Christian in an otherwise highly status-conscious society such as medieval France—might be quite small, but even a serf had rights: the right to practice the Catholic faith and the right to life among them (and the related right not to be reduced to chattel slavery). Custom, of course, also assured the serf in thirteenth- and fourteenth-century northern France considerably more, such as procedural due process in manorial courts, but in theory entitlement to this—by right—was still contested.[13]

By analogy with modern law on aliens, a Jew might be "naturalized" through his or her renunciation of Judaism and acceptance of baptism. As long as Jews remained Jews, however, they enjoyed their benefits solely at the pleasure of princes.[14] These benefits could be considerable and were often enunciated in solemn acts of state.[15] They might privilege Jews above particular groups of Christians, but the benefits so bestowed were not regarded as unassailable in law. Although custom had seriously eroded the ability of lords to deal with serfs contrary to conventional legal procedures in manorial courts, Jews remained liable to arbitrary arrest, imprisonment, physical punishment, and confiscation of goods by the prince throughout the thirteenth century.[16] The distinction between alien and "subject" with inherent rights was and remained firm down to the modern period.[17]

According to the solemn royal pronouncement that defined the range of privileges of (and the limitations on) the new Jewish settlers in France, they were as a protected alien minority permitted to consecrate cult sites and burial places, and they were otherwise allowed to practice their religion (though with no public or private disparagement of the Christian faith).[18] Presumably this privilege applied only as long as the Judaism practiced conformed to the religion described in scripture or could easily be inferred from scripture. The French crown had long before taken the position that accretions to the religion, especially as embodied in the text of the Talmud, were both blasphemous to the Christian faith and perverted biblical Judaism.[19] Consequently, the bringing of books of the Talmud into the kingdom was proscribed.[20]

The alien character of the Jews was further emphasized by provisions in the charter of settlement that discouraged contact between Christians and Jews. Residence was restricted to areas ("és Villes & és lieus") where Jews lived before 1306.[21] In all public spaces Jews were obliged to wear badges on their clothing that were large and easy to recognize and that identified them as Jews.[22] Additionally, except in one area of economic life, Jews were to sell goods and provide services solely to their coreligionists. At least this is my interpretation of the chapter in the charter that repeats language associated with ordinances of Saint Louis requiring Jews to labor with their own hands ("Il laborront de leurs mains") or to vend acceptable products ("marchanderont de bonnes, & loyals marchandises").[23] There had never been any expectation that such *loyal* (in the sense of honest or legal) work was a license for Jews to service or sell products to the Christian community, although presumably there was no objection to the Jews spending their own money to buy Christian products.[24]

Although lending on bond was prohibited, the exception referred to above was pawnbroking with high levels of permitted interest[25] (in the specialized language of the scholastics, the lending done by "manifest usurers"),[26] a fact that clearly hints at part of the substance of the negotiations that took place between the king's agents and the Jewish leadership in the spring before the edict permitting settlement was issued. The benefit provided departed from an old prohibition in France, going back to the early period of Saint Louis's reign, that had emasculated the legal pawnbroking business by restricting profits to the sale of unredeemed pledges.[27]

The benefits listed were undoubtedly conceived as free-will offerings, boons, granted by the king, but can the charter bestowed on the Jews be assimilated to *acta* made for his Christian subjects? Insofar as he was bound to uphold the latter, it was because every regulation, ordinance, or statute implied a promise or oath to enforce the law,[28] even though few pieces of legislation explicitly use such language. Indeed, it would have been slightly jarring for a French king to supplement a *stabilimentum* with the words, "I promise before God that I will effect this law." It would be tantamount to an admission of incompetence or malfeasance in the past.[29]

Clearly, the charter for the Jews, though negotiated, would be hard to categorize as a contract pure and simple, although negotiation in that it implies mutual "agreement" (OF *convenance*) lends certain contractual aspects to it;[30] so, it may be wise to pursue the analogy with "ordinary" legislation. The charter, then, like ordinary legislation, lacks an explicit oath on the part of the king promising enforcement. By analogy, this absence is insufficient grounds for inferring that the king felt free to change it at will.[31] If, on the other hand, Jews who were coming under his *dominium* believed there was an implicit oath in the granting of the charter, we can be fairly sure that they also recognized its limitations. They had learned through bitter experience that legists could concoct arguments that effectively annulled even explicit oaths (or contracts) if enforcing them could be regarded as "immoral."[32] The charter seemed to the Jewish leadership as good a guarantee as could be achieved in 1315, but it was not necessarily an ironclad agreement. After all, contractual agreements were voidable or unenforceable at law under many conditions.[33] As we shall see momentarily, the experience of resettlement made it necessary to clarify the otherwise lucid charter, and at that time the Jewish leadership was able to extract a formal binding promise, extraordinary evidence of the government's continuing crisis.

Sojourners

The hesitancy that many Jews had in returning and, therefore, the low rate of return are themselves evidence that they had forebodings of the likely failure of the experiment and its temporary character. To some degree, even those who were most optimistic must have had apprehensions, and to this extent all the settlers were sojourners of a sort. When social scientists use the word *sojourners,* however, they mean to categorize people who will remain in contact with societies and cultures physically at a distance from the districts of residence in which they temporarily reside. It is these districts that are "home," even if certain individual sojourners never really intend to return. It may be from these home societies that spouses will come, or prolonged visits to them may be necessary for cultural reasons.[34]

It was the prohibition on possession of the Talmud that provided a strong incentive for young men to travel back to what had once been lands of exile for study with masters of Jewish law.[35] Effectively, the homecoming of 1315, given the conditions of the return, had a transforming effect on the image of the lands of exile themselves. In 1306 the expellees, judging from the plethora of remembrances they would write, looked upon many of the lands of exile as hostile places.[36] Differences of language, physical environment, and culture made adjustments difficult. Poverty made the exiles dependent on the goodwill of their coreligionists; and the flip side of the acts of charity was a sense of weakness and incapacity. A decade in exile, for many of the expellees, had softened the experience; for others it had not. But for all of them it had made the terrain less foreign. The necessity for small communities of resettled Jews in France to reach out to these larger former exile communities in order, at the very least, to maintain talmudic study inexorably reconfigured concepts as fundamental as "personal identity," "loyalty," and "home."

The legal charter of resettlement reinforced the sojourner mentality of the immigrants by putting a twelve-year limit on settlement, "jusques a douze ans."[37] The readmission, in other words, was to be an experiment, the phrase "jusques a" suggesting but not mandating that it last until 1327. A year before the expiration of the agreement, the Jewish leadership was to be informed by the crown whether the agreement would be renewed or the Jews expelled: "Nous ne les pourrons chacier arrieres hors de nostre Royaume, que Nous ne leur donnons temps convenables, c'est assavoir un an."[38] It would have been hard not to regard this as a threat.

Nevertheless, the more optimistic among the Jewish leaders expected the experiment to be a success. After all, in evident contempt of Philip the Fair, Louis, long before he was king of France, had actually permitted residence to those expelled by his father in 1306. He had opened the borders of Navarre to them, where, from 1305, he was king in his own right.[39] A young and vigorous man in his twenties when he became king of France, he could be expected to have a long and prosperous reign. Why not be optimistic? Here was a trustworthy man. Undoubtedly this was the heartening hope.[40] But it was only a hope. It could not of itself eliminate that lingering sense that the twelve-year time limit might actually be enforced. And what happened—almost from day one of resettlement—did nothing to weaken that sense.

If even the most hopeful Jews could not ignore the fact that there was a danger that resettlement would be temporary, Christians opposed to the resettlement for whatever reasons could take some pleasure in the charter's stipulation of the twelve-year limit. One can imagine a kind of calculus informing considerations of the significance of the clause. If social, economic, or political conditions in the kingdom grew bad, it would be possible to blame the Jews, but also to look forward to (and indeed to argue for) their reexpulsion at the end of the twelve-year period. Moreover, some Christians with real or imagined grievances against Jews might have no compunction about carrying out acts that would contribute to that end.

Enemies

The year 1306 had been an immense relief for most of the Christian population in France.[41] To be sure, the immediate reaction to Philip's expulsion of the Jews was muted by the apprehension among some poor people that Christian moneylenders, in the absence of competition, might treat them worse than had the Jews.[42] But the making of an unfavorable comparison of Christian usurers to Jewish usurers is hardly evidence of wistful pining for the Jews to return.[43] As time went on, even those who were professionally ambivalent about the theological appropriateness of expelling the Jews probably came to see the expulsion of 1306 as bringing an end to a hitherto intractable social "problem."[44] Louis X's agreement to let the Jews return would be seen by many as a betrayal, the capricious re-creation of a problem that had effectively been solved.

Of course Louis was not so stupid or naive as to admit this. Quite the contrary, the preamble to the charter of resettlement sets out *positive* reasons for granting permission to return. There was the "common clamor of the people"—a cry, it was said, supported by theology and devotion to the memory of Saint Louis. *Theology* meant the Augustinian theory of the necessity of having the Jews around at the end of time as witnesses to Christian truth. The appeal to the memory of Saint Louis (that is, to what were regarded as the best impulses of all good Christians) recalled the desire of the saint-king to convert the Jews. Had not the blessed predecessor himself thought better of expelling the Jews? All this is expressed or implied in the charter of settlement.[45] To take these words from the preamble of the charter at face value, however, and to conclude that there was "euphoria" at the readmission of the Jews (even if it supposedly died rapidly) is unconvincing.[46]

Evidence that the return caused serious consternation is not hard to find. The chroniclers were just plain baffled by the king's decision.[47] Moreover, from the moment immigrants crossed the borders to return to their old homes, there were nasty incidents, assaults, and intimidation.[48] Indeed, life among the resettled refugees continued to be marred throughout late 1315 and 1316 by repeated indignities and outrages. Local royal officials who had jurisdiction over the Jews with respect to their dealings with Christians were under pressure from the crown to keep order and protect the settlements, yet they were also under pressure from Christians who had been forced to resell to the Jews—and without any profit—property that had been confiscated in 1306. There were resentments, too, among the hordes of debtors who had been forced in 1306 to pay to the crown the outstanding principal of the money they had originally borrowed from Jews. For these people the presence of Jews stirred hateful memories of their dependency on a group of people who were—in the prevailing ideology of the time—not supposed to have dominance of any sort over Christians, the people of God. And it reanimated hatred of an authoritarian state that enforced the payment of these debts more systematically than Jews had been able to do.

On top of everything else, the crown granted Jews the right to collect any old debts (not interest) that it had failed to collect through ignorance in the period of their exile. In other words, any Christian debtors who had, to the crown's detriment, successfully hidden their obligations were to be punished, if the Jews could provide evidence, by being forced to pay the full debt that was proved against them. The "take" was to be split, one-third for the Jewish lender, two-thirds for the crown. Although provision was made for the punishment of malicious accusations, few clauses in the charter of resettlement could have had greater potential for provoking anger,[49] yet various royal letters of 6 August, 15 August, and 18 August 1315 reveal that the crown took very seriously the matter of collecting on these debts.[50] Animosities lingered.[51]

Local royal officials sensed the hostility in their communities. They acted in ways that seemed both to obey the crown and to pander to the indisputable resentments of Christians. They seem to have been very conscientious about investigating alleged instances of Jewish illegalities. Even if they were biased and sometimes unscrupulously clever—and there seems little reason to doubt that they were biased against the Jews and too clever by half—what could the crown do when these local officials claimed merely to be enforcing the letter of the law? If the putatively comprehensive charter of 1315 did not mention a privilege explicitly, did it exist? To be sure, it generally granted to the Jews the privileges enjoyed under Saint Louis, but we need to know what was remembered or recorded in the provinces about the extent of these privileges. Could Jews be forced to go to judicial battle? Did royal Jews have absolute immunity from baronial jurisdiction in the franchises of lords with high justice? Could they be assessed arbitrarily—irrespective of the size of their "estates"? Could they be deprived of inheritances (were they mainmortable) as serfs were?[52]

The fact is that all these matters were in dispute or, better expressed, it was possible to see flaws in the original charter or to quibble about each of them and many more. In a peculiar way, this fact put the Jews in a favorable negotiating position. So much was going bad so quickly that the crown looked upon the suspicious behavior of people—including its officials—toward the Jews as an affront to the royal majesty. There was something repugnant about the recalcitrance and stonewalling against the direct orders of the crown.[53] The optimists among Jewish leaders could only expect that a strong king who was committed to protecting the Jews would eventually get effective control of the realm and, without necessarily responding to every incident of harassment, at least set the tone for a "normalized" way of life between Jews and Christians in the kingdom at large. When the harassment continued, the government in 1317 (after the death of Louis X the year before, an event to which we shall return) moved with firmness to denounce it. And it went even further, for the Jewish leadership must have threatened to abandon the experiment themselves if they were so persistently harassed. How else to explain the introduction of a strong promissory oath in the decree that the crown issued? "Et promettons de nostre certaine science pour nous, & pour nos successeurs Roys de France garder & tenir, & faire garder & tenir toutes les choses dessudites octroyées à nosdits Juifs."[54]

While these events were playing themselves out, something far more serious was undermining the crown's ability to rule. Already in the spring of 1315, just as negotiations between the crown and the Jewish leadership over the readmission of the exiles reached completion, it had started to rain, and for months it did not stop. The rains pounded all of northern Europe. Harvests were sharply off. The spring, summer, and fall of 1316 were worse, the rains relentless and the impact on crop production disastrous. Extended and bad winter weather and lack of fodder decimated the flocks and herds. Modest ameliorations in the weather were only temporary over the next several years, with the consequence that northern Europe suffered famine on a scale the like of which had not been seen for half a millennium or more. The famine persisted in most of northern Europe until at least 1322 and in many regions until 1325.[55]

The famine provides a fundamental context for life among resettled Jews in the kingdom of France after 1315. Resettlement coincided with the very first inklings that a natural catastrophe of nearly unparalleled proportions was befalling Europe. The Jews, permitted the occupation of moneylending through pawnbroking, were obvious targets during the crisis as exploiters of the poor and the vulnerable. Medieval European society was one in which "warnings against avarice and usury" infiltrated all genres of art.[56] These warnings reflected and enhanced hatred of moneylenders in general. The role of Jews as purveyors of credit in the dire necessity of famine inevitably compounded the power and persuasiveness of these images of avarice.

Moreover, the crown became profoundly concerned about the leverage that moneylenders now had over a population in great distress from high prices.[57] Suspecting that illegal practices were on the rise, investigators, commissioned by the king, were at work in the latter half of 1315 and in early 1316 collecting evidence of usurious lending.[58] In the midst of this campaign, on Christmas Eve 1315, Louis issued an order to carry through "appropriate" prosecutions; evidently, in their zeal to discipline certain "manifest usurers" his commissioners had violated ecclesiastical jurisdiction.[59] These usurers would have been Christians (hence, the ecclesiastical rights of justice over them). The king also issued special year-long respites to farmers suffering from the bad grape harvests around the same time. These respites were to apply both to debts owed to manifest usurers under his jurisdiction (by inference, Jews) and to other creditors.[60]

In addition, the government in its efforts to control speculation and hoarding articulated normative standards of behavior in its legislation

(September 1315) that effectively reinforced the perception of the creditor and the classic middleman as evil.[61] It is unlikely that the legislation had as its specific object the regulation of Jewish brokers. After all, brokerage was not a permitted occupation, and Jews would have had insufficient funds in 1315 to broker in a big way anyway. Still, it does not seem unreasonable to suggest that the popular perception of them as part of the general problem of life in famine times would easily promote the assimilation of the caricatured portrait of the avaricious Christian middleman to that of the Jew.

A Franciscan of Spanish extraction, William of Rubio, who was a student in Paris during the famine (1315–25) would a few years later publish a commentary on the *Sentences* of Peter Lombard. His extended discussion of usury to be found in the commentary reflects his observations of the famine. He exhorts the sovereign to enforce on wealthy subjects the duty of succoring the poor in direst necessity. By this, of course, he means encouraging charity but also enforcing the just price, preventing hoarding, and punishing speculation. Clearly, however, what he saw or heard a great deal about was the moneylending that was going on in the city. It depressed him on two accounts. First, usurers were sinning mortally in exploiting the misery of their neighbors and in contravening divine law (Luke 6.35). Second, by paying usury, people in need, even though unwilling participants in the transactions (who would willingly be exploited, after all?), were contributing to bringing the moneylenders into mortal sin. No need for money to save the body could justify imperiling another's soul. The most recent commentator on the Franciscan's analysis concludes that in "this bleak doctrine there is little left of the economic optimism of the preceding generation."[62] The conditions induced by the famine had killed it.

If it seems certain that the mood was bleak, it also seems certain that the role of the resettled Jews as pawnbrokers gave rise to the belief not only that they were prospering from the anguish of Christians who felt compelled to turn to them, but that they were becoming fabulously wealthy. Undoubtedly some Jews did do well. Within a few years one Sance de Dole, *juyf*, became a creditor for the important fair town of Provins in Champagne.[63] Although this kind of success seems to have been rare, a kind of "retributive justice" began to be played out in which gangs of scoundrels went around harassing Jews for "mulcting" Christians and threatening to slander them unless they paid up. If they did not, it was easy enough, say, to plant a counterfeit coin or two in a Jew's house and then accuse the owner and his business associates of being false moneyers. The charge could have terrifying consequences. An order to inquire into one such accusation reminded the investigators that if they were satisfied about its truth they should order "exemplary" punishment.[64] It may be the case that in France the notion that counterfeiting was an act of treason was still contested, but the leading voices in holding that it was treason were those of the judges in Parlement, men like the ones who issued this order.[65] To them exemplary punishment meant public hanging or perhaps something more, such as boiling an offender alive.[66]

Extortion of Jews becomes a leitmotiv in the records. Any number of Jews still had the courage to complain to the crown, and it issued orders to protect the communities or to arrest the perpetrators of false accusations if they were known.[67] A variant in the portfolio of extortion and perhaps the most outrageous incident in the period of resettlement involved a large ring of scoundrels who evidently went around the country and managed to convince authorities that they had a mandate to impose levies on the local Jews. How did they get away with this? The answer seems to be suggested by the very names of the malefactors who were ultimately identified. At least a couple of them were converted Jews. They could have come into a local community, claimed royal backing by means of a forged writ, showed Hebrew documents that convinced officials of their expertise, and then hounded the Jews without any external interference.[68]

The other factor that disturbed the resettlement, to which I referred earlier, was the death of the king. Young and vigorous though he was, Louis X fell ill in 1316 and died the same year. It was an ominous sign so soon after a period of rebellion. Rumors circulated that he had been poisoned.[69] A comet in the heavens was said by some to have heralded the king's untimely death and the ruination of France ("denonçant le detriment du royaume").[70] He was succeeded by a brother, Philip V, who reigned only until 1322, and another brother, Charles IV, who survived only until 1328. Whatever the views of these two kings (and Philip V certainly favored holding to the agreement with the Jews),[71] the situation grew increasingly desperate for the settlers.

Legal records document a crescendo of nasty incidents that disturbed relations between Christians and Jews. The spring of 1317, for example, saw a lynch-mob mentality sweep through the castle town of Chinon when rumor had it that Jews had murdered a Christian child. The *bailli* or provincial administrator of the Touraine was caught up in the fervor and moved swiftly to arrest four Jews, put them to torture, extract two confessions, and hang the allegedly guilty parties. Other Jews managed to bring a complaint to the crown.[72] It was only discovered in July, after the royal investigation requested by the Jews was completed, that the child had died at the hands of a gang of Christians. Orders went out to arrest them.[73]

Elsewhere the situation was similar. We learn, for example, that in the fall of 1317 a Jewish doctor was solicited illegally by an infirm Christian for treatment and then was accused of poisoning him. The Jew was said to have had an accomplice in the murder; the accomplice was accused also of being a coin-clipper. A royal order to inquire into the charges was issued on 12 October 1317.[74] A few months later in Château-Thierry a gang broke into the local synagogue, smashed the tabernacle, and stole the rolls of the Law, which would have been kept in a precious container. An investigation of this incident, at the request of the Jews of the town, was ordered on 6 March 1318.[75] As one discovers in reading through the criminal records, accusations—true and false—about sexual misconduct were also bruited about and on at least one occasion with capital punishment as a consequence for the Jewish man so accused.[76]

All of this, we need to recall, had as its backdrop the famine. What was causing the terrible weather, the pestilence affecting herds and flocks, the human deaths, even cannibalism (as some asserted was taking place)? God was using nature to discipline sinners.[77] Appeasing God required recommitting the kingdom to the work of God, including the crusade. Louis's successor issued a preliminary call for a crusade, which he promised to lead in 1320. But the tax base had been seriously eroded in the long series of crises that beset the French kingdom, and it proved to be impossible to put together an expedition. When word spread that despite the call there would be no crusade, poor and disillusioned shepherds, artisans, rural laborers, and, later, urban artisans and workers made up their own motley bands of crusaders. Preachers claimed divine inspiration, and the mobs in 1320 responded by beginning a crusade at home in France against all those whom they regarded as enemies. Sometimes this meant churchmen with wealth and power; sometimes it meant nobles and rich merchants feasting while the poor starved. Frequently it meant Jews (with their loan registers). A wave of massacres swept France.[78]

For many Jews who had resettled, these incidents were sufficient. A new "voluntary" exile began: we have evidence of flight to Lorraine, Alsace, and to what we would now call Belgium.[79] Simonsohn has suggested that other refugees went to the Comtat-Venaissin, papal territory, only to be expelled from there along with native Jews a few months later.[80] It is the case that the government was trying and ultimately succeeded in suppressing these rowdy mobs of crusaders and seemed on the verge of restoring at least a superficial peace to the kingdom. However, there were still seething anger and deep hatred of Jews. Accusations of blasphemy, for example, gained currency. Jews were said to have been caught "mocking the Most High Creator our Lord Jesus Christ and his majesty in contempt, scorn and disdain ('in contemptum, spretum et vituperium') of the Lord's Passion and of the whole Christian faith."[81] The kingdom was like a time bomb waiting to explode.

The occasion for the explosion was a rumor that there was a plot among Muslims in Granada, the Jews, and lepers to bring Christendom and especially the kingdom of the Franks to its knees by poisoning the water supply. In the heightened state of collective nervousness—the continuing famine, the failure to appease God by mounting a crusade, the recent violence—the rumor won believers. Again a wave of atrocities overwhelmed the kingdom: thousands of lepers were burned alive, and the same fate befell hundreds of Jews. One site for the revenge was a little island situated beneath the Loire-valley castle town of Chinon, the same Chinon that had seen the judicial murder of Jews wrongfully convicted in the death of a Christian child four years before. In the summer of 1321, as many as 160 victims were immolated.[82]

The Leper Plot massacres were the next to the last straw for the remnant of resettled Jews who had persisted in remaining in France. The last straw was a fine of 150,000 pounds for participating in the plot. In fact, the Jewish communities were so weakened that they could pay almost nothing, and those members who could pay tried not to.[83] It is likely that some Jewish immigrants to the city of Besançon, now in France but at that time in the Holy Roman Empire, made the decision to migrate in reaction to the Leper Plot accusations and massacres and the financial exploitation of the crown.[84] Whether the crown believed in the justice of the fine and therefore the reality of the plot may be doubted, but official pronouncements certainly asserted its belief. And although there were rather severe denunciations of the violence against the Jews and lepers as a usurpation of the royal right of doing justice, the righteous zeal of the killers who ostensibly wanted to protect the Christian people was also lauded.[85]

A few thousand Jews were probably still resident in France as the year 1321 came to a close and in the first several months of 1322. We have extensive records of the systematic attempt to collect the fine (and of the paltry amounts the collectors managed to obtain).[86] The bankruptcy of the Jewish communities, coupled with the obvious undermining of Jews' respect for the crown that its actions were causing, encouraged further emigration.[87] The experience of resettlement effectively (if not officially) came to an end in 1322. If it is true, as Elizabeth Brown has argued, that there was no formal order of expulsion in 1322,[88] it would nevertheless be the case that only a very tiny remnant of the original Jewish settlers continued to live in the kingdom until 1327, when the twelve-year agreement expired. It was not renewed.

Conclusion

Much of what we know about the position of the Jews in medieval France at any time in the history of the Middle Ages comes from sources such as tax records and court cases, made by and for the politically dominant population of Christians. The records are in Latin or Old French and they invoke all the beliefs (and prejudices) of the majority population. On rare occasions, it is true, it is possible to get beyond these kinds of records and to reconstruct Jewish voices from Hebrew or French documents made by Jews themselves. It is necessary and beneficial to do this systematically and, where possible, regularly. But it is not the case, as some scholars have argued, that it is absolutely impossible to get at the authentic voice of the Jewish population in the (far too frequent) absence of such records. That, in part, is the historiographical importance of studying the Jews' return to France in 1315. The episode, from 1315 to 1322, must be reconstructed almost entirely from Latin and Old French documents of an administrative character, but read closely, these reveal a great deal about Jewish calculations, expectations, and hopes.[89]

First, Jews' willingness to return was based on rational calculations (tinged, to be sure, by an optimism that proved unreliable), rational calculations about the quality of political leadership likely to be in place after the death of Philip the Fair in 1314 and about the importance of the kind of negotiated obligations that marked the return of the Jews to France in 1315. What neither side—Christian royal authorities nor Jewish leadership—fully realized or faced up to, if either did realize it, was how tenuous and fragile the power of the crown was to control popular outpourings of anger and violence. To this extent both Jews in leadership positions and the French crown and its most intimate advisers were deluded by recent history: the expulsion of the Jews in 1306 was a magisterial act of state that seemed to testify to the awesome power of the crown. It did so, but only (or largely) because what the crown attempted did not elicit the active hostility of the populace at large. (One could mention a number of similar cases, such as the destruction of the widely suspected Templar Order in 1308, that fed the notion of the unchallengeability of royal power.) Superficially, the decision made by Louis X in 1315 to reverse the expulsion of the Jews—to turn back the clock—looked equally magisterial and definitive and seemed, again superficially, to confirm the authority of the crown.

In fact, the resettlement of Jews as privileged aliens and the raising of the possibility that their sojourn might be brief combined to give inspiration to those who looked on the Jews as their enemies to subvert the experiment. Even without the ecological catastrophe of the famine years, the experiment might not have been renewed. The famine, and the impetus it gave to people to act on their often paranoid fears of middlemen, speculators, and enemies of Christ and of France, more or less ended the resettlement by 1322. The fact—if it is a fact—that even a few Jews stayed in their "homeland" after that date, perhaps until 1327 and the formal conclusion of the experiment, seems remarkable in this light. But, perhaps, for a few families who had made their homes in France for a thousand years before 1306, not even the tragedies of expulsion or the murderous resettlement could utterly extinguish hope.

Notes

I wish to thank Mr. Benjamin Weiss for commenting on this paper in an earlier draft. I also wish to express my gratitude to the organizers of this conference for providing the incentive to rethink, revise, and expand on some of my earlier published conclusions on the return of the Jews to France in 1315.

1. Charles Baudon de Mony, "La Mort et les funérailles de Philippe le Bel, d'après un compte rendu à la cour de Majorique," *Bibliothèque de l'École des Chartes* 58 (1897): 12;

André Artonne, *Le Mouvement de 1314 et les chartes provinciales de 1315* (Paris: Alcan, 1912).

2. The most comprehensive studies of the development of the kingdom under Philip Augustus and Saint Louis are John Baldwin's *The Government of Philip Augustus: Foundations of French Royal Power in the Middle Ages* (Berkeley: University of California Press, 1986) and Jean Richard's *Saint Louis, roi d'une France féodale, soutien de la Terre sainte* (Paris: Fayard, 1983). The latter is now available in an abridged English translation, *Saint Louis: Crusader King of France,* ed. Simon Lloyd, trans. J. Birrell (Cambridge: Cambridge University Press, 1992).

3. *Ordonnances des rois de France de la troisième race,* ed. E.-J. Laurière, vol. 1 (Paris, 1723), 595–97.

4. Inferred from *Ordonnances,* 1:571–72, cap. 24.

5. William Jordan, *The French Monarchy and the Jews from Philip Augustus to the Last Capetians* (Philadelphia: University of Pennsylvania Press, 1989), 239–40.

6. Elizabeth Brown, "Philip V, Charles IV, and the Jews of France: The Alleged Expulsion of 1322," *Speculum* 66 (1991): 325. The record is inventoried in Paris: Archives Nationales (AN) JJ54 B no. 16, fol. 8 v., dated 29 August 1316, in French, this way: "concession d'un delai de paiement (déjà consenti par Louis le Hutin) aux juifs rentré dans le royaume de France pour les 22,500 l. qu'ils auraient dû acquitter à Louis le Hutin à la Saint-Remi dernierement passée, en recouvrant pour cela le tiers de créances qu'ils détenaient dans le royaume avant leur expulsion." I want to thank Ms. April Shelford and Ms. Leslie Tuttle for help in establishing that the inventory listing corresponds to Isidore Loeb's notice in "Les Expulsions des juifs de France au XIVe siécle," in *Jubelschrift zum siebzigsten Geburtstage des Prof. Dr. H. Graetz* (Breslau: S. Schottlaender, 1887), 41 n. 1, where he gives JJ542B no. 26 as the reference.

7. The estimate of annual royal income, roughly 450,000 pounds *parisis* (562,500 pounds *tournois*), is based on Borrelli de Serres's estimate as revised by Joseph Strayer, "The Costs and Profits of War: The Anglo-French Conflict of 1294–1303," in *The Medieval City,* ed. Harry A. Miskimin, David Herlihy, and A. L. Udovitch (New Haven, Conn.: Yale University Press, 1977), 273. For a fuller discussion of the complex calculations behind such estimates, see Joseph Strayer, *The Reign of Philip the Fair* (Princeton, N.J.: Princeton University Press, 1980), 146–51. The expulsion of 1306 had brought the crown approximately one million pounds, and barons with lordly rights over Jews benefited as well; see Jordan, *French Monarchy and the Jews,* 211–12.

8. Paris: AN, JJ54 B no. 16, fol. 8 v.: "Les Juifs paieront chaque année, à la Toussaint 10,000 l. jusqu'à concurrence de la somme prévue dans les conventions passés avec Louis le Hutin; au bout de 12 ans, ils paieront lesdites 22,500 l. en renonçant audit tiers de leurs anciennes créances les autres conventions restant inchangés"; Loeb, "Expulsions des juifs," 41 n. 1. For evidence of these apportioned periodic payments, see Robert Fawtier, ed., *Comptes du Trésor (1296, 1316, 1384, 1477)* (Paris: Imprimerie Nationale, 1930), no. 504, which records a total payment of 2,700 pounds for the Saint-John (24 June) financial term (the actual deposits were made on 29 May and 30 June): "De compositione facta per gentes Regis domini Ludovici cum Judeis qui fuerunt a regno expulsi anno ccc° vi° super regressu dictorum Judeorum ad regnum."

9. *Ordonnances,* 1:571–72, cap. 24.

10. This number (or percentage) is not quite arbitrary, but it is not firm either. Most scholars would probably agree that resettlement was on the modest side; see Philippe Wolff, "Quelques documents concernant les juifs de Toulouse," in *Les Juifs au regard de l'histoire: Mélanges en l'honneur de Bernhard Blumenkranz,* ed. Gilbert Dahan (Paris: Picard, 1985), 204. Yet good scholars like Béatrice Leroy ("Entre deux mondes politiques: Les Juifs du royaume de Navarre," *Archives juives* 20 [1984]: 35–40) and Yom Tov Assis ("Juifs de France réfugiés en Aragon XIIIe–XIVe siècles," *Revue des études juives* 142 [1983]: 309–10) suggest that much larger numbers returned.

11. I am using the word *stranger* in this paragraph and throughout the essay as it is now used in ordinary speech and was familiar in the Middle Ages in its various Latin and vernacular forms. *Advena* is the word used in the famous text in the Vulgate, "stranger in a strange land" ("advena . . . in terra aliena," Exodus 2.22; echoed in Acts 7.29). Although I will discuss legal issues repeatedly in this essay, I will not invoke the juristic usage of *stranger,* that is, a legal person without responsibilities to help others, sometimes employed in modern American jurisprudence; see Mary Ann Glendon, *Rights Talk: The Impoverishment of Political Discourse* (New York: Macmillan, 1991), 77. The precise meanings of the other categories—alien, sojourner, and enemy—will become clear in the course of the essay.

12. Gavin Langmuir, " 'Tanquam servi': The Change in Jewish Status in French Law about 1200," in *Toward a Definition of Antisemitism* (Berkeley: University of California Press, 1990), 190.

13. For a good general discussion of serfdom, see Guy Fourquin, "Serfs and Serfdom: Western European," in *Dictionary of the Middle Ages,* ed. Joseph Strayer (New York: Charles Scribner's Sons, 1988), 11:199–208. Of course, serfdom varied widely over time and region. The statements in the text are best applied, as indicated above, to northern France and England in the thirteenth and early fourteenth centuries. On contemporary notions of procedural due process, see Kenneth Pennington, *The Prince and the Law, 1200–1600: Sovereignty and Rights in the Western Legal Tradition* (Berkeley: University of California Press, 1993), 156–57, 161–63.

14. I treat the theme of *dominium* over Jews in a paper titled "Jews, Regalian Rights and the Constitution of Medieval France," which is to appear in the *AJS Review.*

15. In general, the models for such general charters (as opposed to those for individual Jews) were those granted in the eleventh century by Bishop Rudiger of Speyer for the Jews of that city and by Emperor Henry IV for the Jews of Worms. See Kenneth Stow, *Alienated Minority: The Jews of Medieval Latin Europe* (Cambridge: Harvard University Press, 1992), 98.

16. I have tried to bring together a large amount of evidence of this theory and its application in France and England in *French Monarchy and the Jews,* 30–213. Early modern jurists and scholars on the English side of the Channel read the fragmentary evidence about the status of the Jew (as against that of the serf) in the Middle Ages in the same way; see Jonathan A. Bush, " 'You're Gonna Miss Me When I'm Gone': Early Modern Common Law Discourse and the Case of the Jews," *Wisconsin Law Review* 1993, no. 5 (1993): 1254.

17. See Bush, " 'You're Gonna Miss Me When I'm Gone,' " 1257 (discussion of Sir Edward Coke's analysis of the medieval precedents).

18. *Ordonnances,* 1:596, caps. 7–8. Across the Channel in England the classification of the Jews as "aliens" was stimulated by their expulsion in 1290. Discussions of Jews—where these exist in English legal manuals written after that date—treat them explicitly as aliens or as assimilable to aliens and explain their historic status in England before the expulsion, despite obvious anomalies, in terms of "alienage"; Bush, " 'You're Gonna Miss Me When I'm Gone,' " 1231, 1251, 1255–65. It is certainly possible that the expulsion from France in 1306 encouraged a similar "simplification" of classification with regard to the legal status of Jews. If true, this might help explain the clarity and precision of doctrine and the effort at comprehensiveness in the charter of resettlement of 1315.

19. William Jordan, "Marian Devotion and the Talmud Trial of 1240," in *Religionsgespräche im Mittelalter,* ed. B. Lewis and F. Niewöhner, Wolfenbüttler Mittelalter-Studien 4 (Wiesbaden: Harrassowitz, 1992), 61–76.

20. *Ordonnances,* 1:596, cap. 9.

21. Ibid., 1:596, cap. 1.

22. Ibid., 1:596, cap. 3.

23. Ibid., 1:596, cap. 2. For Saint Louis's intent, see Jordan, *French Monarchy and the Jews,* 148–49.

24. See *Ordonnances,* 1:646.

25. Ibid., 1:596, caps. 12–16.

26. John Baldwin, *Masters, Princes and Merchants: The Social Views of Peter the Chanter and His Circle,* 2 vols. (Princeton, N.J.: Princeton University Press, 1970), 1:300.

27. Jordan, *French Monarchy and the Jews,* 134, 151.

28. This is one theme in the profound studies of Gaines Post on Bracton and various canonists, Romanists, and theologians of the twelfth and thirteenth centuries. See "Bracton on Kingship," *Tulane Law Review* 42 (1968): 519–54; and "Bracton as Jurist and Theologian on Kingship," in *Proceedings of the Third International Congress of Medieval Canon Law* (Vatican: Biblioteca Apostolica Vaticana, 1971), 113–30.

29. The closest one usually comes to such language in the Middle Ages is in charters of reconciliation following a rebellion—at least when the reconciliation was brought about by a concession or concessions from the crown. This, for example, is the flavor of Louis X's own charter to the nobility of Berry; see Artonne, *Mouvement de 1314,* 185–94.

30. See F. R. P. Akehurst's translation of cap. 34 of Beaumanoir's *Coutumes de Beauvaisis* (Philadelphia: University of Pennsylvania Press, 1992).

31. Pennington, *Prince and the Law,* 125–29, shows how strongly most Italian civilians and canonists held that the prince's free entering into a (morally acceptable) contract was absolutely binding, but they were enunciating these views in reaction to those who held contrary ones. Was this a mere "academic" argument? It is hard to say. French jurists, including those, like Pierre de Belleperche, associated with the court of Philip the Fair, also struggled over the issue, although, so far as I can determine, their views have to be inferred from discussions of the prince's right to seize private property. At least Pennington makes this inference (129 n. 37). See the very compressed and technical (not to say opaque) discussion on which he depends in Ennio Cortese, *La Norma giuridica spunti teorici nel diritto comune classico,* Ius Nostrum, Studi e Testi Pubblicati dall'Istituto di Storia del Diritto Italiano dell'Università di Roma, 6, 1 (Varese: Giuffré, 1962), 1:135–36. (I wish to thank my former colleague Professor Eugenio Biagini for helping me to make some sense of Cortese's remarks.) One may get a taste of the career of Pierre de Belleperche by pursuing the references in Strayer, *Reign of Philip the Fair,* index s.v. "Pierre de Belleperche."

32. On the "impervious" nature of moral precepts (that is, the view of many jurists that one category of duly sworn contracts, namely, those against divine law, lacked validity), Pennington, *Prince and the Law,* 130, has some good words. On the Jews' perception that the French kings did not feel bound by an oath of their (illustrious) predecessors where this oath did not accord with their contemporary moral views, see Joseph Shatzmiller, "Politics and the Myth of Origins: The Case of the Medieval Jews," in *Les Juifs au regard de l'histoire: Mélanges en l'honneur de Bernhard Blumenkranz,* ed. Gilbert Dahan (Paris: Picard, 1985), 56–58. I treat this theme at somewhat greater length in "Identity, (Self-) Fashioning and the 'Other' in France in the High Middle Ages" (in Russian), *Almanach: Odysseus* (1995): 79–91.

33. Beaumanoir, *Coutumes de Beauvaisis,* cap. 34, sec. 1000–1003, etc.

34. This concept has been applied, for example, to alien traders in modern Ghana; see Margaret Peil, "Host Reactions: Aliens in Ghana," in *Strangers in African Societies,* ed. William A. Shack and Elliott P. Skinner (Berkeley: University of California Press, 1979), 123–40. See also in *Strangers in African Societies,* Donald Levine, "Simmel at a Distance: On the History and Systematics of the Sociology of the Stranger," 21–36.

35. A similar pattern had existed in the eleventh and twelfth centuries, when "French" Jews, like the famous exegete Rashi, went to study in the Rhineland with the great sages there (and vice versa), thereby creating ties of affection that in many cases must have softened, without entirely eliminating, the sense of foreignness of the communities of learning. See Stow, *Alienated Minority,* 140; Colette Sirat, "Les Bases de la communication: Édition et circulation des textes manuscrits dans le monde juif," in *La Société juive à travers l'histoire,* vol. 4, *Le Peuple-Monde,* ed. Shmuel Trigano (Paris: Fayard, 1992–93), 219;

and, in the same volume of the collection of articles in which the Sirat essay appears, Gérard Nahon, "La Dimension du voyage," 340.

36. Jordan, *French Monarchy and the Jews,* 234–35. Similar patterns of behavior and feeling have been documented among other exile communities; see, for example, Cesare Colafemmina, "The Jews of Reggio Calabria from the End of the XVth Century to the Beginning of the XVIth Century," in *Les Juifs au regard de l'histoire: Mélanges en l'honneur de Bernhard Blumenkranz,* ed. Gilbert Dahan (Paris: Picard, 1985), 256–60.

37. *Ordonnances,* 1:596, cap. 1. Here, as elsewhere, I have adopted de Laurière's transcriptions and his use or, in this case, nonuse of diacritical marks such as the accent that would conventionally be put over the *a.* Such twelve-year periods for permitted residence of aliens were not uncommon; Lombards in Hainaut enjoyed similar privileges at about the same time. Léopold Devillers, ed., *Monuments pour servir à l'histoire des provinces de Namur, de Hainaut et de Luxembourg,* vol. 3 (Brussels: M. Hayez, 1874), 701.

38. *Ordonnances,* 1:596, cap. 10.

39. Jordan, *French Monarchy and the Jews,* 232–33.

40. One Hebrew source translated by Assis ("Juifs de France réfugiés," 310) expressed the sentiment in these words, "Allons, retournons vers les terres de notre patrie car elle est notre mère, et le roi est un prince bon et droit et il accomplira ce qui a été dit par sa bouche."

41. In a sense, we are moving here from legal to social history. Indeed, many authoritative canonists insisted that the legal category "enemy" (*hostis*) could not be applied to a Jew simply because he was a Jew ("Judaei vero non reputantur hostes"), although this insistence itself may be an indication of the desire of other lawyers to apply it; Bush, "'You're Gonna Miss Me When I'm Gone,'" 1258 n. 102. According to Hostiensis, perhaps the greatest of the thirteenth-century canonists, "Even if (*or* although) [Jews] are enemies of our faith [et si (*or* etsi) sint fidei nostrae hostes]," no Christian has the right ipso facto to violate the terms of toleration and protection under which they are permitted to live (as expressed in the famous and frequently reissued papal bull *Sicut judeis*); Hostiensis, *Decretalium Commentaria* (Venice, 1581), lib. V, De iudaeis, et saracenis, etc., cap. ix.

42. The texts are quoted in Joseph Shatzmiller, *Shylock Reconsidered: Jews, Moneylending, and Medieval Society* (Berkeley: University of California Press, 1990), 98.

43. This problematic interpretation is nonetheless offered by Shatzmiller: "After the expulsion of the Jews in 1306, the mood in France became almost nostalgic. The Jewish usurer, once hated and resented by so many, was now missed by all." Ibid., 98.

44. See Gilbert Dahan, *Les Intellectuels chrétiens et les juifs au moyen âge* (Paris: Editions du Cerf, 1990), 547–48.

45. *Ordonnances,* 1:595–96, preamble.

46. Contra Shatzmiller, *Shylock Reconsidered,* 98.

47. The chronicle evidence is discussed in William Jordan, "Princely Identity and the Jews in Medieval France," to be published in the proceedings of the Thirty-Fourth Wolfenbüttler Symposium, "Juden und Judentum in der Sicht der christlichen Denker im Mittelalter."

48. Assis, "Juifs de France réfugiés," 310.

49. *Ordonnances,* 1:596, cap. 4; Gustave Saige, *Les Juifs du Languedoc antérieurement au XIVe siècle* (Paris: Picard, 1881), 330–31 no. 57; Joseph Petit, ed., *Essai de restitution des plus anciens mémoriaux de la Chambre des Comptes de Paris* (Paris: F. Alcan, 1899), 24 no. 28.

50. *Ordonnances,* 1:604–5.

51. See Paris: AN, JJ54 B no. 16, fol. 8 v. (see note 8, above), dated 29 August 1316. See also Saige, *Juifs du Languedoc,* 333–34 no. 59, dated 1320, for evidence that the vigor of governmental enforcement was even then a continuing bone of contention.

52. Most of these questions or points of contention can be inferred from a later decree of the year 1317 that tries to clarify the situation; *Ordonnances,* 1:646, caps. 1–5. For a court case in 1319 in which some of the still-lingering issues were discussed, see Edgar

Boutaric, ed., *Actes du Parlement de Paris,* 2 vols. (Paris: H. Plon, 1863–67), 2:291 no. 5848.

53. The sentiment is expressed forcefully in a royal admonition to local officialdom on 23 June 1317; Boutaric, *Actes du Parlement,* 2:188 no. 4909.

54. *Ordonnances,* 1:647, cap. 13.

55. William Jordan, *The Great Famine: Northern Europe in the Early Fourteenth Century* (Princeton, N.J.: Princeton University Press, 1996).

56. See, for example, Priscilla Baumann, "The Deadliest Sin: Warnings against Avarice and Usury on Romanesque Capitals in Auvergne," *Church History* 59 (1990): 7–18.

57. "Chroniques de Saint-Denis," in *Recueil des historiens des Gaules et de la France,* ed. M. Bouquet and others, 24 vols. (Paris, 1738–1904), 20:698; and also in the same collection, "E Chronico anonymi Cadomensis," 22:25; "Excerpta e Memoriali historiarum, auctore Johanne Parisiensi," 21:662.

58. "Chronique rimée attribuée à Geoffroi de Paris," in *Recueil des historiens des Gaules et de la France,* ed. M. Bouquet and others, 24 vols. (Paris, 1738–1904), 22:162; Artonne, *Mouvement de 1314,* 74, 91 n. 2.

59. Artonne, *Mouvement de 1314,* 91, 182–84 no. 18; Charles-Victor Langlois, *Formules des lettres* (Paris: Imprimerie Nationale, 1890–97), art. 1, pp. 20–21 no. 5.

60. Langlois, *Formules des lettres,* art. 1, pp. 31–32 no. 10 (36).

61. *Ordonnances,* 1:606–8.

62. Odd Langholm, *Economics in the Medieval Schools: Wealth, Exchange, Value, Money and Usury according to the Paris Theological Tradition, 1200–1350,* Studien und Texte zur Geistesgeschichte des Mittelalters 29 (Leiden: E. J. Brill, 1992), 533–35.

63. Maurice Prou and Jules d'Auriac, eds., *Actes et comptes de la communauté de Provins de l'an 1271 à l'an 1330* (Provins: Imprimerie du Briard, 1933), 259. The reference dates from early 1320.

64. Boutaric, *Actes du Parlement,* 2:263 no. 5613; 22 December 1318.

65. S. H. Cuttler, *The Law of Treason and Treason Trials in Later Medieval France* (Cambridge: Cambridge University Press, 1981), 52.

66. See ibid., 118, on the use of this punishment for a counterfeiter in the later fourteenth century.

67. Boutaric, *Actes du Parlement,* 2:222 no. 5218, 233 no. 5327, 238–39 nos. 5376–77.

68. An investigation (3 March 1319) into the ring's activity is noted in Boutaric, *Actes du Parlement,* 2:274 no. 5713.

69. *Chronique normande du XIVe siècle,* ed. Auguste Molinier and Émile Molinier (Paris, 1882), 32. See Franck Collard, "Recherches sur le crime de poison au moyen âge," *Journal des savants* (January–June 1992): 100.

70. "Chroniques de Saint-Denis," 2:698; "Continuatio Chronici Guillelmi de Nangiaco," in *Recueil des historiens des Gaules et de la France,* ed. M. Bouquet and others, 24 vols. (Paris, 1738–1904), 20:615.

71. This is evidenced by his confirmation of the agreement while serving as regent, 29 August 1316 (Brown, "Philip V, Charles IV," 325), and by his promissory oath of 1317, referred to above (see note 54).

72. Boutaric, *Actes du Parlement,* 2:180 no. 4827.

73. Ibid., 2:191–92 no. 4936.

74. Ibid., 2:201 no. 5023.

75. Ibid., 2:222 no. 5230 (not 3230, as printed).

76. See ibid., 2:459–60 no. 6849, which appears to be a malicious or ignorant accusation against a Jewish man. See also 2:491 no. 7026. The offending couple appears to have been caught in the act. The woman was married and a Christian. The Jewish man was hanged.

77. "Chronique rimée attribuée à Geoffroi de Paris," 22:160.

78. On the events narrated in this paragraph, see Malcolm Barber, "The Pastoureaux of 1320," *Journal of Ecclesiastical History* 32 (1981): 143–66.

79. Émile-Auguste Bégin, "Histoire des juifs dans le nord-est de la France," *Mémoires de l'Académie de Metz* 24 (1842–43), pt. 1, p. 272.

80. Shlomo Simonsohn, *The Apostolic See and the Jews: History,* Studies and Texts 109 (Toronto: Pontifical Institute of Mediaeval Studies, 1991), 62.

81. Boutaric, *Actes du Parlement,* 2:353 no. 6355.

82. I have summarized here my description of these events in *French Monarchy and the Jews,* 245–46.

83. Ibid., 246.

84. See the data assembled in Joseph Morey, "Les Juifs en Franche-Comté au XIVe siècle," *Revue des études juives* 7 (1883): 12.

85. Langlois, *Formules des lettres,* art. 5, pp. 11–12 no. 2.

86. The records are available in *Les Journaux du Trésor de Charles IV le Bel,* ed. J. Viard (Paris: Imprimerie Nationale, 1917). See also Petit, *Essai de restitution,* 127. I have treated some aspects of the matter in *French Monarchy and the Jews,* 246. The problems are explored in Yves Dossat, "Les Difficultés d'un commissaire du roi à Toulouse en 1324–25," *Bulletin philologique et historique du comité des travaux historiques et scientifiques* (1978): 143–53. Dossat concludes that "le désordre et la confusion sont des faits certains."

87. See the evidence of movement to Navarre, for example, assembled by Béatrice Leroy, "Les Relations entre les juifs du Languedoc-Provence et les juifs navarro-aragonais: Quelques exemples aux XIIIe–XIVe siècles," in *Les Juifs à Montpellier et dans le Languedoc à travers l'histoire du moyen âge à nos jours,* ed. C. Iancu (Montpellier: Centre de recherches et d'études juives et hebraïques, 1988), 170.

88. Brown, "Philip V, Charles IV," 294–329.

89. See the encouraging remarks of Sherrill Cohen on doing early modern women's history in *The Evolution of Women's Asylums since 1500: From Refuges for Ex-Prostitutes to Shelters for Battered Women* (New York: Oxford University Press, 1992): "The sentiments of early modern women usually come to us filtered through the writing of others. . . . We must seek women's voices in the documents compiled by male record keepers or in the formulaic writing composed for women by notaries, clergy, and others who helped them to communicate in the styles of official discourse. Sometimes the sentiments of the women themselves come through unmistakably between the lines" (9–10).

CHAPTER 4

Strangers in Late-Fourteenth-Century London

Derek Pearsall

> *Many people—many nations—can find themselves holding, more or less wittingly, that "every stranger is an enemy." For the most part this conviction lies deep down like some latent infection; it betrays itself only in random, disconnected acts, and does not lie at the base of a system of reason.*
>
> Primo Levi, *Survival in Auschwitz: The Nazi Assault on Humanity* (1958; trans. 1961)

The question I ask in this essay is, Who was "the stranger" in the experience and vocabulary of a late-fourteenth-century Londoner, and what was the attitude toward strangers of such late-fourteenth-century Londoners as Chaucer and Langland?

The Words *Strange* and *Stranger* in Middle English

A stranger is one who is identified as "other" in relation to a group that perceives itself or desires to define itself as "one." The concept of the stranger is vital to the creation and preservation of closed communities; as Georg Simmel puts it in the famous essay "Der Fremde" (1908), the stranger is "an organic member of the group," both outside it and necessary to its efficient working.[1] Where a community feels itself to be under threat, the otherness of strangers will be thought of as potentially menacing, and hostility toward them will grow or be fomented. The threat may be perceived to be economic (as, for instance, in a shortage of jobs because of immigrants) or political (as, for instance, in a threat to national security because of the presence of nonnationals); when both fears are combined the outlook for strangers, as outsiders, is bleak. Even where there is no clearly identifiable external threat to a community, one may have to be invented, and continually reinvented, often in the form of demonized racial or religious "others," in order to preserve the established order within that community.

What is "strange," then, is what is construed as "other," and of course the meaning of the word, as it is applied, will vary with the nature of the group that is being defined in relation to the "other." Chaucer provides a convenient archive of examples of the way the Middle English words for "strange" and "stranger" are used, and the connotations and associations they may have.[2]

Chaucer uses the word *straunge* frequently, with a range of meanings that are illustrated also in the Middle English word *straungere.*[3] First, *straunge* means "foreign, from a country not one's own, from abroad," without connotation of odd or weird, and is applied thus to the warriors who come from all over the Near East and the Far East to fight in the lists for Palamon or Arcite in the Knight's Tale. Theseus and his court entertained them, we are told,

> And made revel al the longe nyght
> Unto the straunge lordes, as was ryght.
> (*Canterbury Tales,* I.2717–18)

In the Man of Law's Tale, Constance weeps that she shall be sent to a "strange nacion" (II.268); to her, it is just somewhere abroad. The connotation of hostile alienness is there, however, in the same tale, when Donegyld, Constance's mother-in-law, is said to have thought it an act of "despit" that her son "sholde take / So strange a creature unto his make" (II.699–700). Here *strange* means "alien," distantly and hostilely other, not just foreign but *Christian* as well (an ironic adaptation of the well-evidenced signification *straunge,* "barbarian").

Second, *straunge* means "not a member of one's social group," as more narrowly but still quite broadly defined. The "straunge folk" that Prudence warns Melibeus against in *Melibee* (*Canterbury Tales,* VII.1245) are people not of the family or household, or people who are not friends of the family. All such people one is to be wary of, and the wisdom of Prudence is supported by authorities such as Cato and Petrus Alphonsus (VII.1308–15). A similar meaning may be understood when Criseyde tearfully reproaches Pandarus for encouraging her to get embroiled in a love affair. How can she trust "straunge," she says (using the plural adjective as a substantive) when the one she took to be her best friend betrays her in this way (*Troilus and Criseyde,* ii.411–13). She means, as does Prudence in *Melibee,* those who are not kin or household and not family friends.

Third, *straunge* means "not one of the family," more strictly defined in terms of kinship. In the Clerk's Tale, people are worried that "a straunge successour" may take Walter's heritage if he has no heir (IV.138): they mean someone who is not a member of the ruling family. January has the same concern in the Merchant's Tale lest his heritage "sholde falle / In straunge hand" (IV.1439–40) if he does not marry and beget an heir. Pandarus, when he is organizing Criseyde's visit to Troilus's sickbed, says that she should go in separately because she is "straunge" and Troilus will therefore make an effort for her "to forbere / His ese" (*Troilus,* ii.1660–61). Here it means simply "not one of the family."

The word *straungere* is used only four times in Chaucer, three times in *Boece,* and once in the *Legend of Good Women,* with something of the same range of meanings as *straunge,* though there is a revealing comment on Dido's first taking a fancy to Aeneas in the *Legend of Dido*:

And, for he was a straunger, somwhat she
Likede hym the bet, as, God do bote,
To som folk ofte newe thyng is sote.
(*Legend of Good Women,* 1075–77)

The tone of this suggests that it is a perversity of newfangledness to be attracted to strangers. This comment is not in the corresponding passage in Virgil.

Chaucer does not use *alien* as noun or adjective (he uses it once as a verb, in *Boece*), even though it was quite common in Middle English. It overlapped in meaning with *straunge* and *straungere* but seems, from the citations in the *OED,* to have had a particular and stronger sense—"excluded" (we are made "aliene" from the bliss of heaven through sin, says Rolle), "utterly different in nature" ("we dwell here als aliens"; *Prick of Conscience*).

The word *foreyne,* though it was available as a noun to cover some of the same meanings as *straungere,* is used by Chaucer only as an adjective, and only in *Boece,* as a translation of Latin *alien-*. His one use of *foreyne* as substantive is in the *Legend of Good Women* (1962), where it has the meaning "privy, latrine," being abbreviated from *chambre foreyne,* "a room outside." The word *foreigner* does not become current until the fifteenth century.[4]

There was, one might say, looking at this evidence, a disposition in the language to reinforce and solidify relations within groups. One could call it a verbal architecture of xenophobia, or one could call it a verbal expression of the principle of community, but it seems embedded in the language.[5]

Strangers in London: Noncitizens

If we look now at some of the realities that surrounded late-fourteenth-century Londoners, we find that from the point of view of London citizens a large number of their fellow Londoners were, as far as the record went, "strangers" or "foreigners" (in the Latin of the records usually *forinsecus*). Among the populace there were the enfranchised, who were citizens or freemen of the city, qualified to exercise political rights as well as to pay taxes, and alone legally entitled to buy wholesale for retailing.[6] And then there were the unenfranchised, and mostly unenfranchisable, called "foreigners" or "strangers," even though they came from England and even from London—and not to be confused with "aliens," born overseas, and commonly so called in the London and guild records (in the Latin of the records usually *extraneus*). Foreigners performed menial tasks as porters, water carriers, hucksters, or in casual labor (they are memorably congregated in Glutton's tavern in *Piers Plowman,* C.VI.361–75),[7] or in producing goods on their own premises under the "putting-out" system for sale by citizens; these are the people whose painful life is so sympathetically described by Langland, "the wo of this wommen þat wonyeth in cotes" (C.IX.83). Some jobs, such as basket weaving or the peeling of reeds for the making of cheap tapers (a job mentioned by Langland), fell almost entirely into their hands. They would also sell, semilegally (like modern barrow boys), from market stalls, or they would rent shops, probably no more than about five feet wide and ten feet deep, with just a frontage on the street. Attempts to restrict their retailing activities included prohibiting them from using the street to sell or advertise their wares and, in 1463, moving them all out to an inconvenient district called Blanche-Appleton near Mark Lane.[8]

Distinctions between the *pluis sufficeauntz,* the better people, and the *populo minuto,* the "smale people," between citizens and "foreigners," became sharper as the fourteenth century went on, especially in the larger towns like London, where there was a greater complexity in economic relationships and a consequently greater need, among those who felt that their status was threatened, to signal class distinctions more decisively.[9] It became even more difficult for "foreigners" to get admission to citizenship. They had to secure a broader-than-usual basis of approval, including the assent of a ward meeting and the support of the citizens in the trade they professed.[10] They were most unlikely to get this support unless they were wealthy and could pay for it, and of course they were not in a very good position to become wealthy. It is a familiar trap.

In addition to these "foreigners," and to some extent mixed in with them, there were also the "strangers" who came from out of town to sell their goods. These were a menace to the citizens, as they tended to undercut monopolistic price-fixing, and they needed to be excluded, not just controlled. The guild and municipal records are full of the city's attempts to do this. Country people who brought goods into the city were relentlessly pursued by the city and guild ordinances, the coal vendor because his sacks were too small, the dairywoman because her butter was "corrupt."[11] The fishmongers tried to prevent outsiders from peddling fish in the poorer quarters of the city or from bringing small boats to Billingsgate quay and selling their catch. They secured a retail monopoly in 1364 and managed to keep the price of herring twice as high as it was in the country.[12] John of Northampton, when he was mayor, tried to roll back this legislation, and encouraged country dealers, which is one reason he enraged the powerful victualling companies and their leader, the unspeakable Brembre, and was soon removed. There were physical assaults by London fishmongers on "foreign" fish sellers in 1382, and in the same year a fishmonger called John Filiol vowed he would call the mayor a "falsus scurro vel harelot" and fight him at Horsedoune.[13] We should not assume that Mayor John of Northampton did what he did solely because the care of London's poor was dear to his heart;[14] and even if we think Langland is likely to have shown a more scrupulous concern, we have to recognize that in his constant sniping at "regraterye," or unauthorized retail dealing (e.g., C.III.82, VI.232), he is attacking the very people who were selling more cheaply than the victualling monopolies wanted. Like many people of his (or any other) day, he was influenced by claims that trade needed to be regulated in the interests of the consumer, to ensure fair prices, regular supplies, high quality, and so on.

In contrast to Langland, Chaucer of course hardly recognizes the existence of these "foreigners." His London pilgrims are citizens (Merchant, Man of Law, Guildsmen, probably the Doctor) or they are attached to citizen groups (Cook, Manciple). As far as Chaucer is concerned, "foreigners," a group nearly as large in numbers in London as citizens, are invisible. If they are to be found in his work, it will be in the "suburbes," where the Canon's Yeoman and his master have their "pryvee fereful residence," "lurkynge in hernes and lanes blynde" among robbers and thieves (*Canterbury Tales,* VIII.657–60). Chaucer alludes here to the kind of shantytowns that grew up outside the walls and jurisdiction of medieval cities, with dead-end lanes running between the rough huts and hovels, where petty criminals, secondhand dealers, and tinkers mixed with other "strangers" trying to eke out a living.

Strangers in London: Immigrants from the Provinces

Among these "strangers" there are likely to have been many immigrants newly arrived from other parts of England. Figures for the replenishment rate of recorded Londoners show that without constant immigration there would have been a population decline.[15] But it is hard to get numbers. Names are no certain guide to origin, because place-name surnames were kept for generations and of course apprentices could take the names of their masters (as happened with Chaucer's grandfather), but they are a help. Figures for early-fourteenth-century place-name surnames show half the population of London as being from the home counties, and a fifth from East Anglia (including Lincolnshire), and later in the century London became still more of a melting pot, with a larger proportion of immigrants coming from beyond the home counties.[16] Ekwall points to the emergence of the London dialect as an east midland dialect by 1350 as evidence that there must have been considerable immigration from the east midlands (in which he includes East Anglia) before that point and especially in the early fourteenth century.[17] One important reason for the large scale of immigration from East Anglia (a quarter of Ekwall's names for the east midlands for the period 1250–1350 are from Norfolk) is the expansion of the London cloth trade in the fourteenth century: Norfolk had long been the center of a cottage industry in textiles, and the expansion in London would naturally draw off experienced workers.

Immigrants came from all ranks, walks, and stages of life, tradesmen, clerks, people of means, though many of those recorded came as apprentices, whether as the younger sons of well-to-do families or as sons of less well-to-do families willing to pay a pound or two for the privilege. The city tried to prevent bondmen's sons coming to London to sign up as apprentices,[18] and peddlers and beggars were likewise banned (one remembers Langland's distaste for both groups; *Piers Plowman,* C.V.65,70, IX.61). There were a fair number, according to Ekwall's figures, from the west midlands and the north, as well as some from Scotland, and a sprinkling of Welsh and Irish. They often preserved their dialects, especially when they fell in with people from the same areas, or were taken on as apprentices (or as groups of apprentices) by individuals from the same places. They often kept close connections with their *patria* in the provinces, sending messages and presents to their families and neighbors, retiring there or retreating there in time of plague, though rarely if they came from beyond the home counties, the south midlands, and East Anglia.

One can see here a reason why a poem like *St. Erkenwald,* with a London subject, might have been written in a difficult northwest midland dialect. One can see too the possible reason for a certain patrician quality in Chaucer's provincial references. The northern students of the Reeve's Tale were probably fair game for a laugh for anyone in London who had come across the medieval equivalent of a Geordie, though Chaucer was of course the first to attempt this joking imitation of a provincial dialect.[19] The location of the Reeve himself as coming from Bawdeswell, a village in Norfolk, seems unusually specific. Bawdeswell was a small place, but two of Ekwall's fourteenth-century London immigrants are recorded as having come from there, along, incidentally, with four from the Cambridgeshire village of Trumpington, the setting for the Reeve's Tale, and two from Holderness, the scene of the Summoner's Tale.[20] That one of the nastiest people in the *Canterbury Tales* should come from Norfolk seems a gratuitous slur, and one suspects that Chaucer is playing on Londoners' contempt for parvenu immigrants from that area, especially given that they came into London in such numbers.[21] There is a touch of Norfolk in the Reeve's own speech (e.g., I.3864, 3888), not consistently maintained, but enough to tap the phobia that Londoners had for people from the provinces. Chaucer could rely on a similar metropolitan prejudice when he has the Parson, who declares himself to be "a southren man," speak slightingly of alliterative verse, rhyming "rum, ram, ruf, by lettre" (Parson's Prologue, X.42–43). Alliterative verse, though not unknown in London, was recognized to be a provincial phenomenon, and there would be easy laughs at the expense of someone like William Langland, up from the west country, writing (and probably speaking) alliterative verse, and in every respect a hopeless outsider.

Langland himself, even though a recent immigrant, may not have been entirely free from this prejudice against the provinces (which is still the only quality, in the last analysis, that identifies a Londoner as a Londoner). I have never been quite sure why Langland creates a penitent Welshman,

> ·euan-·elde-a·eyn-yf-y-so-moche-have-
> Al-that-y-wikkedly-wan-sithen-y-witte-hadde (C.VI.310–11),

to reinforce the theme of restitution, whether because he wants to show Welshmen in a bad light, as terrible sinners, or in a good light, as eager to make restitution, or just because "·euan" (Evan) makes a good alliteration with the key word "·elde." But there is a Welshman, "Gryffyth the Walshe," in Glutton's tavern (C.VI.373), and elsewhere Langland clearly voices a common prejudice against Irish priests (C.XXII.221) and uses Norfolk in a contemptuous reference by Covetousness as an example of a remote place where no one knows how to speak French (B.V.239).[22]

Merchant Strangers

A more conspicuous class of strangers in fourteenth-century London was made up of the alien merchants, or "merchant strangers." To use the parlance of the modern U.S. Immigration Department, these were less like resident aliens, holding green cards, than like J-1 visa holders. They stayed in London for quite long periods, certainly longer than the local merchants liked, but they did not live there.

There had long been foreign merchants in London, not so many from Flanders and Gascony, major trading partners where the trade was mostly carried on by English merchants, as from Germany and Italy. Their position was somewhat contested. Generally, they were popular with the king, who extracted higher customs taxes from them, and with the magnates, who were happy to trade directly with foreign merchants and so save the profits that otherwise went to the English middlemen, but they were not so popular with the English merchants. Alien merchants were not unwelcome as long as they restricted themselves to the carrying trade, but they became extremely unwelcome if they tried to trade within England or among themselves.[23] The city of London constantly tried to limit the stay of foreign merchants to forty days; the crown just as constantly tried to set this aside. The London merchants had, of course, ways of persuading the king to put their interests first, at least temporarily. In 1377, Brembre made a large loan to the crown; in the same year Edward III, replying to a petition from the mayor, aldermen, and citizens of London, decreed that alien merchants should not sell to one another for resale within the city, nor should they engage in any retail trade, excepting only for the merchants of the Hanse of Almaine (who had long had a privileged position within the city).[24] But in the Parliament of 1378, John of Gaunt and the magnates gave aliens freedom to trade wholesale and to some extent retail and with each other, and in 1383 it was again promulgated that strange victuallers might come and go and were not to be hindered in their trade.[25] And all the time there was on the London statute books an ordinance of Edward I requiring that an alien merchant who was of sufficient status and repute and who was prepared to pay all customary taxes and charges should be admitted as an equal citizen "and he shall be in every way on an equal footing with them, as well in bearing the charges as in enjoying the franchise."[26] It is true that a few were taken into fraternities and made citizens if they were prepared to forgo royal exemption from taxation, but they were not admitted into livery companies and very few received letters of denization.[27] Jealousy and suspicion were always fostered by the ease with which they won royal favor, and also by their dabbling in the doubtful profession of brokerage. John de Marconovo, a Venetian broker in London in the early 1400s, paid five pounds for honorary membership in the grocers' fraternity (an offshoot of the company) and began to make presents of wine for the company's feasts; one of the wardens noted in the margins of his accounts, "Hit is to drede we bye þylk pipe full dere."[28]

From time to time, open hostility would break out, as much the result of a general animosity against foreigners as of trade rivalry. The Lombard merchants of Lucca, who had taken over many of the banking and moneylending activities of the Jews after 1290, were the object of much hostility, and Reason, recommending to the king in *Piers Plowman* that he should put "love" in charge of his economic affairs, makes a special point of condemning the "Lumbardus of Lukes, þat leuen by lone as Iewes" (C.IV.194; compare C.VI.241). Similarly, in the Parliament of 1376, the Commons pray that the Lombards, having no other business but that of "Brokours," may be banished from the realm, because they practice usury and are often really "Juys, & Sarazins, & privees Espies"; furthermore, they are responsible for having introduced sodomy ("un trop horrible vice qui ne fait pas a nomer") into England (*Rot.Parl.* iii.332). In the romance of *Beues of Hamtoun*, the English translator introduces an exciting passage in which Bevis battles against what seems to be the whole population of London; the people have been deceived by a wicked steward into opposing King Edgar's decision that Bevis's son should be restored to his father's English lands.[29] The battle (4323–538) is against unspecified London people, but toward the climax of the battle (4497) a Lombard emerges as the ringleader of Bevis's enemies, almost as if the translator became aware that he needed to "alienize" this native opposition to an English hero. In the later Chetham manuscript (Manchester, John Rylands Library, MS Chetham 8009), of the fifteenth century, the London opposition to Bevis is dominated by Lombards from the start (4102).

Other Lombard merchants who had received royal license to trade retail in mercery were particularly obnoxious to the London mercers, and were frequently involved in street brawls. On 28 June 1357, there was a vicious and premeditated attack by several London mercers and their servants on two Lombard merchants that clearly had its roots in economic rivalry. The city authorities were more than usually negligent in bringing action, but the Lombards, petitioned the crown. The Council ordered the imprisonment of some of the assailants identified by the Lombards, but they were released soon after. The Lombards petitioned again in 1359, and the procedure was repeated; the assailants were finally brought before the city authorities, at the command of the Council, and fined.[30]

The murder of Nicholas Sardouche, another merchant from Lucca, somewhat later is a more sinister demonstration of the poisonous mix of economic jealousy and xenophobic hatred, and of the lethargy of the authorities in dealing with it. Sardouche had been brought before the mayor's court on 29 November 1368, on the petition of the silkwomen of London, on charges of forestalling the market in silk, buying up all he could find and forcing the price up; he had also been using his own balances to weigh the silk, which was against the city ordinances. The case dragged on, and the silkwomen petitioned the crown; much to the annoyance of the city authorities, the case was now taken into the royal jurisdiction. Sardouche was eventually brought to trial on a whole array of charges, including smuggling, forestalling, and exporting bullion, but he was pardoned on payment of a fee of two hundred pounds. Summoned again before the mayor and aldermen on 22 June 1369, Sardouche produced the writ of protection that he said the king had granted him because of threats against his person. The threats were very real, and the writ of protection little use, because eighteen months later he was killed in a brawl that "arose out of personal animosity but which was undoubtedly inflamed by trade jealousy and ill-feeling."[31] The man who was accused of killing him, John de More, a mercer, was discussing with Sardouche how to renegotiate a debt that he owed to Sardouche but was offended by the Italian's "unseemly and insulting boasting,"[32] and in the brawl that followed Sardouche was killed by two men who happened to be passing and whom John de More claimed not to know. De More was tried and acquitted.

There is a puzzle here, in the dilatoriness of the two rival jurisdictions: one would have expected at least that each would wish to assert the primacy of its own juridical authority. But it appears that neither the royal nor the city authorities had much at heart the execution of justice upon native-born Englishmen for killing foreigners.

Tolerance of alien merchants was particularly sorely tested, as we have seen, in the late 1370s, when there was particularly rapid growth in foreign trade.[33] There are some circumstances relating to the expansion of the wool trade, specifically, that have to do with the fate of one important and representative "stranger" and that need to be explained.

The English wool trade was the basis of English prosperity in the thirteenth and early fourteenth centuries. It was very largely the export of unmade wool, principally to the cloth-making centers of Flanders. Because of their monopoly of the trade, English wool exporters were able to charge a high price, and their profits were enormous. In the end, the huge differential in wool prices between England and Flanders (a sack that sold for four pounds in England might fetch twelve pounds in Flanders) was bound to result in the growth of an indigenous cloth industry to take advantage of low prices at home. The Flemish industry, meanwhile, already forced to concentrate on the luxury trade (like the Merchant's "Flaundryssh bever hat"; General Prologue, I.272) because of the high cost of raw materials, had to drive down wages to cope with high costs; this resulted in urban revolutions against the patriciate throughout the early fourteenth century, a steep decline in production, further accelerated after the Flemish civil war of 1379–85, and the movement of cloth production to other parts of the Low Countries, as well as its expansion in England. Contemporary chroniclers and later historians attribute the growth of the native cloth industry to the wise economic policy of Edward III, but in fact all the crown did was to interfere, in what it saw as its own short-term interests, in these large-scale shifts in patterns of industry and commerce.[34] At best one could speak of a royal policy of fitful protectionism; at worst, and more commonly, Edward was prepared to raise money for his French wars by any expedient that suggested itself.

England was now the clothiers' promised land, and many Flemish immigrants came over to swell the number of native cloth workers who were coming into London, as we have seen, from other parts of England. Cloth exports expanded dramatically, from two thousand cloths at the beginning of the fourteenth century to fifty thousand by the middle. Meanwhile, wool exports declined from thirty thousand sacks to ten thousand by the end of the fourteenth century.

There was a particular expansion of the cloth industry in the west of England, working directly with high-quality Cotswold wool, and when Chaucer declares that the Wife of Bath's cloth making surpassed that of Ypres and Ghent (General Prologue, I.448), he is not unaware that he is doing a bit of useful propaganda for home industry and the export drive. It is this export drive that led indirectly to the murder of Janus Imperial, a Genoese merchant, on 26 August 1379. Paul Strohm, in a brilliant essay on the facts and implications of the murder, shows how the murder appears to have been very much in the interests of the London wool merchants, the Merchants of the Staple, and against the interests of the crown.[35] Janus Imperial was in London to negotiate a deal with the crown to have wool exported from Southampton in Genoese ships and to pay the customs duty to the king directly and not to the Staple at Calais.[36] Many wool growers, including magnates with estates in the south and west, stood to profit from such a deal, and so did the growing cloth industry around Bath. So the London wool merchants had Janus Imperial murdered, it appears, by a couple of hit men who started a quarrel by pretending to trip over the Genoese merchant's outstretched foot and then stabbed him in the ensuing brawl. The case was a cause célèbre. The strange thing is the lassitude with which the murder was followed up. One would have expected a fierce determination on the part of the king and his justices to bring the instigators of the murder to trial, but in the end only one of the small-fry was executed. The crown was perhaps of two minds: there were the immediate profits to be obtained from the Genoese connection, but on the other hand the Staple was a regular and reliable source of income and the merchants of the Staple were a handy source of loans. But there was something else, not entirely rational in economic or any other terms, what Paul Strohm calls "the idiot wind of the inexplicable" that blows through the gaps in the record. Janus Imperial was murdered, but there was no great concern about his being dead. He was, after all, a foreigner, and foreigners step in and out of cultural systems at our convenience. They are always liable to be randomly persecuted or done away with, depending on the particular circumstances of their presence in the host body. Gospel exhortations to universal brotherhood (Matthew 12.50), Christian recognition of universal strangerhood ("We dwell here als aliens"), even Paul's very practical recommendations about showing hospitality to strangers ("for thereby some have entertained angels unawares"; Hebrews 13.2), are likely to have little effect in combating the economic and social imperatives to keep strangers "strange." In history, Christian communities practiced an exclusivism only slightly less intransigent than that of the people from whom they inherited much of their traditional practice.

The Massacre of the Flemings, and Chaucer's Allusion to It

The Jews should provide us here with our prime examples of the racial hatred that is always ready to break out in closed communities, but they of course had been expelled from England in 1290. Chaucer's Prioress's Tale and other anti-Jewish stories of the fourteenth century express something of the virulent hatred of the Jews that persisted, but, in the absence of actual Jews to vent it on, it was in many ways a form of rhetoric.

But there was a community in London that was destined to endure, in reality, the Londoners' hatred of foreigners. I have described how large numbers of Flemish weavers and other cloth workers came over, from the 1350s on, to work in London's rapidly growing textile industry. There were other continental immigrants, especially Germans from Cologne come to work as goldsmiths, woodworkers, and cheese makers, but the Flemings were much the largest community; there were probably nearly a thousand of them, many of them poor and most of them without families.[37] They were needed by the growing textile industry, but they were distrusted and persecuted with regulations. They were imprisoned for acting as brokers, for selling wine and cheese retail, and for keeping lodging houses for aliens to which they admitted "men of ill-fame, evildoers, thieves and prostitutes";[38] Flemish women were commonly accused of being prostitutes, like Langland's "Purnel of Flaundres" in Glutton's tavern (C.VI.367).[39] The mayor and aldermen wanted to lay down regulations to control the Flemings and place them under the direct jurisdiction of the city; a major concern seems to have been that they would make common cause with native workers in the trade and so set up a coven or conspiracy (that is, go on strike) to the inconvenience of the masters.[40] The weavers' guild wanted them made subject to their own ordinances and taxes, but they were exempted by royal letters patent in 1352 and allowed to form their own guild. An added complication was that the immigrant weavers themselves did not always get along. Special arrangements were made in 1370 for unemployed Flemish weavers to assemble at the churchyard of St. Lawrence Pountenay to seek employment, whereas the workers from Brabant were to gather at St. Mary Somerset.[41] This was because of friction and outbreaks of rowdiness between the two groups.

Agitation and conflict continued, and in 1378, when feeling against foreigners was running high because of fears of invasion, the London weavers demanded again that Flemish weavers should be placed under their direct control, insinuating that the Flemish were "for the most part exiled from their own country as notorious malefactors."[42] Such slanders are of course the common currency of anti-immigrant propaganda, and one can see more of it in the comment from two centuries later of John Stow, who on the whole is pleased to report from his researches any strong action against the menace of immigrants. In a reference to the London of his own day, he comments that Billingsgate ward has fifty-one households of strangers, who give twenty pounds a year for a house formerly let for four marks, because it is so conveniently close to the waterside. This of course is very inconvenient for the locals. Furthermore, thirty years before, when there were only three Netherlanders in the ward, it used to yield twenty-seven pounds a year for poor relief, but now barely eleven pounds, "for the stranger will not contribute to such charges as other Citizens doe."[43]

The fiercest outbreak of anti-immigrant hatred came on Friday, 14 June 1381, the day in London when the villagers and craftsmen from Kent had their rebellion hijacked by local workers, journeymen, apprentices, and malcontents. Excited by their success in killing the Archbishop of Canterbury in the Tower and scaring the life out of the king and his company, the rioters descended on John of Gaunt's palace of the Savoy and scattered through the city, looking for anyone who was hated or despised or feared. Immigrant workers were obvious targets, and every chronicle reports the massacre of the Flemings that ensued. Here is the brief account in *The Anonimalle Chronicle,* generally accepted to be the most reliable of the chronicle accounts of the Peasants' Revolt:

> This done [the setting of the head of the Archbishop above the gate on London Bridge], they went to the church of St. Martin's in the Vintry, and found therein thirty-five Flemings, whom they dragged outside and beheaded in the street. On that day were beheaded 140 or 160 persons. Then they took their way to the places of the Lombards and other aliens, and broke into their houses, and robbed them of all their goods that they could discover. So it went on for all that day and the night following, with hideous cries and horrible tumult.[44]

The *London Letter Book H* reports similarly on the massacre of the Flemings in the Vintry Ward and adds that "in one heap there were lying about forty headless persons who had been dragged forth from the churches and from their houses."[45] The *Polychronicon* adds the detail that the rioters made for the banks of the Thames, where most of the Flemings lived (in Stow's day, too, as we have seen).[46] Walsingham, generally less reliable, speaks of Flemings being dragged out for beheading from the church of the Austin Friars as well as from an unnamed parish church, and Froissart, not reliable at all, speaks of a general slaughter, and, more plausibly, of the rioters looting the houses of the Lombards and making free with their taverns.[47]

The circumstances were indeed ideal for attacks on foreigners. The Poll Tax may have triggered the revolt in Essex and Kent, but by now, in a London temporarily liberated from customary restraints, we are watching the acting out of pent-up hatreds, feuds, and discontents. There were economic reasons for the attacks on the Flemings, in the Londoners' jealousy of what they perceived as economic privileges granted to the aliens and in their fear of lost jobs, and there were political reasons, too: French and Castilian fleets had been raiding English coastal towns and penetrating right up into the Thames estuary. They were not Flemish fleets, but they were foreign fleets, and the Flemings were foreigners, and they were handy, and that was enough. We have to allow too for that "idiot wind of the inexplicable," or, as it may appear, if we think of xenophobia as "like some latent infection," the all too explicable.

Chaucer, of course, in his account of the matter, disappears in a luminous cloud of enigma, like some Homeric deity on the battlefield. For him the shouts of the London rioters as they pursue the Flemings are like the cries and caterwauling of the farmyard beasts and workers as they chase the fox in the Nun's Priest's Tale:

> Certes, he Jakke Straw and his meynee
> Ne made nevere shoutes half so shrille

> Whan that they wolden any Flemyng kille,
> As thilke day was made upon the fox. (VII.3394–97)

It is a brutally trivializing reference, and cruelly suggestive of the glee that some Londoners may have felt at the fortuitous removal of a public nuisance.[48] Most critics have been silent about the passage. Strohm argues that the "troubling social implications" of the passage are evaded through the dehistoricizing effects of the tale's stylization; others have tried more implausible rescue acts, or have concentrated on other interesting aspects of the passage.[49] But it is disturbing that Chaucer allows his poetry here to become associated with an unthinking dehumanization of a whole group of "strangers." In some real sense what he does is unpardonable, or rather, as we have learned to say, with Derrida when he speaks of Paul de Man's excursion into anti-Semitism, at least "disastrous."[50]

Notes

I am grateful to Barbara Hanawalt, Paul Strohm, David Wallace, and particularly to David Aers, for reading this paper and making many valuable suggestions for improving it.

1. Georg Simmel, "Der Fremde" (The stranger), in *Introduction to the Science of Sociology,* ed. Robert E. Park and Ernest W. Burgess, 3d ed. (Chicago: University of Chicago Press, 1969), 322–27. Simmel writes elsewhere, "The Stranger is an element of the group itself," and continues, "Mutually repulsive and opposing elements here compose a form of joint and interacting unity" (322).

2. The convenience has to do with the availability now of the excellent new concordance by Larry D. Benson, *A Glossarial Concordance to the Riverside Chaucer,* 2 vols. (New York: Garland, 1993). Quotations from Chaucer in this chapter are from Larry D. Benson, ed., *The Riverside Chaucer* (Boston: Houghton Mifflin, 1987).

3. The senses of *stranger* current in Middle English, as given in the *OED,* are (1) foreigner; (2) newcomer, not a native; (3) visitor; (4) unknown person; (5) nonmember of a society or group, such as a guild; (6) person not of one's kin. These correspond to senses a, e, f, b, c, d, respectively, in the *MED.* There are of course other uses of the word *straunge* (to mean "unusual," "extreme," "abnormal or surprising," "distant or unfriendly") that do not have exact parallels in the uses of the word *straungere,* though they may have connotative associations.

4. Chaucer does not have the wonderful word *outcomlyng,* used in *Cleanness* in the vivid description of the attack upon Lot's house by the people of Sodom, who hate him, they suddenly find, because he is an alien: "Wost thou not wel that thou wones here a wyye strange / An outcomlyng, a carle? We kylle of thin heued!" Malcolm Andrew and Ronald Waldron, eds., *The Poems of the Pearl Manuscript,* York Medieval Texts, 2d series (London: Edward Arnold, 1978), 875–76.

5. It is to be a long time before *l'étranger* will be celebrated as a cultural hero (by Albert Camus) or as "the Outsider" (by Colin Wilson). When that happens, it will not be because words have changed meaning, or because attitudes toward "strangers" have changed, but because the qualities of excludedness and differentness are being paradoxically reappropriated for the purposes of a specific political agenda.

6. The ranks of the enfranchised (and, of course, the unenfranchised) included women as well as men, but women, though they could be citizens, members of guilds, and freewomen, were not allowed to participate in urban government. See Kay E. Lacey, "Women and Work in Fourteenth and Fifteenth Century London," in *Women and Work in Pre-Industrial England,* ed. Lindsey Charles and Lorna Duffin (London: Croom Helm, 1985), 24, 45–47.

7. Langland is quoted from William Langland, *Piers Plowman: An Edition of the C-Text,* ed. Derek Pearsall, York Medieval Texts, 2d series (London: Edward Arnold, 1978).

8. The information in this paragraph is mostly from Sylvia L. Thrupp, *The Merchant Class of Medieval London (1300–1500)* (Chicago: University of Chicago Press, 1948), 3. See also Elspeth M. Veale, "Craftsmen and the Economy of London in the Fourteenth Century," in *Studies in London History Presented to Philip Edmund Jones,* ed. A. E. J. Hollaender and William Kellaway (London: Hodder & Stoughton, 1969), 142–43. There is an important essay by Sylvia Thrupp, "Aliens in and around London in the Fifteenth Century," in the same volume, but it is a specialized study based on the fragmentary exchequer records of the subsidy on aliens introduced in 1440 and on a comparatively small number of alien wills surviving from after 1417, and it is not immediately relevant in the present context.

9. Thrupp, *Merchant Class,* 14–16.

10. Ibid., 70–71

11. Ibid., 25

12. Ibid., 95–96

13. A. H. Thomas, ed., *Calendar of Select Pleas and Memoranda of the City of London, 1381–1412* (Cambridge: Cambridge University Press, 1932), 22, 36.

14. For the background in city politics to these and other conflicts involving "strangers," see Ruth Bird, *The Turbulent London of Richard II* (London: Longman, Green, 1949); and the further investigations in Pamela Nightingale, "Capitalists, Crafts and Constitutional Change in Late Fourteenth-Century London," *Past and Present* 124 (1989): 3–35.

15. Thrupp, *Merchant Class,* 206.

16. Ibid., 209.

17. Eilert Ekwall, *Studies in the Population of Medieval London.* Kungl. Vitterhets Historie och Antikvitets Akademiens handlingar, Filologisk-filosofiska Serien 2 (Stockholm, 1956), xi–xii, lx–lxiii.

18. Thrupp, *Merchant Class,* 216–17.

19. See N. F. Blake, *Non-Standard Language in English Literature* (London: Andre Deutsch, 1981), 28–33. The classic essay is J. R. R. Tolkien, "Chaucer as Philologist: *The Reeve's Tale,*" *Transactions of the Philological Society* (1934): 1–70. Chaucer's innovativeness should be recognized; generally speaking, linguistic tolerance of other dialects was high in London until the establishment of Chancery as standard during the second quarter of the fifteenth century. See A. I. Doyle, "The Manuscripts," in *Middle English Alliterative Poetry and Its Literary Background,* ed. David Lawton (Cambridge: Brewer, 1982), 90.

20. Ekwall, *Studies in the Population of Medieval London,* 37, 118.

21. See Thomas Jay Garbaty, "Satire and Regionalism: The Reeve and His Tale," *Chaucer Review* 8 (1973): 1–8.

22. There are two further anti-Norfolk satirical remarks in the "Z-text" (MS Bodley 851): see *William Langland, Piers Plowman: The Z Version,* ed. A. G. Rigg and Charlotte Brewer, Studies and Texts 59 (Toronto: Pontifical Institute of Mediaeval Studies, 1983), 16–17. For the B-text, see A. V. C. Schmidt, ed., William Langland, *The Vision of Piers Plowman: A Complete Edition of the B-Text* (London: J. M. Dent, 1978).

23. On the economic privileges and disabilities of alien merchants, see Alice Beardwood, *Alien Merchants in England 1350 to 1377: Their Legal and Economic Position,* Monograph Series No. 3 (Cambridge, Mass.: Mediaeval Academy of America, 1931), 39–58. On the earlier period (to 1336), see T. H. Lloyd, *Alien Merchants in England in the High Middle Ages* (Brighton/New York: Harvester/St. Martin's, 1982).

24. Henry Thomas Riley, ed., *Liber Albus: The White Book of the City of London,* compiled 1419 by John Carpenter and Richard Whitington (London: Richard Griffin, 1861), 234, 422–24. The privileges of the German Hanseatic merchants included a guildhall of their own and the responsibility of keeping Bishopsgate in good repair; see *Liber Albus,* 417–18.

25. Ibid., 401–2.

26. Ibid., 250.

27. On the legal status of alien merchants in relation to denization and taxation, see Beardwood, *Alien Merchants,* 59–75. Beardwood also gives lists of aliens who became London freemen in the period 1350–77 (196–99).

28. Thrupp, *Merchant Class,* 221

29. Eugen Kölbing, ed., *The Romance of Sir Beues of Hamtoun,* EETS, e.s. 46, 48, 65 (1885, 1886, 1894). The earliest manuscript, and Kölbing's primary copy-text, is the Auchinleck manuscript (Edinburgh, National Library of Scotland, Advocates' MS 19.2.1), dated about 1330.

30. See Beardwood, *Alien Merchants,* 92–97; the record of the affair is printed in full at 189–96.

31. Ibid., 14.

32. Ibid. One does not know to what degree differences of language and misjudgments of tone of address were an aggravation in these confrontations. In York in 1360 two Lombard merchants who had been "wandering in the city for three days" were arrested after it was ascertained that no one could understand what they were saying; ibid., 91.

33. See T. H. Lloyd, *England and the German Hanse, 1157–1611* (Cambridge: Cambridge University Press, 1991), 55.

34. See M. M. Postan, *The Medieval Economy and Society: An Economic History of Britain in the Middle Ages* (London: Weidenfeld & Nicolson, 1972), 191–95. For a detailed account of the royal initiative, see E. B. Fryde, "Edward III's Wool Monopoly of 1337: A Fourteenth-Century Royal Trading Venture," *History* 37 (1952): 8–24, reprinted in his *Studies in Medieval Trade and Finance* (London: Hambledon, 1983). The fullest account of the English medieval wool trade is T. H. Lloyd's *The English Wool Trade in the Middle Ages* (Cambridge: Cambridge University Press, 1977).

35. Paul Strohm, "Trade, Treason, and the Murder of Janus Imperial," *Journal of British Studies* 35 (1996): 1–23. I am very grateful to Professor Strohm for letting me see a copy of this paper before its publication. The story of the murder is in *Select Cases in the Court of King's Bench, under Richard II, Henry IV and Henry V,* ed. G. O. Sayles, vol. 7 (London: Bernard Quaritch, 1971), 15–21, 40–41.

36. See E. B. Fryde, "Italian Maritime Trade with Medieval England (c.1270–c.1530)," *Recueils de la Societe Jean Bodin* 32 (1974): 291–337, reprinted in *Studies in Medieval Trade and Finance.* Fryde describes how from about 1370 onward Genoese ships put in at southern and southwestern ports, especially Southampton, to collect wool from the Cotswolds and cloth from the Bath area, and to bring in dyes and alum for the textile industry. The avoidance of the Staple was made possible by special royal license, something the Good Parliament of 1376 complained about bitterly. We remember how Chaucer had been instrumental in initiating and developing this policy during his visit to Genoa in 1372–73, and how in 1373 he had been in Dartmouth, another south-coast deepwater port that was not London, to negotiate the release of a Genoese ship that had been overenthusiastically "arrested" by the authorities. See M. M. Crow and C. C. Olson, *Chaucer Life-Records* (Oxford: Clarendon, 1966), 40.

37. See Thrupp, *Merchant Class,* 8, 51, 222. The fact that most poor immigrants were single men in itself served to make them objects of suspicion as "strangers," given that they were "outside the family, which was the basic social cell"; see the evidence for Paris presented by Bronislaw Geremek, *The Margins of Society in Late Medieval Paris,* trans. Jean Birrell (Cambridge: Cambridge University Press, 1987[1971]), 254.

38. A. H. Thomas, ed., *Calendar of Select Pleas and Memoranda of the City of London, 1364–1381* (Cambridge: Cambridge University Press, 1929), 151, 227.

39. See Lacey, "Women and Work," 49–50. It may not be irrelevant to remark that "strange woman" is the phrase used in the Wycliffite Bible to translate an expression (Vulgate, *mulier aliena*) commonly used in Proverbs (2.16, 5.3, and others) and occasionally elsewhere in the Old Testament to mean "prostitute."

40. Henry Thomas Riley, ed., *Memorials of London and London Life in the XIIIth, XIVth and XVth Centuries. Being a Series of Extracts, Local, Social, and Political, from*

the Early Archives of the City of London. A.D. 1276–1419 (London: Longman, Green, 1868), 307. Two bailiffs of the Flemish weavers were imprisoned in 1366 for failing "to inform the Mayor and Aldermen of divers evildoers among the Flemish weavers, who made covins and assemblies in the City and suburbs... and for having told the above weavers that they need not work, thus allowing them to wander about the City to the grave damage of the common people"; Thomas, *Calendar of Select Pleas and Memoranda, 1364–1381,* 65–66. The enforced separation of the two groups of workers, who after all had the same basic interests, created a fertile breeding ground for racial hatred.

41. Riley, *Memorials of London,* 346.

42. Reginald R. Sharpe, ed., *Calendar of Letter-Books, Preserved among the Archives of the Corporation of the City of London: Letter-Book H, circa A.D.1375–1399* (London: John Edward Francis, 1907), 94.

43. John Stow, *Survey of London,* ed. Charles Lethbridge Kingsford, 2 vols. (Oxford: Clarendon, 1908), 1.208. On the regulation and repression of strangers and foreigners in sixteenth-century London, see Steve Rappaport, *Worlds within Worlds: Structures of Life in Sixteenth-Century London* (Cambridge: Cambridge University Press, 1989), 42–47. It is a painfully familiar story.

44. I quote from the excellent collection of primary sources in translation in R. B. Dobson, *The Peasants' Revolt of 1381,* 2d ed. (London: Macmillan, 1983), 162. The original French can be found in V. H. Galbraith, ed., *The Anonimalle Chronicle, 1333–1381* (Manchester: Manchester University Press, 1927), 145–46.

45. Dobson, *The Peasants' Revolt,* 210.

46. Ibid., 201.

47. Ibid., 175, 188–89.

48. Chaucer's poetry elsewhere is expressive of a cultivated English contempt for the Flemish. Flanders is the setting for the Pardoner's Tale (VI.463), as a place notorious for drunkenness, and is the home of Sir Thopas (VII.719), presumably in mockery of the aspiration to knightly manners of the bourgeois Flemings. See Geoffrey Chaucer, *Canterbury Tales,* ed. John Matthews Manly (London: Harrap, 1928), 616–17, 628–30; see also Dorothy Macbride Norris, "Chaucer's *Pardoner's Tale* and Flanders," *PMLA* 48 (1933): 636–41.

49. Paul Strohm, *Social Chaucer* (Cambridge: Harvard University Press, 1989), 165. Susan Crane, for instance, in "The Writing Lesson of 1381," in *Chaucer's England: Literature in Historical Context,* ed. Barbara A. Hanawalt (Minneapolis: University of Minnesota Press, 1992), writes of the passage as "another instance of the commons' racket, silence, or misspeaking" that "remanipulates incoherence as a touchstone of low status" (214). The Flemings seem somehow to have become invisible.

50. Paul de Man, "Les Juifs dans la littérature actuelle," *Le Soir* 4 (March 1941): 45; Jacques Derrida, "Like the Sound of the Sea Deep within a Shell: Paul de Man's War," *Critical Inquiry* 14 (1988): 623.

CHAPTER 5

Knights in Disguise: Identity and Incognito in Fourteenth-Century Chivalry

Susan Crane

My subject is how romances and historical imitations of romance define identity in moments when knights disguise themselves or dress up in the badges and regalia of orders of knighthood. Literary characters express chivalric ideology through the poetics of a genre; historical knights who imitate them are similarly engaged in a rhetoric of gestures and appearances, in a metonymic self-presentation that depends for its meaning on literary and social conventions and precedents.[1] It is on this rhetorical plane of self-dramatization that I will associate a few historical and literary instances of chivalric behavior.

Initially, I suspected that the knight who chooses to disguise himself seeks to conceal a part of his identity from scrutiny and judgment, to make himself a stranger to his own chivalric community. For this conference on strangers in medieval society I planned to claim that chivalric disguise estranges the knight by removing him from public view, making him an outsider even as he engages his peers in tournaments or fights alongside them in war. I have come to believe, however, that chivalric incognito, as a motif of romance and as a historical practice, amounts to a peculiar kind of self-presentation, a self-dramatization that invites rather than resists public scrutiny. This function of incognito becomes clearer when placed in relation to other means by which knights display their identity, in coats of arms, badges, and the insignia of orders of chivalry. All these gestures, I believe, construct an identity that calls persistently on the chivalric community's recognition in order to constitute itself, but that retains as well a suppressed and threatening potential for alienation from that community.

My reading of chivalric dress and disguise reconsiders a familiar dispute about medieval and modern selfhood. Renaissance scholars have long characterized the Middle Ages as the time before individuality. Stephen Greenblatt writes that in the Renaissance, people began to fashion individual identities self-consciously, to choose and value "a distinctive personality, a characteristic address to the world, a consistent mode of perceiving and behaving."[2] Jacob Burckhardt much earlier argued that in the Middle Ages "man was conscious of himself only as a member of a race, people, party, family, or corporation—only through some general category."[3] That "only," that dichotomy between identity conceived independently of others and in terms of others, has also conditioned medievalists' counterclaims that individuality is a medieval phenomenon as well as a modern one. With regard to romance, my primary interest, Robert Hanning argues that the driving tension of the genre is between the striving hero's private desires and his social commitments. The protagonist's sense of self precedes encounters with the world: "The great adventure of chivalric romance is the adventure of becoming what (and who) you think you can be, of transforming the *awareness* of an inner self into an *actuality* which impresses upon the external world the fact of a personal, self-chosen destiny, and therefore of an inner-determined identity."[4] Peter Haidu, in contrast, argues that the opposition between inner self and external world is an entirely modern conception: "Le Moyen Age nous lisant ne peut que s'émerveiller à la vue d'un système social produisant des sujets s'opposant, aux meilleurs moments de la vie, à la société et au système de valeurs encodées qui les fondent en tant que Sujets." Looking specifically to Chrétien de Troyes's *Yvain*, Haidu argues that the choice that text offers is between a fully integrated social identity and no identity at all.[5]

For both sides of this debate, a division, indeed an irreconcilable opposition, distinguishes the individual from society: medieval subjectivity is either determined by social forces or confronts them in a dialectical struggle over that determination. But this oppositional conception itself has a history, one moment of which is articulated with particular clarity in the work of John Locke. Locke and his contemporaries convinced the architects of the American Revolution that each and every "man" had a primary duty to question "received Opinions" on every matter of importance to his daily conduct; each man's reason was his means to liberation from "the secret motives, that influenced the Men of Name and Learning in the World, and the Leaders of Parties" to further their own interests.[6] Locke is the first theorist to propose that everyone, not just the philosopher, must take a dialectical stance to social precedent and authority, and that to resist and interrogate is the essence of liberty: "He is certainly the most subjected, the most enslaved, who is so in his Understanding."[7] Students of the novel will recall Ian Watt's argument that Locke's version of the autonomous individual in confrontation with the social world is crucial to the generic shift from romance to novel in the eighteenth century.[8]

Locke's skeptical, questioning relation between the self and the world is so natural to us that it may constrict our ability to imagine other moments in the complex history of subjectivity.[9] Indeed, my argument concerning chivalric identity should not be taken to propose a globally "medieval" self. A particular fascination of chivalric literature for me has been that it appears to imagine identity quite differently from the learned religious writing on which medieval studies tend to ground general claims about premodern self-conception.[10] All positions in this debate recognize that the forms self-conception takes are ideologically conditioned; one implication of ideology's role is that identity might be multiform even in one era, differently configured, for example, in clerical and secular circles or in popular and elite ones. These circles interpenetrate, of course, in chivalric literature itself, where authors' clerical or reformist impulses cannot be fully disentangled from their representations of an ideology specific to chivalric practice. But something of that ideology can be recovered by cross-reading the more clerically oriented works, such as *Sir Gawain and the Green Knight,* against more secularly invested ones, such as Geoffroi de Charny's *Livre de chevalerie* and the statutes of chivalric orders.

In considering chivalric identity, we might imagine Locke's premises stood on their heads—or, from the medieval perspective, righted from their postmedieval inversions. Precedent and social consensus become reliable measures of merit rather than dangerously misleading "Opinions," and the relation between the self and those measures becomes largely mutual and interpenetrating rather than oppositional. Independent selfhood is not the goal of social life but a threat to it, a state of alienation that is to be avoided rather than sought out. And the isolated self does not precede confrontation with the world—is not the starting point for building an identity—but is rather an effect, and a largely negative one, of the quest for renown.

My argument contrasts with the two current kinds of argument on chivalric behavior specifically. Louise Fradenberg's analysis of tournaments brilliantly exemplifies the position that personal identity is threatened by external perception; for her the jousting knight is involved in a continuous process of self-dramatization through which he attempts to match up his own self-perception with public measures of honor.[11] In contrast, on the issue of chivalry Lee Patterson argues for an undifferentiated, publicly defined subjectivity: "It is essential to grasp, as our initial premise, that chivalry entailed a form of selfhood insistently, even exclusively, public. It stressed a collective or corporate self-definition and so ignored the merely personal or individual."[12] In my view, Fradenberg's *City, Marriage, Tournament* and Patterson's *Chaucer and the Subject of History* are superior to other recent studies of the literary and historical intersections that determine subjectivity, and their virtually diametric conclusions on the nature of chivalric identity are the more striking for the many consonances of approach they share. I will argue here for a third view, that an individual identity can be founded in renown in this period when the individual had not yet become the questioning opponent of social precedent. Accorded by the chivalric community, this individuality derives from, rather than precedes, public judgment. I will first outline several cases that locate identity in renown, in the estimation of the community, and then go on to argue that chivalric ideology sustains a peculiar kind of individuality based on one's capacity to win renown. A brief third section points to the risk in this identity system that misjudgment may produce a premodern version of the alienated self.

Incognito and Renown

Literature, and especially romance, begins to inspire chivalric behavior extensively in the later thirteenth century, for example, in Edward I's Round Table celebrating the conquest of Wales (1284) and in the Picardy tournament (1278) presided over by a Dame Courtoisie and a Queen Guinevere who welcomed to the lists a "Chevalier au Lyon," a suite of damsels he had rescued, and his lion.[13] The Knight of the Lion imitates Chrétien de Troyes's disguised hero Yvain, in disgrace and attempting to remake his reputation as the "Chevalier au lÿon . . . / qui met sa poinne a conseillier / celes qui d'aïe ont mestier [þe knight with þe lyown: / He helpes al in word and dede, / Þat unto him has any nede]."[14] The historical impersonation of Yvain's impersonation illustrates the double attraction that the motif of incognito holds for the late medieval audience: literary disguises not only stimulate the creation of similar disguises in imitation of romance, but inspire as well the direct imitation of literary figures by historical persons. "Incognito" in its many fourteenth-century manifestations encompasses both concealed identity modeled after romance plots and fictive identity borrowed from them.

A striking instance of the latter, if we accept Juliet Vale's compelling interpretation of the records, is provided by Edward III: having participated in the 1334 Dunstable tournament as "Monsr. Lyonel" (a Round Table knight and cousin to Lancelot, chosen perhaps for the "lions"—actually leopards—on the royal coat of arms), Edward extended the impersonation of Lionel in so naming his third son in 1338. Vale further suggests that the green hangings ordered for Lionel of Antwerp's betrothal recall the green ground on which the "arms of Lionel [schuchon' de armis Lyonel]" were embroidered on hangings of 1334, and that those tournament arms were perhaps passed on to Lionel of Antwerp at his birth.[15] Edward continued to participate incognito in later tournaments, as a simple knight bachelor at Dunstable in 1342 and in the arms of his followers Stephen de Cosington and Thomas de Bradstone in 1348.[16] And at least one English knight of the period, Sir Thomas Holand, used adopted arms reminiscent of those in romance: although he bore his family's coat of arms in his early twenties, his later armorial seals of 1354 and 1357 as well as the Antiquaries' Roll (no. 106, c. 1360) record his use of a plain sable shield.[17] Perhaps Holand used his plain arms only in tournaments, but in any case they seem likely to refer to the plain arms often used by disguised knights in romances.

The kind of disguise at issue here is the most common of all in romance: protagonists adopt plain or fabricated arms in combat, often just for the space of a decisive tournament. The narrative pretexts for such disguises are various. Chrétien's Cligés and Hue de Rotelande's Ipomedon are new knights seeking to prove themselves as they enter adulthood; Partonope of Blois and Chrétien's Yvain have committed offenses against their lovers that they are striving to redress. In all these cases, chivalric incognito is a public act, one of definition and redefinition that speaks to onlookers. Incognito does conceal information, but does so only temporarily in order to focus attention on the judgment of present actions without regard for lineage, past achievements, or past failures.

Winning renown (los, pris, name, renommee) requires submitting to a semiosis of performance and display. The protagonist of the fourteenth-century *Ipomadon* uses multiple disguises, yet his layered self-presentation, which the English redactor attributes to his perpetual sense that he is not yet worthy of his lady, culminates in major scenes of revelation linking his screen identities together. For example, after a three-day tournament designed to find a husband for his lady, Ipomadon intends to "wend my way / To gette me more worshipe, yff I may," but he sends his burgess host to court with the red, white, and black horses he used in the tournament and two more horses won from two rivals there.[18] Presenting each major figure in the narrative with one of these equine tokens of achievement, the burgess claims the renown for Ipomadon that Ipomadon is reluctant to claim for himself. At this point Ipomadon's three tournament disguises and two of his court personae come together, but his name and lineage remain concealed: his chief rival, Cabanus, tries to find out "where he was borne & what he hatte," but in the absence of that information he must still concede that "a wortheer knyght þen he is one / Vnder the cope of heyven is none."[19] Ipomadon's merit in arms is the more firmly established for its independence from his lineage, although his lineage, discovered much later, consolidates his meritorious performances. As each disguise is changed for another, reassumed, and ultimately lifted, Ipomadon seems less to conceal himself from others than to articulate his construction of an identity fully constituted in renown, in the perception and judgment of his society.

Incognito serves Partonope much as it does Ipomadon, concentrating the public eye on the moment of action in order to establish an identity independent of affiliations with the past. In contrast to Ipomadon, Partonope is afflicted with failure when he attends the three-day tournament that will determine Melior's husband: he has disobeyed Melior's magical interdiction, exposing their love to public shame, and must now appear in disguise because, he believes, Melior has rejected contact with him forever. His plain silver shield becomes the metonymy for his superior performance: in the bon mot of a participant praising one of his victories, "The white shelde þinketh not to dey / At þis tyme [The white shield isn't thinking of dying just yet]."[20]

Where a past fault is the motive for disguise, there is a refashioned identity concealed beneath the incognito, but the strategy of romances is typically to externalize both the fault and the penance. Yvain's recollection that he has forgotten to return to his wife coincides exactly with a public reproach for his oversight, transforming what could be an occasion for private guilt into a public scene of shame. The Middle English adaptation of Chrétien's work *Ywain and Gawain* does away more thoroughly than its source with Ywain's prior identity by insisting that his fault negates it altogether. His wife's messenger calls into question his knighthood and his lineage:

> It es ful mekyl ogains þe right
> To cal so fals a man a knight
> . . .
> Sertainly, so fals a fode
> Was never cumen of kynges blode,
> Þat so sone forgat his wyfe.[21]

No wonder this "unkind cumlyng [unnatural little upstart]" runs maddened from court and later declares, "I am noght worthi to be sene...I was a man, now am I nane."[22] Ywain, like Partonope, reconstructs his manhood in deeds of chivalry, disguised as the Knight of the Lion.

These literary instances clarify Edward III's adoption of a chivalric disguise when his city of Calais was in danger of being recaptured by the French. Edward's exploit is noted in several chronicles, but Jean Froissart's most fully elaborates the interactions between English and French combatants.[23] When Edward learned that Geoffroi de Charny had offered money to the captain of the garrison at Calais in return for access to the city, the king (together with the Black Prince and certain reinforcements) came in secrecy from England to Calais, instructed the garrison captain to appear willing to admit the French, and fought against the French force "sans cognissance de ses ennemis, desous le banière monsigneur Gautier de Mauni" [without the knowledge of his enemies, under the banner of Sir Walter Manny]."[24] Froissart makes much of this incognito, pointing it out repeatedly in the course of his account; the Rome version adds the comment, "Bien monstra la li gentils rois Edouwars que il avoit grant desir de conbatre et amour as armes, qant il s'estoit mis en tel parti et tant humeliiés que desous le pennon mesire Gautier de Manni, son chevalier [There the noble King Edward showed well that he had a great desire for combat and love of arms, when he took part in such an action and so humbled himself under the banner of his knight Sir Walter Manny]."[25] Edward fights hand to hand particularly with Eustache de Ribemont; again Froissart insists, "Mesires Ustasses ne savoit a qui il se conbatoit; mais li rois le sçavoit bien, car il le recongnissoit par ses armes [Sir Eustache did not know with whom he was fighting, but the king knew him well, for he recognized him by his arms]."[26] Edward's disguise works, like those of romance, to concentrate attention on his chivalric skill and courage independent of his established status as sovereign and military leader. The initial effect is paradoxical—the leader now a follower, the sovereign on a footing with the soldier—but Edward integrates his disguise with his kingship by staging a scene of revelation and judgment to follow the scene of incognito, inviting the captured knights to a dinner on the night of their defeat at which he mingles with them, wearing not a crown but a chaplet of silver and pearls. In Froissart's text, Edward reproaches Geoffroi de Charny and praises Eustache de Ribemont:

> Adonc prist li rois le chapelet qu'il portoit sus son chief, qui estoit bons et riches, et le mist et assist sus le chief à monsigneur Ustasse, et li dist ensi: "Messire Ustasse, je vous donne ce chapelet pour le mieulz combatant de toute la journée de chiaus de dedens et de hors, et vous pri que vous le portés ceste anée pour l'amour de mi. Je sçai bien que vous estes gais et amoureus, et que volentiers vous vos trouvés entre dames et damoiselles. Si dittes partout là où vous venés que je le vous ay donnet. Et parmi tant, vous estes mon prisonnier: je vous quitte vostre prison; et vous poés partir de matin, se il vous plest."[27]

> [Then the king took the chaplet that he was wearing on his head, which was fine and rich, and put it on Sir Eustache's head, and said to him, "Sir Eustache, I give you this chaplet for being the best combatant of the entire day of those within and those without, and I beg you to wear it this year for love of me. I know well that you are gay and amorous, and that you willingly find yourself in the company of ladies and maidens. So say wherever you come that I gave this to you. During this time you are my prisoner; I excuse you from imprisonment, and you may leave in the morning if you please."]

Edward reconstitutes the military encounter as a festive occasion, an event very like a tournament, of which he is the judge in apportioning the honors. War and tournament reveal here their close allegiance, their shared preoccupation with honor (versus Charny's attempt to suborn) and with testing and measuring participants.[28] Edward adopts the role of sovereign observer of the day's events (as if despite his participation in the field he was nonetheless aware of all the action "dedens et de hors"), but he simultaneously enhances his exploits in the field by choosing his own adversary as the best combatant. Eustache, in heralding his reward, will publish as well the exploit of Edward and the victory of Edward's party.[29]

Froissart, and presumably Edward before him, seems to have in mind not only the semiosis of disguise in tournaments but also its roots in romance. Edward conceals his identity in combat as do Ipomadon and others, but, as in those cases, the incognito is ultimately lifted and renown credited to the unknown knight. In Froissart's account the crucial revelation to the French, noble adversaries, has a romantic resonance with the transnational pursuit of chivalric renown; the "dames et damoiselles" who are to be the audience for Eustache's narrative recall the feminine associations of romance: beyond as well as within the genre, women are said to have a special susceptibility to romance and tend to be invoked for an audience in fact more mixed. Edward's imitation of literary incognito provides a second level of disguise for the English king as a hero of romance, and his exploit's literary origins prepare for its return to narrative in the accounts of Eustache de Ribemont and Froissart.

The pivotal function of chivalric incognito, then, is to establish or revise the perception of others concerning the disguised knight's merits. That is, incognito is not significantly self-concealing and self-protecting, but the reverse: the disguised knight draws the curious and judgmental eye and stands clear of his past to be measured anew. Moreover, the full semiosis of incognito requires that the knight complete his adventure by giving up the disguise and incorporating the renown he has won into his earlier identity. As *Ywain and Gawain* summarizes, "þe knyght with þe liown / Es turned now to Syr Ywayn / And has his lordship al ogayn."[30] This trajectory toward revelation echoes that of adventures in general in romance: the wandering knight, isolated from the court's view, fully achieves his adventures only when they are reported—whether by himself or by his captives and emissaries—back to the courtly audience.

Limitations of Renown

By reading chivalric disguise as a language of self-presentation rather than as a means of self-concealment, it becomes clear that incognito is only the end point on a continuum of visible signs through which knights perform and manipulate their identities. Now I will turn from disguise to other adopted marks of identity on that continuum, and extend my argument from the claim that the chivalric self is first of all in the gift of the community to claim as well that this selfhood is ultimately divided—indeed, estranged—from the community that established it.

The public nature of chivalric identity does not do away with tensions analogous to those that complicate the modern struggle between "individual" and "society." A kind of individuality—though I would mark it off from modern individuality—comes into play at the point of opposition between the ideology of chivalric brotherhood and that brotherhood's charge to each knight to distinguish himself. The chivalric community both asserts its seamless accord and demands differentiation. The Order of the Garter, for example, represents the equivalence of its members in their shared regalia and a nonhierarchical organization. Yet it also institutionalizes its members' difference from those knights not admitted to the order and further from each other, in that their original seating arrangement in the choir of St. George's chapel seems to reflect two tournament teams of twelve members each, one under the Black Prince and the other under Edward III.[31] In founding the order in part to declare the unity of interests among his most loyal supporters and in part to foster contests among them, Edward followed the design of tournamenting confraternities generally, and perhaps specifically that of the Order of the Band, whose statutes require each new member to run two courses against two members of the order at the first tournament held after his initiation.[32] The regalia worn by members of Jean II's Order of the Star unites them visibly in the colors vermillion, black, and white, which probably carried the significances contemporaneously ascribed to them in Geoffroi de Charny's *Livre de chevalerie* for the dress of squires about to receive knighthood: white for sinlessness, vermillion for the blood a knight is prepared to shed, black for mortality.[33] The order's robes and the colors of investiture urge a spirit of common purpose and shared identity. Yet each member was charged at the order's annual feast to recount his "aventures, aussy bien les honteuses que les glorieuses [adventures, the shameful as well as the praiseworthy]" for the purpose of designating "les trois princes, trois bannerez et trois bachelers, qui en l'année auront plus fait en armes de guerre [the three princes, three bannerets, and three bachelors who during the year have accomplished the most in the arms of war]."[34] Charny's *Livre* similarly posits both a universal "ordre de chevalerie" made up of all true knights and the principle "qui plus fait, miex vault [he who accomplishes more is more worthy]," which becomes the refrain of his opening pages.[35]

The Orders of the Garter and the Star established in midcentury by Edward III and Jean II overtly imitate Arthur's Round Table, implying their founders' imitation of Arthur and their members' imitation of his knights. The Arthurian inspiration for the orders of chivalry licenses a turn to literature for some insight into the paradoxical relation between injunctions to chivalric fellowship and to individual distinction. *Sir Gawain and the Green Knight,* particularly because it ends with the founding of an order of chivalry, might be expected to comment on this double imperative. Throughout the poem, Gawain is declared the paradigm of knighthood. His pentangle illustrates the virtues to which all knights might aspire. To Bertilak's courtiers he is "þat fyne fader of nurture"; in Bertilak's assessment, "As perle bi þe quite pese is of prys more, / So is Gawayn, in god fayth, bi oþer gay knyȝtez."[36] Both metaphors assert relation as well as superiority; Gawain is comparable to other knights but also excels on all the scales of commitment and achievement implicit in the pentangle's mathematics. In Charny's terms, he surpasses the *preux* and the *souverainement preux* to count among *les plus souveraine.*[37] When Arthur's courtiers adopt Gawain's green girdle on his return, they honor Gawain's superiority in the same gesture that strives to reintegrate him into the "ordre de chevalerie" in general and this new order in particular.

The court's response, however, is problematic. Gawain asserts that the green lace is the bend of his blame and the token of his transgression, but the courtiers laugh loudly and found a brotherhood whose members will each wear this "bende abelef hym aboute of a bryȝt grene" (2517). Are the courtiers *over*estimating Gawain's success, carelessly laughing and failing to recognize the spiritual fault he sees emblematized in the "token of vntrawþe" (2509)? Or are they rather *under*estimating Gawain's success, presumptuously adopting as their own this "pur token / Of þe chaunce of þe grene chapel" (2398–99) to which only Gawain's extraordinary adventure can give the right? Even if they are perceptively asserting their own inferiority in adopting the baldric, thereby declaring their aspiration to become as "imperfect" as Gawain, they are reinterpreting his own version of his achievement. The interpretive impasse that Gawain—and each reader—faces in this scene foregrounds the problem of interpretation itself that is the weak link in a system of individual honor dependent on public recognition. Misrecognition is always possible. The court's perhaps insightful, perhaps ignorant judgment and Gawain's contrasting judgment of his performance raise questions about how accurately deeds get translated into renown.

It is immediately tempting to attribute the gap between Gawain's and the court's assessments of his adventure to a fundamental alienation of the private self known only to itself from the ignorant outside world. Casting Gawain's predicament as a dichotomy of "inner" and "outer" identities is natural to the modern view of selfhood, but I believe Gawain throughout the romance is identified with his public reputation alone, and that the sense of interiority arising at the work's end derives from the conflict over what measure of renown to accord his most recent exploits.

The tests of courage and courtesy Gawain undergoes in his adventure were, according to Bertilak, designed "to assay þe surquidré, ȝif hit soth were / þat rennes of þe grete renoun of þe Rounde Table" (2457–58), echoing his declared motive at the poem's outset (258–64) and his taunt, "Now is þe reuel and þe renoun of þe Rounde Table / Ouerwalt wyth a worde of on wȝes speche" (313–14). As the Round Table's representative, Gawain even in his intimate conduct with Bertilak's wife is subject to constant measurement against the standards of—and his own prior reputation for—courteous and chivalric behavior. "Þou art not Gawayn" is the persistent reproach of Gawain's male and female challengers as they demand that he live up to the ideals of his court (1293, 1481, 2270). His challengers speak as if "Gawain" were simply metonymic for an ideology of knighthood. His identity is articulated and judged by others; his task is to perform the chivalry and courtesy imputed to him as perfectly as possible.

The signs of identity Gawain bears further emphasize its public nature. The pentangle on Gawain's shield blazons his virtues in a visible calculus of fives and in a narrative register that appears to be beyond counterinterpretation. Many critics have noted the firmness and stability with which the pentangle's "endeles knot" (630) of interlocked virtues is "harder happed on þat haþel þen on any oþer" (655) and the contrasting mobility with which the green girdle is draped, knotted, and interpreted.[38] I have not seen commentary on the heraldic resonance of Gawain's final way of wearing the girdle "Abelef as a bauderyk bounden by his syde, / Loken vnder his lyfte arme" (2486–87). The pentangle has made a muted but I think unmistakable return in Gawain's second arming, when he completes his preparations for meeting the Green Knight by donning "his cote wyth þe conysaunce of þe clere werkes / Ennurned vpon veluet"—his badge or cognizance having been the pentangle at his first arming (2026–27).[39] In this period, armed knights typically bore their coats of arms on their surcoats as well as their shields.[40] When Gawain arms for the second time, the girdle maintains something of its character as a belt, wrapped twice around Gawain's waist, but after he comes to see in it the "syngne of my surfet" (2433) he takes to wearing it crosswise. It is possible that for a fourteenth-century audience the "bende abelef" that Gawain ties across his "cote wyth þe conysaunce" would have recalled a heraldic bend, a deliberate revision Gawain has blazoned on his earlier "bytoknyng of trawþe" (626).[41]

That Gawain blazons a new identity reflective of his adventure breaks the pentangle's "endeles" stability and reasserts the performative nature of chivalric identity. But the difference between the meaning Gawain attributes to the girdle and the meanings urged by Bertilak and Arthur's courtiers mark the point where Gawain is, finally, estranged from his community. The text's focus on renown ends in a crisis of renown, as Gawain's sense of shame divides him from both his past position as the Round Table's best representative and the present "broþerhede" of knights in green baldrics (2516). My argument is that Gawain's differing sense of self does not precede but rather derives from his participation in a chivalric economy of identity conceded in return for deeds. His trajectory from an identity fully constituted in renown toward an identity unavailable to public understanding exactly reverses the narrative, familiar to us from a thousand novels, of an independent youth at odds with tradition. For modern sensibility, the kind of estrangement from social consensus that Gawain experiences on his return to court is the universal precondition of individuality; for chivalric ideology, Gawain's estrangement amounts to a failure in the system of renown that has generated his individuality.

Identity beyond Renown

Marked and overwritten with the colors and symbols that convey his identity, Gawain makes himself available to the reading of others, and his own words of shame carry little weight with them. That Gawain's new token is a feminine garment invites Marjorie Garber's thesis on the transvestite: he/she is one who doesn't fit, who embodies a problematic not just of gender but of other classifications—here of the imperfect coordination between exploits and renown.[42] The crisis of interpretation with which *Sir Gawain and the Green Knight* ends could contextualize the motto of the Order of the Garter, "Honi soit qui mal y pense," which appears (possibly in a later hand) at the end of the unique manuscript of *Sir Gawain.*[43] The order's motto recalls a number of parallels between Gawain's experience and the account, perhaps spurious but widely attested, that the Order of the Garter began with Edward III retrieving a garter fallen during a dance at court from a woman's leg. When his courtiers' reactions suggested that such an action was beneath a king, Edward is said to have responded with the order's motto, "Shame to him who thinks evil of this," turning unfavorable interpretations of the act back onto the interpreters and further forestalling criticism by founding an order in which the worthiest men of England and Europe would go about wearing the emblem of the incident.[44]

Historians are suspicious of this account of the order's inspiration, preferring to attribute it to Edward's claim to the French throne and specifically to the Crécy campaign.[45] Yet the earliest surviving accounts of the Garter's origins offer instead the story of the woman's garter. *Tirant lo Blanc,* whose author, Martorell, was in England from March 1438 to February 1439, has it that the dancing woman was of little standing and that the king wore her garter for several months before the protests of courtiers and displeasure of the queen led him to utter the (mangled) motto "Puni soit qui mal y pense" and to found the Order of the Garter to consolidate the merit of his action.[46] In 1534, Polydore Vergil, a reliable historian who spent much of his adult life in England, endorsed the "popular tradition" that the Order of the Garter began with the king's retrieval of "a garter from the stocking of his queen or mistress"; Vergil comments, "English writers have been modestly superstitious, perhaps fearing to commit lèse-majesté if they made known such unworthy things; and they have preferred to remain silent about them, whereas matters should really be seen otherwise: something that rises from a petty or sordid origin increases all the more in dignity."[47] The scribal notation in the Gawain manuscript, which makes best sense in terms of the "popular tradition" about the Garter, may indeed be that tradition's earliest trace—earlier by a few decades than the English material published in *Tirant lo Blanc.*

Here I am arguing neither that the Garter foundation story is necessarily true, nor that the Gawain poet alludes to it, but rather that the Garter motto written at the end of the Gawain manuscript suggests a contemporary perception of similarities between the foundation stories of the two brotherhoods. According to these stories, both orders begin with interpretive crises in which Edward and Gawain understand the feminine token differently from their courts. Both men can be said to cross-dress, although not simply because they transfer a woman's garment to their own bodies. Edward's and Gawain's gestures recall the common practice among knights of wearing bits of feminine clothing as love tokens. Such tokens do not disturb the gender binary but on the contrary assert the knight's heteronormativity, signaling even on the battlefield that he is actively engaged in courting a woman.[48] In contrast, the garter and girdle narratives carry a potential for shame: Edward stoops to retrieve an intimate garment as his courtiers titter; Gawain succumbs to cowardice as he accepts the lady's girdle. At the point where shame still inheres in the action and the garment, Edward and Gawain could be said to cross-dress, with all the loss of status that represents for men in the heterosexual paradigm.[49] As Gawain explains his plight to himself, "wyles of wymmen" have brought down mankind from the first (2415). The potential shame is suppressed as the feminine garment becomes a token of honor for a new chivalric brotherhood. It is this trajectory from shame to honor that involves the adopted garments in the gender hierarchy and invites the notion of cross-dressing.

In that moment when they can be described as cross-dressing, Edward and Gawain dramatize the risk of submitting to public judgment and the gap where their interiority might be distinguished from their renown. But the pressure of chivalric ideology is against such interiority. According to Polydore Vergil, Edward "showed those knights who had laughed at him how to judge his actions" by transforming a sexually charged situation into an affair of state that actively defends against illicit interpretation.[50] Stephen Jaeger cites Vergil's account of the Order of the Garter in a compelling argument that medieval courts persistently fabricate a public, asexual discourse from the language of sexuality and intimate interactions.[51] In support of Jaeger's argument, I would point out that Edward's two most durable mottoes, "Hony soit qui mal y pense" and "It is as it is," embroidered again and again on his tournament costumes and hangings, his beds and tents, assert control over interpretation and deny that multiple interpretations might have merit.[52]

Similarly, Gawain's apparently private interactions with Bertilak's wife, as noted above, are immediately generalized by reference to courtly standards and turn out to be not a genuine seduction but a test of *treuþe* that Gawain goes about confessing and signaling with the girdle. The court's reading of his adventure, and the Garter motto appended in the manuscript, deny the shameful potential in Gawain's interactions with Bertilak's wife. Yet this is not to say that the potential was never there at all. The feminine associations of the two garments are not completely erasable—they persist at least in the foundation stories of each order—and their persistence dramatizes the more visibly how powerful the court's ability to suppress and redefine can be. In the garter and girdle narratives the illicit holds an important role as that which is repressed and denied in order to establish that which constitutes noble identity: the illicit is the trace of a potential for private identity that the court quickly rejects in favor of a public identity constituted in renown.

Gawain's green baldric, blazoned over his pentangle, represents a belated interiority that amounts to the difference between his sense of shame and his court's admiration. Edward's and Gawain's situations differ in that the king asserts sovereign control over his court's interpretation, whereas Gawain finds his self-assessment overridden by Arthur's and the court's approval of his performance. The private sense of self his adventure has produced in him is marginal, and perhaps fleeting as well, as he faces the court's conclusion that the green baldric is to represent "þe renoun of þe Rounde Table" (2519). The semiotics of chivalric dress and incognito insist first of all that measures of honor and dishonor, renown and infamy, are in the gift of the community. Far from negotiating a tension between private self-perception and a potentially contradictory public perception, chivalric dress and disguise seek to move from one public estimation to a higher one; far from valuing and sheltering an inner self from misestimation, the disguised knight generates a public dialectic concerning his two or several identities. But where there is conflict within the community's judgment, or between the adventuring knight's self-assessment and the assessment of his peers, a space opens up for an identity that is beyond the reach of public determinations.

Notes

I am grateful to Tom Hahn, Richard Kaeuper, and David Wallace for helpful comments on this essay.

1. Michael Herzfeld bases his work on the rhetorical nature of behavior in *The Poetics of Manhood: Contested Identity in a Cretan Mountain Village* (Princeton, N.J.: Princeton University Press, 1985); also of interest to medievalists are some intriguing similarities between Cretan manhood as Herzfeld analyzes it and medieval chivalric masculinity (for example, a self established in competitive performance that is also invested in the community—"One has *egohismos* on behalf of a collectivity"; 11).

2. Stephen Greenblatt, *Renaissance Self-Fashioning: From More to Shakespeare* (Chicago: University of Chicago Press, 1980), 2.

3. Jacob Burckhardt, *The Civilization of the Renaissance in Italy,* trans. S. G. O. Middlemore (London: Phaidon, 1965 [1860]), 81, quoted in Lee Patterson, *Chaucer and the Subject of History* (Madison: University of Wisconsin Press, 1991), 7. See also Patterson's discussion of subjectivity in relation to Chaucer and his work (3–46).

4. Robert W. Hanning, *The Individual in Twelfth-Century Romance* (New Haven, Conn.: Yale University Press, 1977), 4. Colin Morris, *The Discovery of the Individual, 1050–1200* (London: S.P.C.K., 1972), holds a similar view, although he finds that the "self" is a more accurately medieval concept than the "individual" (e.g., 64–95).

5. Peter Haidu, "Temps, histoire, subjectivité aux XIe et XIIe siècles," in *Le Nombre du temps: en hommage à Paul Zumthor,* ed. Emmanuèle Baumgartner et al. (Paris: Champion, 1988), 120. For similar views, see Douglas Kelly, *The Art of Medieval French Romance* (Madison: University of Wisconsin Press, 1992), 54–58, tracing rhetorical and philosophical pressures against individuality; and Paul Zumthor, *Essai de poétique médiévale* (Paris: Éditions du Seuil, 1972), 351: "Une exigence profonde de la mentalité de ce temps et de la

société courtoise en particulier" determines that "les valeurs de l'individu n'ont d'existence que reconnues et visiblement manifestées par la collectivité."

6. John Locke, *An Essay concerning Human Understanding,* ed. Peter H. Nidditch (Oxford: Clarendon, 1975), 718–19.

7. Ibid., 711.

8. Ian Watt, *The Rise of the Novel: Studies in Defoe, Richardson and Fielding* (Berkeley: University of California Press, 1957). Michael McKeon urges the continuing indebtedness of the novel to romance in *The Origins of the English Novel, 1600–1740* (Baltimore: Johns Hopkins University Press, 1987).

9. The shaky fortunes of postmodern attempts to reimagine identity as a social construction or a deconstructed nonidentical field testify as well to the effectiveness of the modern paradigm. I plan to treat postmodern theories of the self in an expansion of the third section of this essay; see also my *Gender and Romance in Chaucer's "Canterbury Tales"* (Princeton, N.J.: Princeton University Press, 1994).

10. For example, Patterson's proposition that, in general, medieval identity is grounded in a "dialectic between an inward subjectivity and an external world that alienates it from both itself and its divine source" (*Chaucer and the Subject of History,* 8) contrasts with his view of chivalric identity (see note 12, below).

11. Louise O. Fradenberg, *City, Marriage, Tournament: Arts of Rule in Late Medieval Scotland* (Madison: University of Wisconsin Press, 1991), e.g., 205–7.

12. Patterson, *Chaucer and the Subject of History,* 168.

13. Sarrazin, *Roman de Ham,* in *Histoire des ducs de Normandie et des rois d'Angleterre,* ed. Francisque Michel (Paris: Renouard, 1840), entry of Yvain, 315–16. On thirteenth-century engagements with literary models, see Juliet Vale, *Edward III and Chivalry: Chivalric Society and Its Context 1270–1350* (Woodbridge, Suffolk: Boydell, 1982), 4–24.

14. Chrétien de Troyes, *Le Chevalier au Lion (Yvain),* ed. Mario Roques, C.F.M.A. 89 (Paris: Champion, 1960), ll. 4810–12; *Ywain and Gawain,* ed. Albert B. Friedman and Norman T. Harrington, EETS, o.s. 254 (London: Oxford University Press, 1964), ll. 2804–6. In order to concentrate on the English fourteenth century, where they exist I will cite Middle English versions of romance texts, many of which have French or Anglo-Norman antecedents.

15. Vale, *Edward III and Chivalry,* 64, 68–69.

16. Juliet R. V. Barker, *The Tournament in England, 1100–1400* (Woodbridge, Suffolk: Boydell, 1986), 86; Adam Murimuth, *Continuatio Chronicarum,* in *Adae Murimuth Continuatio Chronicarum. Robertus de Avesbury De gestis mirabilibus Regis Edwardi Tertii,* ed. E. M. Thompson, Rolls Series 93 (London, 1889), 123–24.

17. Gerald Brault, *Early Blazon: Heraldic Terminology in the Twelfth and Thirteenth Centuries with Special Reference to Arthurian Literature* (Oxford: Clarendon, 1972), 31–32, 36. For an instance of a family adopting arms from romances, see Max Prinet, "Armoires familiales et armoires de roman au XVᵉ siècle," *Romania* 58 (1932): 569–73.

18. *Ipomadon,* in *Ipomedon in drei englischen Bearbeitungen,* ed. Eugen Kölbing (Breslau: Koebner, 1889), ll. 5044–45.

19. Ibid., ll. 5189, 5200–5201. J. A. Burrow, "The Uses of Incognito: *Ipomadon A,*" in *Readings in Medieval English Romance,* ed. Carol M. Meale (Cambridge: D. S. Brewer, 1994), 25–34, argues that Ipomadon engages in a "curious honorific calculus" whereby unclaimed glory continues to accrue to his merit (30).

20. *The Middle-English Versions of Partonope of Blois,* ed. A. Trampe Bödtker, E.E.T.S., e.s. 109 (London: Kegan Paul, 1912), ll. 9868–69. A courtier in *Ipomadon* similarly subsumes the protagonist into his disguise by announcing to his lady, "The blake baner hathe brought you blis" (l. 8682). On the moral implications of colors chosen for heraldic incognito, see Michel Pastoureau, *Figures et couleurs: Etudes sur la symbolique et la sensibilité médiévales* (Paris: Léopard d'or, 1986), 193–207.

21. *Ywain and Gawain,* ll. 1611–12, 1621–23; compare *Yvain,* ll. 2718–75.

22. *Ywain and Gawain,* ll. 1627, 2096, 2116.

23. Long versions by Froissart are *Chroniques,* ed. Simeon Luce et al., Société de l'Histoire de France, vol. 4 (Paris: Renouard, 1873), 70–84; and *Chroniques: Dernière rédaction du premier livre. Edition du manuscrit de Rome Reg. lat. 869,* ed. George T. Diller (Geneva: Droz, 1972), 861–76. Another long account is Geoffrey le Baker de Swynbroke, *Chronicon,* ed. E. M. Thompson (Oxford: Clarendon, 1889), 103–8. The episode is briefly mentioned in William Worcestre, *Itineraries,* ed. John H. Harvey (Oxford: Clarendon, 1969), 346–49; Thomas Walsingham, *Historia anglicana,* ed. H. T. Riley, 2 vols., Rolls Series (London, 1863–64), 1:273–74; and Robert de Avesbury's *De gestis mirabilibus Regis Edwardi Tertii,* in *Adae Murimuth Continuatio Chronicarum. Robertus de Avesbury De gestis mirabilibus Regis Edwardi Tertii,* ed. E. M. Thompson, Rolls Series 93 (London, 1889), 408–10.

24. Froissart, *Chroniques,* ed. Luce, 79.

25. Froissart, *Chroniques,* ed. Diller, 870. Peter F. Ainsworth comments on revisions to this episode in *Jean Froissart and the Fabric of History: Truth, Myth, and Fiction in the* Chroniques (Oxford: Clarendon, 1990), 299–300.

26. Froissart, *Chroniques,* ed. Diller, 870; compare the briefer version in *Chroniques,* ed. Luce, 80: "non qu'il le cognuist, ne il ne savoit à qui il avoit à faire [not that he (Eustace) recognized him (Edward), or knew with whom he was dealing]."

27. Froissart, *Chroniques,* ed. Luce, 83.

28. Richard Kaeuper has pointed out to me that Edward's use of the terms *dedens* and *dehors* contributes to the analogy with tournaments. See Vale, *Edward III and Chivalry,* 6: "The notion of two teams, *dedens* and *dehors* is, of course, common in the late thirteenth and the fourteenth centuries."

29. Froissart, *Chroniques,* ed. Diller, 875, further emphasizes the renown accrued by Edward's strategy: Eustace tells the French king and lords "sen aventure" and his wearing of the chaplet produces "grandes nouvelles en France et en aultres pais."

30. *Ywain and Gawain,* ll. 4020–22.

31. Vale, *Edward III and Chivalry,* 86–91; Maurice Keen, *Chivalry* (New Haven, Conn.: Yale University Press, 1984), 196–97.

32. Vale, *Edward III and Chivalry,* 91; Keen, *Chivalry,* 185–86; D'Arcy Jonathan Dacre Boulton, *The Knights of the Crown: The Monarchical Orders of Knighthood in Later Medieval Europe 1325–1520* (New York: St. Martin's, 1987), 109.

33. Geoffroi de Charny, *Le Livre de chevalerie,* in Jean Froissart, *Oeuvres,* ed. Kervyn de Lettenhove, vol. 1, pt. 2 (Brussels: Victor Devaux, 1873), 514–15; see also Charny's probable source for this passage in *L'Ordene de chevalerie,* in *Raoul de Houdenc: Le Roman des eles; The Anonymous Ordene de chevalerie,* ed. Keith Busby (Amsterdam: John Benjamins, 1983), ll. 137–88.

34. Léopold Pannier, *La Noble maison de Saint-Ouen, la villa Clippiacum, et l'Ordre de l'Etoile d'après les documents originaux* (Paris: Aubry, 1872), 90, 93n; Malcolm Vale, *War and Chivalry: Warfare and Aristocratic Culture in England, France and Burgundy at the End of the Middle Ages* (Athens: University of Georgia Press, 1981), 54.

35. Charny, *Livre de chevalerie,* 464–72, 513–19.

36. *Sir Gawain and the Green Knight,* ed. J. R. R. Tolkien and E. V. Gordon, 2d ed. rev. Norman Davis (Oxford: Clarendon, 1967), ll. 919, 2364–65. Subsequent line references appear in the text.

37. Charny, *Livre de chevalerie,* 502–5.

38. For me the most illuminating discussion of the pentangle and girdle in relation to questions of identity is Geraldine Heng's "Feminine Knots and the Other *Sir Gawain and the Green Knight,*" *PMLA* 106 (1991): 500–514; and the most useful discussion of chivalric identity as a performance in *Sir Gawain* is Carolyn Dinshaw's "A Kiss Is Just a Kiss: Heterosexuality and Its Consolations in *Sir Gawain and the Green Knight,*" *diacritics* 24 (1994): 205–26.

39. *Ipomadon* uses *conusaunce* in this sense when a young knight recognizes an adversary by his coat of arms: "Jasone wold no lengur byde, / To the knyght can he ryde, / He knewe his conusaunce" (ll. 4417–19).

40. The effigy on the Black Prince's tomb and the Luttrell Psalter's image of Sir Geoffrey Luttrell are two familiar examples. Compare "þe pentangel nwe / He ber in schelde and cote," *Sir Gawain and the Green Knight,* ll. 636–37.

41. *Sir Gawain and the Green Knight,* ll. 2517, 2026, 626. Altered arms were a regular feature of tournaments: knights used blank and fabricated arms, quartered their arms with those of a leader, or adopted a label or difference marking allegiance (Barker, *Tournament in England,* e.g., 87); Gawain's gesture recalls more closely an augmentation such as might be adopted or granted to commemorate particular feats of arms (A. C. Fox-Davies, *A Complete Guide to Heraldry,* rev. ed. J. P. Brooke-Little [London: Thomas Nelson & Sons, 1969], 456–64).

42. Marjorie Garber, *Vested Interests: Cross-Dressing and Cultural Anxiety* (London: Routledge, 1992), e.g., 36–37.

43. The motto "Hony soyt qui mal pence" at the end of the manuscript is "possibly by a later scribe," according to Israel Gollancz, *Sir Gawain and the Green Knight,* E.E.T.S., o.s. 210 (London: Oxford University Press, 1940), 132n; other scholars tend to assume the hand is not that of the scribe, although of approximately the same period.

44. Like the order sketched in *Sir Gawain* (2515–18), the Order of the Garter initially included women members, "lordes and ladis," though it was always understood as a "broþerhede."

45. In this interpretation, the blue garter may appropriate the blue ground of the French royal arms, the French motto may recall Edward's lineal claim to the throne, and the garter's design as a small belt (rather than the knotted strips of cloth that both men and women used in the period as garters) may imitate the knight's sword belt, one of his insignia of rank: e.g., Vale, *Edward III and Chivalry,* 79–85. Michael Packe, *King Edward III,* ed. L. C. B. Seaman (London: Routledge, 1983), 170–74, adduces evidence that may sustain the fallen garter story; the color blue would then indicate loyalty (to women or to sovereign), a significance much attested in the later fourteenth century: Stella Mary Newton, *Fashion in the Age of the Black Prince* (Woodbridge, Suffolk: Boydell, 1980), 46; Boulton, *Knights of the Crown,* 246 (use of blue by Order of the Sword, with motto "C'est pour loiauté maintenir").

46. Joanot Martorell and Martí Joan de Galba, *Tirant lo Blanc,* trans. David H. Rosenthal (New York: Schocken, 1984), ix–x, 121–23.

47. Quoted in Richard Barber, *Edward, Prince of Wales and Aquitaine* (New York: Scribner, 1978), 85. Barber also quotes the 1463 comment of Mondonus Belvaleti that "many assert that this order took its beginning from the feminine sex, from a lewd and forbidden affection" (86).

48. Eliduc wears a girdle sent to him by Guilliadun: Marie de France, *Les Lais de Marie de France,* ed. Jean Rychner, C.F.M.A. 93 (Paris: Champion, 1983), *Eliduc,* ll. 380, 407–10.

49. Vern L. Bullough, "Transvestites in the Middle Ages," *Journal of Sociology* 79 (1974): 1381–94; Michèle Perret, "Travesties et transsexuelles: Yde, Silence, Grisandole, Blanchandine," *Romance Notes* 25 (1984–85): 328–40.

50. Quoted in Barber, *Edward, Prince of Wales and Aquitaine,* 85.

51. C. Stephen Jaeger, "L'Amour des rois: structure sociale d'une forme de sensibilité aristocratique," *Annales: Economies, Sociétés, Civilisations* 46 (1991): 547–71.

52. On appearances of the mottos, see Vale, *Edward III and Chivalry,* 57–91; Newton, *Fashion,* passim.

CHAPTER 6

The Sexual Stranger: The Sexual Quest in Wolfram's *Parzival*

Edward R. Haymes

Sex is knowledge. This equation, at least as old as the Old Testament, lies at the basis of much literature, both fictional and scientific. In the original Hebrew and in all translations I have been able to check, the Old Testament uses *to know* as a euphemism for "to have sexual intercourse with." Or is it a euphemism? The itch to gain a certain piece of information, to find out how a story comes out, is often remarkably similar to the desire for sexual union. The unraveling of a mystery is often accompanied by a *jouissance* akin to the pleasure of sex. It is no wonder that Roland Barthes uses that term to describe the pleasure of unraveling a difficult text, of being led by what he calls the "hermeneutic code, [where] we list the various (formal) terms by which an enigma can be distinguished, suggested, formulated, held in suspense, and finally disclosed."[1] In a later work, Barthes identifies the most erotic part of the body as that place where the garment parts—that is, where knowing ends and unknowing begins.[2] I think these are important points about narration, and about romance narration in particular.

Many romances involve quests. In fact, the expression *quest romance* is almost pleonastic for the Middle Ages. The quest may claim to be for some object, classically the Holy Grail, but if we look more closely we can see that the quest is really for knowledge and that this quest is almost always associated with a quest for sexual union with the sexual stranger, the sexual other, as well.

If we narrow our focus to the classic Arthurian romances of Chrétien de Troyes and their reception in Germany, we can observe this quest in operation. Hartmann von Aue established the baseline for Arthurian romance in Germany with his adaptations of *Erec et Enide* and *Yvain.* Hartmann's adaptations differ very little from their originals in the points I am making here, so I will use them to represent both Chrétien and his reception. Erec wins Enite almost as a by-product of an adventure he embarks on to avenge an insult to Ginover. He only "falls in love" with Enite on the way back to Arthur's court after actually "winning" her at a tournament. When he returns to his own lands, he spends all of his time in bed with her. Hartmann describes their getting out of bed only for the Mass in the morning followed by a meal, and then:

swie schiere man die tische ûf zôch,
mit sînem wîbe er dô vlôch
ze bette von den liuten.
dâ huop sich aber triuten. (2948–51)[3]

[As soon as the table was carried away, he fled from the people with his wife to bed. Then began again the lovemaking.]

Hartmann exaggerates the time the couple spends in bed (Chrétien had them remain in bed only until noon). When Enite's incautious complaint makes Erec aware of his having lost the respect of his society, he sets out to engage in knightly adventures designed to restore his good name. He takes Enite along to serve as his squire. The adventures prove her worth to him and allow him to find the proper balance between chivalric service and love service. Following the main sequence of adventures, the couple spends a week at a castle, during which their relationship is reestablished on a new basis. The sexual stranger has become the sexual partner in perfect balance with the other duties of chivalric life.

The story of Iwein is almost exactly the opposite. Iwein sets out to avenge a shameful defeat suffered by his cousin some ten years earlier. He challenges and kills the knight of the adventure and manages to win the hand of the widow through the intercession of the lady's chambermaid. After the wedding, Iwein asks leave to spend a year at chivalric tournaments with his friend Gawein. He forgets to return, and, when reminded of it by a visit to Arthur's court by the chambermaid, he loses his mind. The remainder of the story involves his gradual return to normality. He rescues a lion from a dragon and the beast becomes his inseparable companion. The two undergo adventures in which Iwein shows again and again his commitment to helping those in need. He wins great fame anonymously as the "Knight of the Lion." The couple is reconciled when the chambermaid convinces her lady to accept the Knight of the Lion as her protector and husband. The lady does not know that the man she has accepted is the Iwein who had betrayed her long before. She thus accepts the sexual stranger for a second time.

Although both romances involve a love relationship that has already been consummated, the behavior of the respective hero-knights makes it clear that the woman in each case is still a sexual stranger—a person who is not yet truly known—and the quest has as its goal the establishment of a new relationship built on mutual respect and an ideal balance of love and chivalry.

The third romance by Chrétien to be adapted into German adds great complication to this scheme. In *Perceval,* Chrétien allows his hero to achieve an ideal sexual union with his lady before the adventures that will test and educate him. The poet may have hit on a novel method of dealing with this anomaly, but the incomplete condition of the text only allows us to guess what he might have done with this ambitious double romance. Wolfram von Eschenbach did far more than simply adapt Chrétien's story, as Hartmann had done. He provided a prologue and a conclusion, enriched the story with complexities far beyond anything Chrétien had included in his fragment, and attacked the problem of the sexual quest with unique inventiveness.

In his recasting of Chrétien's romance, Wolfram allows himself an occasional dig at his source. One of these throws the sexual aspect of the tale into relief. After arriving at the castle of Biaurepaire, Chrétien's Perceval is treated to what little hospitality the besieged castle can provide and is shown to bed. The lady of the castle, Blancheflor, goes secretly to his bed to ask his (military) aid and ends up sleeping with him "boche a boche [mouth to mouth]" (2048), which most readers have interpreted as a synecdoche for a more complete union.[4] Wolfram certainly did.

Wolfram begins the same scene with the assertion that "ez prach nicht wîplîchiu zil" (192, 2), which Hatto translates as "There was no breach of feminine decorum" (p. 105).[5] Later we are told that

Si heten beidiu kranken sin,
Er unt diu küneginne,
an bî ligender minne. (193, 2–4)

[They both had little sense, he (Parizival) and the queen, about lying-together love.]

In other words, they were both ignorant of sex. The possibility of sexual contact is further ironized by Wolfram's description of the lady's white silk shift as "werlîchiu wât," or "defensive clothing" in the sense of armor. (Wolfram also distances himself from his source by giving the queen a far more distinctive name, Condwiramurs, which might be translated as "leading [or attracting] love.")

The attention paid to sex in this passage makes it clear that Wolfram expected at least a part of his audience to expect the chivalric couple to consummate their love at this point, an expectation they would have gained from a knowledge of Chrétien's text as well as from Wolfram's protestation that nothing untoward took place.

Wolfram does allow his hero and heroine the pleasure of "bî ligen" after Parzival has defeated the seneschal of the unwelcome suitor besieging the castle, lifted the siege, and provided the townspeople with their first meal in a long time. We are told that he spent two additional chaste nights with her, although she considered herself his wife and changed the way she wore her hair to symbolize the change to the public. Finally, on the third night, things change and

von im dicke wart gedâht
umbevâhens, daz sîn muoter riet:

Gurnemanz im ouch underschiet,
man und wîp waern al ein.
si vlâhten arm unde bein.
ob ichz iu sagen müeze,
er vant daz nâhe süeze:
der alte und der niwe site
wonte aldâ in beiden mite.
im was wol und niht ze wê. (203, 2–11)

[He often thought about embracing as his mother had advised him. Gurnemanz had also taught him that man and wife were one. They entwined arms and legs. If I have to tell you, he found the nearness sweet: The old and new custom dwelled between them there. It was delightful to him and not at all painful.]

Almost immediately after enjoying his wife for the first time, he tells her of his wish to go and find out how his mother is faring. He then embarks on the journey that will take him to his first fateful encounter with the Gral and its world and will take him away from her for more than four years.

Chrétien's romance of Perceval is a strange double structure, with the second part concentrating on the exploits of Gauvain. Wolfram turns this doubling into a sophisticated structure that allows Gawan to function as Parzival's surrogate in the more traditional kinds of chivalric adventures. Unlike Chrétien, Wolfram reminds us frequently of his absent hero so that the passage of time will apply to him as well as to Gawan. The technique used here is interesting in its own right, but it would draw us too far from our quest for the sexual stranger.[6] What is important for our purposes is the recognition that Gawan is Parzival's surrogate and that his quest for his sexual partner is a parallel, one could almost say an "objective correlative," of Parzival's spiritual search. Parzival will recover his sexual Other when he reaches his goal, the Gral, but Gawan's unattached status allows him to explore the sexual world Parzival is no longer free to experience.

Wolfram arranges for Gawan a sequence of variations on the theme of sexual relations between knights and ladies. In the first, Gawan serves a child named Obilot in a parody of courtly love service. It is clear that the child is too young to grant sexual favors to the knight, but all the externalities of a courtly love relationship are observed. When she offers her love in exchange for his service, Gawan points out that she is much too young to offer *minne,* by which he clearly means sexual favors:

ê daz ir minne megt gegebn,
ir müezet fünf jâr ê lebn. (370, 15–16)

[Before you are able to grant love, you would have to live five (more) years.]

This element is totally lacking in Chrétien, who seems content to let the comedy of the child-lover stand on its own.

In the second sexual variation, Gawan meets a woman at the court where he is to fight a duel to defend his honor and the two are drawn to each other immediately. They have already kissed and exchanged caresses when they are interrupted by members of the court intent on avenging their late lord, whom Gawan had been falsely accused of killing. If the first variation involves a "lady" who is not yet ready to be a sexual partner, the second involves a lady who is far too ready. Here Wolfram again thematizes the overt sexual nature of the encounter to a far greater extent than his source. Chrétien's narrator speaks only of the two being "antrebeisant" (kissing one another). The irate "vavasor" who interrupts adds "conjoir" and "acole" (greeting and hugging) to the kissing to make his accusation of the nameless princess that much more damning.

Wolfram names her Antikonie and allows the scene to expand exponentially. Gawan comes into her presence and tells her that her brother had sent her word through him to accede to all of his wishes. She specifically offers to kiss him if he feels it is appropriate. His response combines with the narrator's remark in an image that is both humorous and sensual:

> Gâwân sprach "frouwe, iwer muont
> ist sô küssenlîch getân,
> ich sol iweren kus mit gruoze hân."
> ir munt was heiz, dick unde rôt,
> dar an Gâwân den sînen bôt.
> da ergienc ein kus ungastlîch. (405, 16–21)
>
> [Gawan said, "Lady, your mouth is made so kissable, I should have your kiss with your greeting." Her mouth was hot, full and red, to which Gawan offered his own. A kiss took place that was not (merely) hospitable.]

After the initial kiss, the princess sends her attendants out of the room. Matters quickly progress beyond the kissing stage:

> er greif ir undern mantel dar:
> Ich waene, er ruort irz hüffelîn.
> des wart gemêret sîn pîn.
> von der liebe alsölhe nôt gewan
> beidiu magt und ouch der man,
> daz dâ nâch was ein dinc geschehen,
> hetenz übel ougen nicht ersehen. (407, 2–8)
>
> [He reached under her clothing there, I think he touched her thigh. From this his suffering was increased and they gained such pain from love, both the girl and the man, that a thing would have taken place, if evil eyes had not seen them.]

The evil eyes belong to townspeople who interrupt their lovemaking and demand that Gawan be punished for killing the king.

The third variation is represented by the lady who will become Gawan's wife. She is appropriate in terms of age and station, but she is unwilling because of her arrogance. She sends Gawan on a series of deadly adventures. Stretching (or perhaps misunderstanding) the descriptive epithet Chrétien had fashioned for her (l'Orgilleuse de Logres; i.e., the Proud Lady of Logres), Wolfram calls her Orgeluse, using it simply as a proper name. We shall return to Gawan's relation to her after we glance at two further examples of Wolfram's thematization of sex that are bracketed within the Orgeluse adventures.

Gawan is tricked off his horse by a wounded knight whose life he had saved. The scoundrel turns out to be Urjans, who had been humiliated at Arthur's court by being forced to live with the dogs. Gawan had brought about this punishment in lieu of the death penalty after Urjans had been convicted of rape. Chrétien speaks only of his having "done his will" with the girl, whereas Wolfram makes it clear that the knight had taken "ir kiuscheclîchen magetuom [her chaste virginity]" (526, 5).

In a later episode, Wolfram invents a young woman where there had been none in Chrétien. After winning the joust with Lischoys Gweljus, Gawan spends the night at the home of a rich ferryman. The ferryman sends his daughter in to make sure that all of Gawan's wishes are fulfilled and in the morning she returns and watches over him as he awakens. His request for information about the magical castle across the river causes her to burst out in tears because of the danger to his life. At this point the father enters and assumes that Gawan has taken advantage of her sexually. He tries to comfort the girl:

> dô sprach er 'tohter, wein et niht.
> swaz in schimpfe alsus geschilht,
> ob daz von êrste bringet zorn,
> der ist schier dâ nâch verkorn.' (555, 27–29)

> [Then he said, "Daughter, do not weep. Whatever has happened here in sport, even though it may make you angry at first, it will quickly pass."]

Gawan is quick to declare their innocence and to tell him that his question in regard to the castle had caused this outburst.

Through this series of adventures Gawan is exposed to a wide range of sexual possibilities, some of which are open to him and others of which are not. It is the contribution of Wolfram that each of these is made sexually explicit in those passages where the reader is left with a nudge and a wink from Chrétien to fill in the blanks. Gawan encounters a girl who is too young for him to possess sexually;

a woman who is almost instantly willing to take Gawan to bed with her;

a woman who rejects love from all men, but allows them to humiliate themselves in her service;

a reminder of a rape in the form of a renewed crime by a rapist; and

a girl who is sent by her father to grant *all* of Gawan's wishes.

The one area in which Wolfram does not add sexually explicit material is in the Schastel Marveile episode. The reason for this is clear. Gawan is too closely related to the queens for them to be sexual candidates, and the other women at the castle are their inferiors, and thus Gawan's as well. Gawan knows about the relationship even if the women do not. Apparently incest was not one of the sexual variants Wolfram felt compelled to illustrate.

When Gawan has established himself through numerous acts of prowess to be worthy of Orgeluse, the woman who is appropriate to him but resistant, she breaks down and weeps for the pain and danger she has caused him, showing her noble nature. Gawan offers her love on the spot, but she puts him off on the grounds that "an gîsertem arm / bin ich selten worden warm [I have never warmed to an ironclad arm]" (615, 2–3). She does teasingly point to the future when he can claim his prize.

The two return to Schastel Marveile so that Gawan can recover completely from his wounds. He suffers a lover's torments in his dreams, and we are told that he is actually so well bandaged that

ob friundîn waer bî im gelegen,
het er minne gepflegen,
daz waere im senfte unde guot. (628, 5–8)

[If a lady friend had lain by him, he would have made love, that would have been comfortable and good.]

Obviously, sex is not to be lost as a goal here. Chrétien does not even insert a night of rest here, much less a reference to potential lovemaking.

When Gawan and Orgeluse finally reach their sexual goal, Wolfram suddenly becomes coy and teases us with his own winks and nudges:

Die tür beslôz hêr Gâwân.
kunn si zwei nu minne steln,
daz mag ich unsanfte heln.
ich sage vil lîht waz dâ geschach,
wan daz man dem unfuoge ie jach,
der verholniu mære machte breit.

ez ist ouch noch den höfschen leit:
och unsaeliget er sich dermite.
zuht sî dez slôz ob minne site. (642, 30–643, 8)

[Sir Gawan barred the door. The two can now steal love; I can't hide that easily. I (could) tell you easily what happened there, except that a person who talks abroad about what is hidden is always accused of improper behavior. It is also painful to the chivalrous. The person who does this plunges himself into sorrow. Let modesty be the bar before the conduct of love.]

Having brought Gawan to the goal of his sexual quest, we can turn back and remind ourselves of the knowledge Gawan's double, Parzival, has gained during this time. Wolfram seems to value three kinds of knowledge highly: knowledge of one's blood ties; "lore" about such things as precious stones, herbs, and the Gral (which seems to be a precious stone for Wolfram); and the "theological" knowledge necessary to participate in a chivalric version of Christianity. Parzival's major scene of enlightenment is placed centrally within the Gawan episodes. His visit with the hermit, who turns out to be his uncle Trevrizent, is one of the most studied portions of both romances. For the modern reader it raises as many questions as it answers.

By the end of his sexual education, Gawan has gained the knowledge that is necessary for his existence. He seems to have already had a wide knowledge of the lore necessary for the chivalric life. His gathering of an herb to heal the injured knight suggests that he is expert in medicine. He has learned the identity of the mysterious four queens at Schastel Marveile—they are his grandmother (Arthur's mother), Arnive; his mother, Sangive; and his two sisters, Cundrie and Itonje—without revealing his own identity. The last hours at Schastel Marveile are spent preparing to bring together all the threads of his knowledge in the form of a huge surprise at Arthur's court. He goes to great difficulty to prepare his surprise without revealing anything to the other interested parties. The climactic, almost musical-comedy-like scene of revelation is, however, somewhat played down because it is only the end of the surrogate plot and there are important revelations remaining in the Parzival story.

The day before he is to defend his honor against a second unjustified challenge, Gawan encounters an unknown knight. For once the audience of the poem is allowed to know more than the participants. The combatants are Gawan and Parzival, two men so bound by love and kinship that they would never have fought if they had known each other's identity. The theme of withheld knowledge is brought to a natural conclusion in this battle. Parzival gets the better of Gawan before the identities are revealed, establishing once and for all Parzival's superiority to the greatest knight of Arthur's permanent circle.

The story of Parzival was one that was very difficult to tell. The tools of chivalric romance did not provide the equipment to tell of an inner journey to self-recognition and spiritual knowledge. Chrétien probably decided to use Gauvain as a Perceval-surrogate in his romance, but its incomplete state leaves the experiment unsatisfactory. Wolfram had the advantage of being able to re-form the material from the beginning, and he was able to strengthen the surrogate plot's relationship to the main plot by having Parzival almost present in scene after scene throughout the Gawan episodes. He is usually referred to only as "der rote ritter" or otherwise identified without mention of his name, but he is present throughout the Gawan portions in a way that demonstrates Wolfram's unique skills as an architect of a giant structure. Perhaps the most striking almost-appearance is the one in which he refuses Orgeluse's proffered love during the Schastel Marveile sequence. His prowess wins her attention, but he remains true to Condwiramurs, whom he has not seen in more than four years. The reader experiences this encounter only in the chagrined narration of the rejected Orgeluse:

> mînen lîp gesach nie man,
> ine möhte wol sîn diens hân;
> wan einer, der truoc wâpen rôt.
> mîn gesinde er brâht in nôt. (618, 19–22)
>
> [No man ever saw me from whom I was unable to win his service, except for one who wore red armor. He threatened my knights.]

We recognize Parzival immediately from his red armor. After all of Orgeluse's knights are defeated, she advances to meet him herself:

> Dô er die mîne überstreit,
> nâch dem helde ich selbe reit.
> ich bôt im lant unt mînen lîp:
> er sprach, er hete ein schoener wîp,
> unt diu im lieber waere.
> diu rede was mir swaere. (619, 1–6)
>
> [When he had defeated all of my men, I rode after the hero myself. I offered him land and my body: He said he had a more beautiful wife, one who was dearer to him. This speech pained me.]

After the duel with Gawan, Parzival is present once more as the central character in the romance. He engages (once again victoriously) in a duel with Gawan's challenger as a surrogate for Gawan, whom he had put *hors de combat* the day before. After the various feuds and love tangles that had hung over the Arthurian court are straightened out, Parzival feels restless and goes for a ride in the forest, where he encounters a strange knight. For the second time the audience is allowed to know more than the protagonists. The narrator tells us that this strange knight is Parzival's half-brother Feirifiz, who is particolored black and white from his mixed parentage. The narration of the battle is peppered with complaints that two such close relatives are engaged in mortal combat. The importance of blood relation is expressed powerfully when Wolfram says of the two that they are "ein verch und ein bluot [one life and one blood]" (740, 3). Only the breaking of Parzival's sword prevents fratricide. The heathen tosses his own sword away and suggests a truce, during which the two men reveal their identities.

Upon his return to Arthur's court with his brother, Parzival is approached by Cundrie la Surziere, the messenger of the Gral, who tells him that his trials are over and that he is to return to Munsalvaesche to free his uncle with the "Question." After doing so, he sets out to meet his wife and sons. Wolfram again makes the sexual element of their relationship explicit. She receives her husband in her tent:

> sie blicte ûf und sah ir man.
> si hete niht wanz hemde an. (800, 29–30)
>
> [She looked up and saw her husband. She had nothing but a shift on.]

She throws the bedclothes around her shoulders and goes to meet her husband. Suddenly, Wolfram steps back from the narration into his ironic pose as narrator: "man sagte mir, si kusten sich [I have been told that they kissed each other]" (801, 5). After Parzival greets his young sons, Kardeiz and Loherangrin, everyone is cleared out of the tent and the pair are left alone. Wolfram tells us that Parzival had had many opportunities to enjoy the love of women, but that he had refused them all. Finally he slips back into his ironic mode to imply what is going on here:

> ich waene er kurzwîle pflac
> unz an den mitten morgens tac. (802, 9–10)
>
> [As far as I know, he disported himself there until towards mid-morning.] (Hatto's translation, p. 398)

Wolfram allows himself an encore in the love story between Feirifiz and Repanse de Schoye, the Gral bearer. Feirifiz is still a heathen, so he is unable to see the Gral, but he is able to see the bearer and he falls in love with her instantly. He accepts baptism in order to win the girl and is immediately able to see the Gral and enjoy its benefits. The two return to the East, where they become the parents of the legendary Prester John.

At the end of the romance all mysteries have been revealed and all couples are sleeping snugly in each other's arms. Are these unrelated conclusions? I think not.

Glancing back at the simpler romances involving Erec and Iwein, we can see the double quest of the romance quite clearly. Both stories identify one goal of the quest as the ideal relationship with one's lady. This identification is lacking in the Perceval/Parzival story, and it is this lack that makes it such a difficult story to transform into a generically satisfying romance. Both Chrétien and Wolfram recognized the lack and transferred the action from the already happily wived Parzival to the surrogate Gawan, who could engage in the sexual adventures denied Parzival. Chrétien was unable to carry out the experiment successfully, but he created a structure that many other poets would find congenial to the development of romance plots of their own.[7] Wolfram recognized the great lack of the Perceval story as he found it and corrected it by tying the pair Parzival/Gawan more closely together through the device of Parzival's frequent background appearances and by making the sexual content, which Chrétien had played down (or neglected) in his version, much more explicit.[8] The sexual content of Parzival's relationship to his wife is also repeatedly foregrounded both through the delay of its consummation beyond the point found in Chrétien and through the explicit mention of their lying together afterward. As if this were not enough, we are told repeatedly that Parzival had no sexual relations with any woman but Condwiramurs.

Sex, implied and explicit, granted and refused, indulged in and avoided, is a major aspect of the romance genre as Wolfram found it, yet it is largely lacking in the quest portion of Perceval's story. The Gauvain plot is also incomplete and lacks a sexual conclusion. Wolfram realized this lack and carefully went through the text establishing the love interests of Parzival and Gawan as authentic sexual strangers, sexual counterparts to be sought and learned about, and making the sexual nature explicit where his source had little or nothing. In so doing, he transformed an incomplete work that failed to satisfy the generic expectations of the chivalric romance into a consummation of the genre, a work that would be the model for German Arthurian romance throughout the later Middle Ages.

Notes

1. Roland Barthes, *S/Z*, trans. Richard Miller (New York: Hill & Wang, 1974), 19.

2. "L'endroit le plus érotique d'un corps n'est-il pas *là où le vêtement baîlle*?" Quoted by Jonathan Culler in *Structuralist Poetics: Structuralism, Linguistics and the Study of Literature* (Ithaca, N.Y.: Cornell University Press, 1975), 255.

3. Quotes are from Hartmann von Aue, *Erec*, ed. Albert Leitzmann, 4th ed. Ludwig Wolff, Altdeutsche Textbibliothek 59 (Tübingen: Niemeyer, 1963). Translations are mine.

4. All quotes from *Perceval* are from Chrétien de Troyes, *The Story of the Grail (Li Contes del Graal), or Perceval*, ed. Rupert T. Pickens, trans. William W. Kibler (New York: Garland, 1990).

5. All quotes from *Parzival* are from *Wolfram von Eschenbach*, ed. Karl Lachmann, 6th ed. (Berlin: de Gruyter, 1926). The translation used here is by A. T. Hatto (Harmondsworth: Penguin, 1980). Unattributed translations are my own.

6. See Hans-Hugo Steinhoff, *Die Darstellung gleichzeitiger Geschehnisse im mhd. Epos* (Munich: Eidos,1963), 44–76, for a discussion of this and other parallel narrations in *Parzival.*

7. See the list of continuations and adaptations in Chrétien de Troyes, *The Story of the Grail,* xxiv.

8. Much of the sexually explicit language in Wolfram is discussed by James Marchand in "Wolfram's Bawdy," *Monatshefte* 69 (1977): 131–49. Marchand does not, however, address the generic function of the passages.

CHAPTER 7

Creating Credibility and Truth through Performance: Kelin's Encomium

Maria Dobozy

The itinerant poet-minstrels, or *Spruchdichter,* of medieval Germany regularly disseminated information and created reputations for wealthy and aspiring members of the nobility. Given their public, political function, it may appear misleading at first to speak of them as outsiders or strangers. However, in sociological terms, entertainers, both individually and as a group, existed in the interstices of society, between the threads that tie people into more stable relationships. For most minstrels, interaction with others was transitory and relationships were temporary. The temporariness of their social ties, an inevitable result of the wandering life, placed minstrels outside the bounds of conventional social interaction. Their resulting outsiderhood limited their ability to interact with the rest of society. Nevertheless, they were able to subsist and, using performance as the primary medium, to make use of several different opportunities to interact with all levels of society in a variety of situations. I hope to show that the more innovative poets were able turn the handicap of being outsiders to their advantage.

The key to understanding minstrels' pariah status can be found in documents in which German society defined itself. The most informative of these for Germany is the law code or customary known as the *Sachsenspiegel.* It mentions minstrels only a few times, which is an indication that they were not fully incorporated into the legal system. According to the *Sachsenspiegel,* legal protection and legal rights of performers were severely limited in comparison to those of freemen: "Kempen unde er kinder, spellude, unde all de <in> unecht geboren sin . . . de sin alle rechtelos [Hired fighters and their children, minstrels, and all those illegitimately born are all without rights]." However, they did retain legal capacity: "It is manich man rechtlos, de nicht is echtlos [A man who is without legal rights is not without legal protection]."[1] Their lack of rights made them ineligible to serve as judge, doomsman, witness, or advocate in a court of law. They also lacked the right to appeal a legal decision. But the greatest restriction to their legal status, and the greatest threat to their safety, was their ineligibility to clear themselves with a cleansing (exculpatory) oath if accused of a crime.[2]

The cleansing oath was central to the entire legal system. It was based on the reputation and social standing of the accused and on his ties first to family and second to members of the community. Clearly, the legal system was able to deal only with those who had close ties in a village or town where every inhabitant knew the family and background of every other person and could be called upon to swear to an individual's personal integrity. As an itinerant, a minstrel remained a stranger to every community. In matters of serious dispute, he simply lacked an identity, and consequently was unable to find any oathhelpers (compurgators). Hence the profession of performer, with the accompanying vagabond status, carried with it lack of credibility.

Usually the *Sachsenspiegel* passages are interpreted as denying minstrels their legal rights and protection, but it appears that the limitations placed on their rights stem from the nature of the legal system itself. It is the task of the customaries to determine what lies within the purview of the system. Minstrels, lacking social ties, stood at the very boundary of legally regulated society. They were thus in constant danger, for without supporters and the protection of a social group they could easily be accused of being threats to the community. How, then, did the poet-singers turn this handicap to their advantage?

There were a number of different kinds of entertainers who fit this description and yet gained temporary access to society by means of their performance. They were all called minstrels, or *Spielleute.* In this essay I concentrate on Kelin (fl. 1250–87), a representative of a relatively homogeneous group of wandering didactic singers (*Spruchdichter*) who composed their own melodies and lyrics. They depended on the generosity of patrons and audiences for their livelihood, and in return, they composed panegyrics and songs with political, religious, and moral themes. We have no evidence of any female poet having been active among them.

Here it is useful to draw an analogy with the operations of contemporary ghostwriters and image makers, who perform the same functions even though they are not considered entertainers. What these people produce can be called art, although it is rarely considered so. This is obvious in the case of Roger Ailes. Roger Ailes is called a media consultant, and as a creative image maker, he has a lot in common with a medieval poet-minstrel like Kelin. He, too, has gone unrecognized.

If we compare them, we find that both are concerned with promoting the reputation (public image) of another individual. This means shaping audience opinion while forgoing an identity of one's own. The difference between the medieval *Spruchdichter* and the modern media consultant, of course, lies in the use of new techniques offered by modern technology. The minstrel was an outsider in his time because of his activities. In our time, image makers such as Roger Ailes are now being discussed and reevaluated as creative artists. It is also appropriate now to reassess medieval singers like Kelin.

The cult of the creative artist has biased us in our aesthetics against anything with specific political or didactic aims. Especially when compositions are created for money, they are suspicious and not considered art. The work of both contemporary artists and singers of the past needs to be reconsidered without such romantic prejudice. Ted Byfield has said of Ailes: "The job of political consultant is to unify politics and aesthetics."[3] This was Kelin's goal as well. For Kelin, however, this unity already existed and was avowedly recognized. His primary task was to make the aesthetic value clear to his audiences.

Only recently has Ailes been called the most successful contemporary American artist, a claim that expands the concept of art to include images that have a strong impact on an audience regardless of their (promotional) purpose.[4] If his skill can be measured by the success of his clients—Richard Nixon, Ronald Reagan, George Bush, and Dan Quayle—this assertion is certainly true. Just how responsible he was for their election is open to debate, but many feel that the images he created for them contributed significantly to their political success. However, Ailes did not have the reputation of an artist because of his lack of public identity and the newness of the profession of image making. He had been working for presidents for many years before anyone considered him an artist.

Like Kelin, Ailes must stay in the background in order for his images to work. All such people lack public identity, as the term *ghostwriter* signifies. The ghostwriter must remain anonymous, hiding in the shadows of the presidential speech or the staged photo opportunity, for after all, the purpose of word or picture is to shape public opinion regarding the public figure who has enlisted the ghostwriter's services. It is inconceivable, for example, that a president would read a ghostwritten speech and give credit to the writer. Such a mistake would completely obliterate his own authority and nullify the rhetorical effect of the speech on the audience—even though everyone knows that speeches are ghostwritten. Richard Nixon himself attempted to deny that his image had been constructed when he said, "If people looking at me say that's a new Nixon, then all that I can say is, well, maybe you didn't know the old Nixon."[5]

The itinerant poet-singers worked to fulfill a similar political function, ably using their negative situation and low status to their own advantage. There are two differences, however. First, unlike ghostwriters, medieval *Spruchdichter* performed their own songs even though they created images for others. And they used the power of their performance to cross the social border and to assume a temporary place within the society that excluded them.

The poet-singers collected material for their songs while in attendance at a court. Occasionally, individual minstrels may have had intimate access to members of the household and may even have acquired private and privileged information. They would then disseminate their material, in the form of panegyrics, on their travels. As they reached the next court, they would sing of their experiences at the previous one and praise or censure the previous hosts. This manner of transmitting information required traveling and justified an itinerant life—although singers made use of other modes of dissemination as well. This third stage of the process was the most critical, because it was necessary for a singer to create credibility by means of the poem and the performance. If the singer struck the right chords in his audience, his message would be embraced and remembered. His success depended upon the quality of the poem as well as on the artistic level of the performance, both of which reinforced the credibility of the singer.

Kelin is a case in point. He composed and sang during and after the difficult years of the Interregnum (c. 1254–72). His poems, like those of other wayfarers, indicate that his travels gave him the opportunity to disseminate commissioned panegyrics, to seek out new audiences, and to choose whom to praise. Thus his outsider status gave him the independence to view society from a distance, yet with familiarity. Furthermore, the very task of composing panegyrics, of choosing whom to praise and whom not, made him a moral critic. The self-assured stance typical of his poems reveals that he was fully aware of his role.

I wish to discuss the poem below first as a text (= poem) and then within the context of a performance situation (= song). In the poem, Kelin relates the process by which he fulfills his obligation to praise Volkmar von Kemenaten.[6] In so doing, he demonstrates that he must interact with many different people in order to be successful. After performing for Volkmar and accepting his gifts, Kelin leaves that court and sings three encomia (*lobeliet*) praising his donor, in two different places. His commission did not necessarily limit or name the kind of poem expected, but he declares that he sang three *lobeliet.* There were apparently three separate performances of at least two, possibly three different songs, because they were sung in two different locations. These specific bits of information, prefaced with his comment that Volkmar outfitted him well ("mit gabe wol bereit"), make clear that gifts given to minstrels were considered not so much remuneration for current entertainment as they were advances or commissions for future laudatory poems. Hence Kelin's specific reference to the number of songs performed indicates that he has indeed accomplished his portion of the contract:

Wil ieman hyn kegen swaben
der sol den edelen sagen
daz ich mit kranken gaben
mich vil lutzel kan betragen.
man sol in sagen man se mich selten riten.

Volcmare von Kemenaten
dem sage er myne leit
Der manigen hat beraten

in hoch gelobeter werdicheit
die ie irstreit vil lobes by synen tziten.

Sit daz ich von dem edelen schiet
der mich unde manigen gerenden da myt gabe wol bereit
sit sang ich yme in tzwen landen dry lobeliet:
zu Wensberg eynez die tzwey dort uf dem sande.

Die ich mit willen bringe viure
des ist Volcmar von Kemenaten
ein of getane tiure
sit ich ir keines milte viur die sine spiure,
so hat er lob unde richeit ane scande.[7]

[Should anyone be going to Swabia, let him tell the worthy people that I cannot get by on shabby gifts. One should tell them I'm seldom seen on horseback.

He should relate my woes to Volkmar, who has outfitted many by reason of his highly praiseworthy nobility, which always achieved much praise for him in his time.

Since I took leave of that noble man, who supported me and many a minstrel with gifts, since then I have sung to him three songs of praise in two lands, one in Weinsberg and two there on the strand.

To those whom I choose to bring forward Volkmar is an open door. Since I do not perceive the generosity of others outdoing his, he rightfully deserves praise and wealth without blame.]

My discussion begins, like the poem, with the topos most consistently associated with minstrels: the singer's complaint of inadequate compensation and an accompanying plea, implicit or explicit, for more generous remuneration. The complaint, expressed by all minstrels, identifies Kelin as an outsider. Such pleas have, because of their frequency, exposed many poet-singers to charges of unashamed begging and greed. Influenced by the cult of the genius, modern scholars have tended to disregard poets who write for money and to dismiss poetry with political content. Unlike the fourteenth-century scribes who compiled the Minnesinger manuscripts, such scholars would not have included panegyrics in the now much-prized collections. Yet if we accept the terms of the contract that require Kelin to perform commissioned encomia before audiences, then perhaps the request for payment is more than a mere formula.[8]

The poem's surface meaning is straightforward. Since leaving Swabia, Kelin has not received adequate compensation. As a result, he is clearly disappointed and wants someone to communicate his plight to the Swabians (str. 1). In a *laudatio temporis acti,* he praises what Volkmar von Kemenaten has done in the past (str. 2). Valued already by Volkmar, he now proves himself by fulfilling his obligation to his benefactor (str. 3). The outdoing topos in the final strophe reassures us that Volkmar is still unsurpassed in his generosity.[9] Kelin argues by implication that his poetry is good—good enough for Volkmar to have commissioned him to sing and laud him on his travels; but now in Bavaria, or wherever he is outside of Swabia,[10] he encounters rejection. From his perspective, he has acquitted himself well as a singer, and suggests, therefore, that it befits his current host to offer him adequate remuneration and a commission.

Right from the beginning, the surface meaning is intended for a divided audience, as we can tell from the general address "wil ieman" in the first line. By enlisting a messenger to take information to the Swabians, Kelin signals that he has three distinct messages that divide his intended audience into three distinct subgroups: the immediate listeners, the potential emissary, and the Swabians who will receive the information. Kelin specifically addresses the potential courier, expressing a message intended for the Swabians and Volkmar, but he also offers specific messages to each of them. The poem carries multiple subtexts, because each group of addressees has its own interests and will find different points to focus on.

Kelin employs the complaint—with its tacit plea for support—to address each audience separately according to its own perspective and interest from which it hears the song. For example, the lack of support Kelin expresses is certainly an appeal to the immediate listeners to be as generous as the Swabians. Although this statement implies praise of Swabian generosity, a compliment that includes some and excludes others is certainly more welcome to the Swabians than to the non-Swabians. Kelin also uses the grievance as a point of departure to honor Volkmar with yet another poem, thus adding a fourth performance (and perhaps even a fourth composition) to his catalog of *lobeliet* to Volkmar. This clever coupling of his charge of inadequate remuneration with a panegyric creates a third level of meaning—the poem itself becomes the message.

One may conclude that the combined complaint and praise implies two ways of affecting the audience on the one hand and of helping the minstrel's own cause on the other. First, it reminds the listeners of the reason for remuneration. Second, the poet-singer illustrates with his poem how well he can weave new encomia into a performance. This sets up his listeners to draw the conclusion that he can work effectively for them, too. Such a claim means that he is less concerned with the explicit complaint of insufficient remuneration than with the implicit advertisement for himself. The result is that the complaint becomes a literary fiction at this point. It leads to the conclusion that his composition and his performance are intended to be understood as an audition. Kelin is thus able to present an example of his encomiastic ability to the audience before him and at the same time assert that his artistic excellence has already been received favorably in Swabia.

By the same token, the introductory missive to the Swabian nobles—Kelin's absent audience—is not merely a pretext for inducing the members of his immediate audience to open up their money bags and commission eulogies. Rather, the enumeration of the *lobeliet* reveals his aim in sending a messenger—to enable that person to report to the nobles that he has indeed sung skillfully the praises of Volkmar in fulfillment of his contract. Beyond the layer of meaning aimed at the entire audience lies the hidden meaning intended for the traveling emissary. Kelin appeals to his listeners to convey his message. But who might take such a missive to Swabia, and who would communicate it most effectively? Obviously, one who hears him perform. This person may be a Swabian visitor or any member of the audience, but the most likely messenger would be a fellow wayfarer. This assumption makes most sense if both content and form—that is, the song itself—is to be transmitted. A minstrel could easily learn and perform the song and would not need to resort to a colorless paraphrase. After all, the poem is far broader and much more engaging than the complaint it voices.

The final lines are even more revealing if they are intended for the ears of a minstrel.[11] According to von Wangenheim, Kelin states that whoever he should choose to bring or present at Volkmar's court will be welcomed by his host.[12] The statement thus implies that if a minstrel arrives with Kelin's song, used perhaps in lieu of a "letter of introduction," then Volkmar will admit him.

Yet if we read the pronoun (*die* in l. 15) as perhaps referring to the songs Kelin composes, then the line can mean that if the songs are welcomed by Volkmar, then Kelin's minstrel-emissary will be, too. Either interpretation is quite plausible because it would be false to assume that composer and singer are always the same person. Furthermore, as it has already been mentioned that Volkmar opens his door to Kelin's colleagues ("mich und manigen gerenden"), it appears that he offers his court as a center for literary and artistic exchange.

Addressing three audiences, Kelin accomplishes several goals in one poem: he praises Volkmar's court, submits his credentials (i.e., previous support of noble patron), auditions for commissions, and notifies his patron that he is indeed singing the commissioned songs. The fact that the poem subsumes multiple messages enables the system to feed itself. The very use of the medium of the encomium to inform the donor that the contract has been satisfied is clever enough, but the poet is even more efficient. He uses the same poem as an audition to acquire an additional commission, either from the praised patron or from a new one. As Kelin demonstrates, the poet can weave into his poem an illustration of his talent for panegyrics.

What Kelin tells us he accomplished may appear simple and straightforward, but its potential for reaffirming and shaping prevailing attitudes and for creating new ones among his listeners should not be underestimated. For example, his praise of the generous Swabians in Franconia or Bavaria works to his best advantage when such an implication of lack of generosity and taste is directed against the listeners' sense of identity, because it attributes to them provincialism, or breach of custom, a disgrace no nobleman is likely to accept. A donor has good reason to commission eulogies, for in this system of oral dissemination the minstrels' songs can have far-reaching influence in the shaping of attitudes toward individual nobles, their courts, and their actions.

Theoretically, then, a performance is also an audition. A good singer displays his talents and considers the performance especially successful if it culminates in a commission. An audition points to the priority of performance and the dependence of a literary work on it, such that the meaning of the work is not determined by the text, but created by the performance. In other words, Kelin's poem exists on parchment merely as text and becomes song only during performance.

If this line of thought is carried one step further, one can say that meaning develops fully only in the performance context, where it unfolds in auditory sequence. During performance, a bond is formed between the spectators and performer that has been referred to as the urge to share an experience.[13] Usually the performer tends to disappear behind the role he plays, but here Kelin does not let the illusion take over. Instead, he accentuates and thematizes the dichotomy between the performer and the role. Then as the performance proceeds, the experiential reality it produces combines with the truth of the words. Listening to this song, the audience should not suspend disbelief. Rather, the spectators must become aware that what the performer demonstrates by singing this composition is exactly what he says he is doing—singing encomia. This announcement enables the listeners to discern the two voices: the individual wayfaring minstrel who appears to speak for himself (but is not identical with the "true" Kelin, who has no identity) and the singer role, namely, the first-person voice. When the voice (= singer) asks for a messenger (ll. 1–4), it appears to be a sincere request that requires a response. But the audience cannot be sure of the sincerity of that request until the next two stanzas. In the second stanza, where the laud of Volkmar begins, the complaint of insufficient remuneration in stanza 1 suddenly falls into the background as a pretext for a panegyric. Once the tribute is recognized, the pose of the performer becomes obvious, and the listener must now reevaluate the sincerity of the first request. The clothing the minstrel performs in can become an additional layer of commentary on the substance of his words: rags would corroborate the complaint, and rich attire would create irony.

If the first stanza appears to reveal the performer's true complaint and the second exposes it as a pose that simultaneously identifies the "I" of the song as the wayfaring minstrel he is, a double perspective has been created that is carried further in the third stanza. Here it becomes clear that the complaint cannot be dismissed as a mere pose. The listener is forced to view both possible interpretations—as pose and as genuine assertion—simultaneously when the singer claims to have sung panegyrics to Volkmar. The listener may recognize the performer's role-playing, but at the same time his assertion is proven true by the fact that he is doing it before his audience.

The claim is that he has sung two songs in praise of Volkmar. Now, the members of the audience have not heard those songs but discern that they are witness to a song of praise. Since the performer actually performs what he claims to have done, the act of praising becomes linked to the words of praise in such a way that the spectators come to experience an encomium through the performance. This correspondence between word and deed at the moment of performance establishes the needed credibility for the performer. The listeners can now accept the veracity of the song's content because they are experiencing one such panegyric. Further, if they respond positively to the performer, if they enjoy the song at all, then they must also accept the assertion that Volkmar valued his songs and performances.

By association, the truth claimed for the content is not merely that Kelin sang the songs, but also that his praise of Volkmar is accurate. Thus we have here the double perspective of knowing that the wayfarer is both playing a role and presenting himself, and it is this perspective that makes possible the claim to veracity that the audience can now accept. They witness precisely what the singer claims to have done because the assertion and the deed have been linked by means of the double perspective. The listeners are then given the task of reflecting upon this link.

In contemporary performance, we are accustomed to the modern avant-garde, which begins with reality and aims to expose the illusion and duplicity created in performance. In contrast, medieval performances, lacking the usual formal physical frames of curtains, stage, lighting, and so on, acknowledge from the very outset the illusion they create. Like ritual, medieval performance aims to transform the role created into a new reality. Medieval audiences knew that the singer is not identical with the first-person voice. Moreover, the success of this song depends on its double perspective's being recognized and maintained by the spectators throughout the performance. The double perspective allows the audience to question the credibility of the song while recognizing that the voice of genuine experience and the pose could well merge into one, and that what the minstrel sings could well be true. Gradually, the congruence of word and deed turns the role-playing into reality to the extent that the listeners experience this unity, and once experienced, it has a life of its own. This is a conjuring trick to be sure, but one that can occur in any society immersed in ritualistic thought. As Tyrone Guthrie has written, "I believe that the theatre makes its effect not by means of illusion, but by ritual."[14]

By making the audience aware of his actions while he executes them, the poet-minstrel creates, like Heinrich von Veldeke, self-conscious poetry. In performance it draws attention to itself, its artistry and craft. The performer uses the two voices and the double perspective consciously, pointing out the simultaneity of the performer and the first-person role. Then, having brought the spectator this far, the first-person singer sets up a second correspondence between word and deed in the third stanza. But this time the "I" of the song is making claims about Volkmar's deeds and not his own. As a result, the boundary between the "apparent" experiential reality and the literary (fictional) pose is made more conspicuous but also more permeable.

The performer must always cross that boundary when he performs a role, but here Kelin thematizes it on two levels: the role of singer and the person of the performer are kept as two separate but interdependent voices, and the content of the song is linked to audience experience. While the performer plays the singer, he forces his listeners to reflect upon the performance world that runs parallel to but also spills over into the "real" world. What the audience experiences as reality is a performance that verifies the content of the song, enabling the audience to experience an event that is true or real and timeless in medieval terms. Because this event is identical to the narrative content, the performance opens the door between fiction and reality. The result is a ritualistic transformation: the song becomes a way to make "true" what the voice claims is true. Thus a performance must be understood as a process and the song it produces yields true learning in the form of audience experience.

My interpretation indicates that the poem and song are intensely concerned with the nature of art. The double perspective reexamines, as epic theater does, the boundary between truth and artifice, art and reality. When Kelin forces his listeners to be aware of the double perspective, he makes them cognizant of his mastery of the art forms that enable the song to spill into their experienced reality. What the song underscores is the poet-performer's art. The intricate multilayered construction (text) can be admired for itself, for its tone is one of lighthearted pleasure, but a performance illustrates for the listeners that the very art and invention of the singer are essential for creating and conveying truth. The process of performance and the first-person account of events go beyond hearsay (no subjunctives are used, for example) because they provide the experience of what the song declares to be true. This art relies on the performer's ability to turn words into reality by crossing the boundary in performance. Kelin's tactic or goal, then, is the valorization of poetry. In addition to pleasure, poetry provides new knowledge and experience. Ultimately, one can make no better argument for a commission than to claim that good poetry serves patron and audience alike because it provides access to truth.

Finally, if we imagine a minstrel taking Kelin's message in the form of the song itself to Volkmar's court, then the message acquires yet another self-referential layer as the second singer plays the role of the first. Removed from its original geographic location and performance context, the performance now takes place in Swabia, where the listeners have different loyalties. Because credibility must be reestablished at every performance, the song still challenges and involves the audience the way the first performance did—it aims again to link word and deed. This time, however, the second performer sings a message that came from elsewhere, while the first-person voice remains the same. In this case, the encomium is sung in Volkmar's presence, but by another performer, one lauding him voluntarily. Once the audience members discover that the song's message comes from outside Swabia, they too, must accept the truth of the content because the performer and singer have executed what the previous singer requested and foretold: the second singer, who is Kelin's emissary, has come to Volkmar's court and has been welcomed.

Thus the song has potential for ever more variations in performance without varying the text in any way. If a song can be passed on from singer to singer, we may conclude that a minstrel can create truth by singing words of praise because the words in the form of song can take on an independent existence. It comes as no surprise, then, to hear another laudatory singer confidently exclaim in praise of Volkmar and another patron, "Ir lib ist tot, ir lob kan niht irsterben [Their body is dead, their praise can never die]."[15]

Each singer, as a new carrier of Kelin's encomium, will play the role of stranger, and indeed must *be* a stranger as he begins his song. The notion of strangerhood is thus here raised to the status of an aesthetic imperative.

Notes

1. From Karl Eckhardt, ed., *Sachsenspiegel. Landrecht, MGH. Fontes Ivris Germanici antiqui,* 1, 1; 3 (Göttingen: Musterschmidt Verlag, 1973), 1:38 para. 1, 1:51 para. 1. See Friedrich Scheele, "'Spillute . . . di sint alle rechtelos.' Zur rechtlichen und sozialen Stellung des Spielmanns in Text und Bild des *Sachsenspiegels,*" in *Der Sachsenspiegel als Buch,* ed. Ruth Schmidt-Wiegand and Dagmar Hüpper (Bern: Peter Lang, 1991), 315–57.

2. See Hans-Peter Hils, "'Kempen unde er kinder . . . de sin alle rechtelos.' Zur sozialen und rechtlichen Stellung der Fechtmeister im späten Mittelalter," in *Zusammenhänge, Einflüsse und Wirkungen,* ed. Joerg O. Fichte (Berlin: de Gruyter, 1986), 255–71.

3. Daniel Hinerfeld reporting on Ted Byfield's evaluation of Roger Ailes's work, taken from transcript of NPR's "Morning Edition," October 29, 1992, 20.

4. Lincoln Tobier, "Morning Edition," 19.

5. Quoted on "Morning Edition," 20.

6. We do not know exactly who Kelin's patron was. Between 1231 and 1282 there were at least four people by the name of Volkmar von Kemenaten. The Volkmar of the poem lived in the castle in (Groß) Kemnat by Kaufbeuren. See *Das Basler Fragment einer mitteldeutsch-niederdeutschen Liederhandschrift und sein Spruchdichter-Repertoire (Kelin, Fegfeuer),* ed. Wolfgang von Wangenheim (Bern: Peter Lang, 1972), 41–43.

7. The text is taken from the Jena manuscript (f. 19 v). I have added the line and strophic divisions. This poem is also in *Minnesinger. Deutsche Liederdichter des zwölften, dreizehnten und vierzehnten Jahrhunderts,* ed. Friedrich Heinrich von der Hagen, 5 vols. (Aalen: O. Zeller, 1962 [1838]), 3:24, poem III, 8; cited hereafter as HMS. The translation is mine.

8. See my article on gift exchange, "Beschenkungspolitik und die Erschaffung von Ruhm am Beispiel der fahrenden Sänger," *Frühmittelalterliche Studien* 26 (1992): 353–67.

9. Apparently, Kelin was able to make comparisons because he knew the High German areas: "mir sint die besten kunt in Swaben unde an dem Rine"; HMS, 3:24, poem II, 3. See also von Wangenheim, *Das Basler Fragment,* 41.

10. In str. 3 Kelin mentions where he sang, but we cannot be sure of the location of "uf dem Sande." It could refer to the bank of the Pegnitz in Nürnberg as in Marner's line "Nüerenberg hat liut und der Sant" or the Danube as Kelin mentions in another poem: "ze Wiene an dem Sant." Von Wangenheim, *Das Basler Fragment,* 133.

11. There are two variants of line 15; von Wangenheim, *Das Basler Fragment,* gives "die" (ms. Basel N13, 145) and HMS gives "diu" as the first word. Although Middle German does not distinguish between the two forms, the meaning of the line is ambiguous.

12. Von Wangenheim, *Das Basler Fragment,* translates this line: "Wen ich von mir aus mitbringe, der ist Volkmar willkomen" (134).

13. J. L. Styan, "The Mystery of the Play Experience," in *Performing Texts,* ed. Michael Issacharoff and Robin F. Jones (Philadelphia: University of Pennsylvania Press, 1988), 13.

14. Tyrone Guthrie, *A Life in the Theatre* (New York: McGraw-Hill, 1959), 350, cited in ibid. See also Anne Righter, *Shakespeare and the Idea of the Play* (London: Chatto & Windus, 1962).

15. Rumslant von Schwaben, HMS, 3:69, poem 3.

CHAPTER 8

The Stranger and the Problematics of the Epic of Revolt: *Renaut de Montauban*

William Calin

In this essay I offer a literary analysis—practical criticism—of one chanson de geste from the period circa 1200: *Renaut de Montauban.*[1] Among other approaches, I examine *Renaut de Montauban* intertextually, with reference to the earlier epic tradition, especially that of *La Chanson de Roland,* and sociologically, with reference to the contemporary historical situation and the aesthetics of reception. Two characteristics stand out in this late chanson de geste: on the one hand, something approximating realism, the probing of questions of feudal ethics and feudal law, the attempt to portray in as authentic a manner as possible the situation created by the clash of feudal and monarchic interests; on the other hand, something approximating melodrama and pure storytelling, an aesthetic of escape designed to distract the implied audience, to release tensions by making listeners laugh and weep. These two characteristics, juxtaposed or synthesized, contribute to the unique "literary reality" of *Renaut de Montauban.* The juxtaposition and synthesis will tell us something about medieval epic and also, I believe, about medieval and modern responses to epic.

Throughout, I use as one means of approach the concept of the stranger with its binary opposite, the native or "he who belongs," with their thematic extensions: outside versus inside, other versus self, and margin versus center. The reader may here interject that I do not, strictly speaking, investigate medieval strangers; I am employing the stranger as a metaphor in critical discourse. This is partially true, although, for medieval man as for modern man, "strangerness" was never limited to spatial extraterritoriality. Anyone who broke feudal law and/or who declared himself a rebel vis-à-vis his lord became legally and morally a stranger to his law and his lord. Furthermore, given that the binary opposition of self and other, or center and margin, is a topos in contemporary criticism, it can do no harm to expand the parameters of this volume by employing it indeed as a metaphor or conceptual device to facilitate scrutiny of the text. I doubt that I am the only contributor to do so.

The relatively late epic of revolt *Renaut de Montauban* is to a large degree a synthesis of much of the preceding epic tradition. The chanson not only alludes intertextually to any number of earlier epic heroes and songs, it also devours, so to speak, a number of earlier narratives. *Renaut de Montauban*'s diegetic universe presupposes the existence of other, extradiegetic stories; without them, it would not exist and cannot be properly understood. For example, *La Chanson des Saisnes* is recapitulated by Charlemagne; it is, so to speak, the *texte générateur* that launches the action. More to my point, Ogier the Dane and the young Roland play important roles in the action; their roles, their functions, are grounded in the implied audience's presumed knowledge of *La Chevalerie Ogier* and *La Chanson de Roland,* sterling representatives of the Rebel Cycle and the Cycle of the King.

Renaut de Montauban thus grows out of two distinct traditions: the "standard" Christian and royal epic (*Roland, Les Saisnes*) and the probaronial epic of revolt, which reacts against the royal epic (*Ogier, Girart de Roussillon*). The intertextual play with *La Chanson de Roland* is especially significant. The narrative time (*erzählte Zeit*) of *Renaut,* as with *Girart de Vienne* and *Aspremont,* is presumed to have occurred prior to the time of *La Chanson de Roland.* These adventures of the young Roland and the young and older Renaud draw inspiration from, and are meant to comment upon, a series of events that have not yet occurred but will occur, in the future, after Renaud's epic has ended.

Whether we deem Roland to be guilty of hubris or innocent from beginning to end, whether we deem the *Chanson* to contain tragic elements or not, Turold's epic depicts a relatively unproblematic universe, the hero embodies the values of the community, and the individual and the social coincide. Although the Franks have invaded Spain and are surprised on the return, they are in no sense strangers. The narrative is almost always focalized through the eyes of Charlemagne, Roland, and Oliver; the world is their world, depicted as they see it, whether it be Aix-la-Chapelle or Rencesvals. They are the self, their adversaries are the other. Well may this be the case, given that, in this unproblematic, militantly Christian and imperial mind-set, just as there is only one God in heaven, so there can be only one emperor, his deputy, on earth. It is his earth. All who claim otherwise are rebels and traitors, to the same extent that Satan is a rebel and traitor. They have made themselves outsiders, as Satan is an outsider. Rencesvals can be envisaged as the borderland between France and Spain, Christianity and pagandom, and good and evil; it is also Roland's true home, where he becomes himself to the fullest. Typologically it *is* his home, just as Jerusalem is Christ's city, prior to the one (and the other's) passion and subsequent entry into the heavenly *civitas Dei.*

In *Renaut de Montauban,* a century later, the Rolandian structures and the Rolandian certainty are reversed, undermined, distorted, decentered, and turned upside down. In Paris (the later equivalent of Aix-la-Chapelle) Charlemagne feels perfectly at home; however, Renaud recognizes that he is a stranger there. He, his brothers, and his father, Aymon, are literally in danger of their lives on the few occasions they do their feudal duty. Renaud the young hero, the Roland figure par excellence, is not allowed to perform the enshrined, expected Rolandian feats in Spain. Instead, he is forced to act and react, fruitlessly, inside the kingdom, where he remains ever a stranger. All he asks is to leave the court, the inhospitable center, and escape somewhere to the fringes of the realm, where he can create his own little center and act as a little Roland (more accurately, a sort of Guillaume) in his turn. So he tries, three times: to Montessor, to Montauban, and to Trémoigne. However, the spatial configuration mirrors, as it must, the feudal-monarchical configuration. Renaud's space is also Charles's space. Three times Charles arrives with an army to dislodge him. From Renaud's perspective, Charles appears as an invading, intrusive stranger, whereas from the emperor's perspective, he is simply (re)asserting his natural rights in his realm (what is not his realm?); and, mirroring the historical actuality of the Middle Ages and Renaissance, the capital or seat of power proves to be wherever the monarch holds court, wherever he chooses to be. Renaud also seeks refuge three times at his father's home in Dordonne and once flees to the Ardennes. In all cases he is forced out or for other reasons cannot remain. As a result, Renaud, ever the outcast, is pushed farther and farther to the limits of the empire and of the Christian, civilized world. In the long run the solution to his problem will be either to leave the empire totally and make a career as a pilgrim and crusader in the East and/or to remain within Francia but to abandon his identity and social class, that is, to become Saint Renaud by building the cathedral at Cologne in the guise of a laborer. Both solutions are wish-fulfillment fantasies in that they remove the protagonist from the spatial reality of his world and the social reality of his class. Both choices involve his becoming an involuntary stranger.

In contrast to the relatively unproblematic and celebratory *Chanson de Roland, Renaut de Montauban* contains powerful tragic elements, grounded in the tragic reality of the later feudal age.[2] The spatial configuration reflects that reality. One aspect of the social is the conflict between blood ties and the feudal bond. Ogier the Dane and Renaud's father, Aymon, are two magnificent Rüdiger figures (as in the *Nibelungenlied*), torn between kin loyalty to Renaud and their feudal oath to Charles. A second social aspect is the problematic nature of the feudal bond itself, especially when it conflicts with the concept of monarchy. As in that other great epic of revolt, *Girart de Roussillon,* the conflict is, I believe, consciously meant to be ambiguous. Is Beuves d'Aigremont Charlemagne's vassal for his lands or does he owe the emperor only symbolic loyalty, the loyalty of any great French baron to a French king? Similarly, to what extent is Renaud, Beuves's nephew and Aymon's son, chased from the court and from his father's lands and disinherited by his father, still Charles's vassal and beholden to Charles, if only symbolically? To what extent then is Renaud free to become the vassal of King Yon of Gascony? Is Yon also the vassal of Charlemagne and is he obliged, if only symbolically, to support the emperor against Renaud? How strong and how binding would the medieval audience have deemed Renaud's (and the others') obligations? I am convinced that the audience response would have been complex and multivocal outside the text, just as Renaud's response is complex and multivocal within the diegesis.

A final aspect of reality concerns the fact that Renaud finds himself locked in a situation, an *engrenage,* not of his own making but from which he cannot extricate himself. The first two thousand lines of the poem form a prologue or introduction that sets the stage for what follows. The Saxon Wars, Beuves's refusal to participate, his failure to go to court, Charles's sending Lohier as ambassador to summon him, Lohier's insults, Beuves's slaying of Lohier, Charlemagne's ambush of Beuves, and the subsequent war between Charles and Renaud's uncles—all this ensures that Charles and Renaud, at their first genuine contact, are driven by suspicion, animosity, guilt, and desire for vengeance. What follows is the inevitable outcome of what has gone before. In the conventional epic chess game, a nephew of Charles (Bertolai) loses his temper and strikes Renaud. Renaud appeals to Charles:

"Sire droiz emperere, je nel vos quir celer,
Mon oncle m'avez mort, donc mult me doit peser;
Et vostre niés meïsmes m'ala hui bufeter:
Quidez que ne m'en poist, droit emperere ber?
La mort Buef d'Aygremont vos vodrai demander
Que vos m'en faciez droit, par le cors seint Omer,
Ou se ce non, dans rois, il m'en devra peser." (2178–84)

["Rightful emperor, sire, I do not wish to hide it from you,
  that you have killed my uncle, which should sadden me greatly;
  and your nephew himself came up to me today and struck me.
Don't you think this grieves me, mighty, rightful emperor?
I want you to give me restitution, by the body of Saint Omer,
for the death of Bueves d'Aigremont.
Or if not, sir King, I will be greatly grieved."]

Charles responds brutally and with contempt:

"Malvais garçon, dist il, par le cors seint Omer,
A poi que ne vos vois de ma paume doner?" (2187–88)

["Wicked youth," he said, "by the body of Saint Omer,
I am coming close to slapping you myself."]

Renaud slays Bertolai. The rest will occupy twelve thousand lines in the Thomas edition, sixteen thousand lines in the old Castets edition.

One aspect of this psychological *engrenage* is that, once it is unleashed, there is no way out. Even so, over the course of years, reacting to it, the two adversaries evolve in time; they grow. Growth is represented in symbolic terms: Renaud's return to the mother after his dehumanizing experience as an outlaw in the Ardennes, or his winning a city and a bride in Gascony. In addition, the hero slowly, surely learns the lesson of maturity and sacrifice. In the end he is willing to recognize Charles's hegemony, to abandon all feudal rancor and desire for vengeance, to abandon his feudal and princely identity, and, for the sake of peace and to save his soul, to leave the space of the realm. Renaud discovers that to become other (to become a Christian stranger) is most truly and nobly to transform his self. Charles, on the other hand, grows in the opposite direction. Under the pressure of the Aymon family's unexpected resistance, above all riled by Maugis's tricks, Charles becomes a fanatic, declining all efforts at reconciliation, determined to hang Renaud and Maugis at any price and in the face of the absolute opposition of his barons.

These features or elements of the text function in and contribute to a total ambience that, to some extent, resembles what in nineteenth-century fiction we call realism. Compared to *La Chanson de Roland*—for that matter, compared to many an Arthurian romance—*Renaut de Montauban* is a work of realism. It probes social and class tensions (the high aristocracy versus the monarchy) within France, and it probes the human reaction to these tensions over a period of years. Compared with Turold and with many an Arthurian romancer, the *Renaut* poet is concerned with history, with movement in history, with exceptional people who face the most severe and ambivalent of moral choices in a problematic universe; he creates what Auerbach has called contemporary secular tragedy. I use the term *contemporary* given the fact that, although the action is displaced onto the Carolingian past—the conventional past of chanson de geste—it mirrors, glosses, and addresses any number of contemporary problems, including the rise to power of the Capetian kings of France and the ensuing loss of power on the part of the baronry.

It is true, a number of medievalists would fault the previous analysis on the grounds of medieval alterity: that the medieval mind-set was not that of the nineteenth century and, therefore, that terms such as *realism,* for that matter the notion of a character evolving in time, are inappropriate for medieval texts, which are largely conventional in nature. My response is that nineteenth-century texts are also conventional, that nineteenth-century realism and the *Bildungsroman* are also massively grounded in convention. All literature is conventional. All literature is also created by human beings and mirrors the human condition. To the extent that narrative literature is mimetic—that it tells a story involving people and participates in the representation (*Darstellung*) of people, places, and things—some texts will be more mimetic than others, and issues of mimesis, psychology, and social commentary will be valid in texts and in our discussion of them. Furthermore, whatever its faults, the new historicism is right to emphasize that all texts—of high culture and low culture, of the present and the past—mirror history and help create it, just as history itself functions as a text.

The social analogy, feudalism, evolution in time, contemporary tragedy—these are elements of *Renaut de Montauban* that, together, form a structure or pattern. However, they are not the only elements or pattern. I return to the observation that, in willed antithesis to Renaud, who learns to renounce lands, title, and feudal honor, Charles becomes more and more intractable in his hatred of the Aymon family and in his absolute refusal to make peace with them. Yes, the family of traitors counsels the emperor badly; however, he is eager to receive their wicked counsel, and often he acts entirely on his own. The real traitor is he who breaks the feudal bond—Charles. Years ago, Bender postulated in the history of chanson de geste a shift from good Charlemagne to weak Louis to evil Charlemagne, the stages corresponding to the *prise de conscience* on the part of the feudal nobility of its weakened status vis-à-vis the monarchy, the final stage (evil Charlemagne) reflecting the reign of Philip Augustus.[3] I agree. I should add, however, that the depiction of a pure and good Renaud opposed to a tarnished and wicked Charles inevitably draws the implied audience away from the careful, evenhanded scrutiny of the feudal dilemma and of man's problematic destiny in the feudal world toward a very different literary climate: melodrama.

As I see it, the most powerfully emotional scenes and the most poetically convincing passages evoke melodrama: pathos, not tragedy; emotion, not analysis. The battle for Montessor itself is of no great literary weight. Massive, on the other hand, and powerful in its overtones, are the consequences of the fall of Montessor: the sons of Aymon starving in the Ardennes, surviving on wild game and water, bloated, stinking, their skin turned black, and their clothes turned to rags and rotting on their rotting flesh. They are reduced to the life of beasts:

La grasse char et l'eve les a si engrotez
Que il sunt tuit enflé par flans et par costez;
Mult les a maubailliz li venz et li orez:
Par .i. poi que chascun n'est mort et afolez,
Fors que li .iiii. frere, cil puent mal assez.
. . .
Chascun n'est pas el bois ne logiez ne travez:
De fuilles et de branches se sunt tuit aünbrez.
Lor garnement ont toz ronpuz et depanez,
Tant ont sor les chars nues lor garnement portez
Qu'en plus de .ii.c. leus lor est li cuirs crevez,

Et tot parmi les mailles lor est li poil volez,
Et ont les chars plus noires qu'arrement destrenpez,
Et si sont plus velu que .i. gaignon betez. (3425–29, 3457–64)

[The fat flesh and water has so sickened them
that their sides and ribs are all swollen
the wind and the storm has done them great harm:
almost every one is dead or wounded
except the four brothers, and they smell pretty bad.
. . .
No one has a hut or a tent in the forest:
they are all sheltered by leaves and branches alone.
Their armor is all rent, and pieces torn off.
They have worn their armor so long on their bare skins
that their skin is pierced in more than two hundred places,
and their hair has grown out between the links of their mail,
and their flesh is darker than diluted ink,
and they are more hairy than a matted dog.]

Similarly, the war in Gascony is touched upon lightly. It serves as a frame for two great sequences of events. The first is the betrayal at Vaucouleurs, when the four brothers ride forth alone, without armor, dressed in red cloaks, promised a treaty of peace only to be assaulted by armies. The pathos of their martyrdom—Renaud wounded, his horse slain, Guichard captured then recovered, Richard wounded—leads to other events of pathos, when King Yon and then Richard and still later Maugis are captured and condemned to execution, Richard's neck actually placed in the noose, before the victims all return safe and sound to Montauban. The second sequence, a reflection of the flight to the Ardennes, recounts the siege of Renaud's citadel from the perspective of the besieged. They starve to death, the little people perish, Clarisse and Renaud's two boys are famished, each brother sacrifices his horse in turn, Renaud even bleeds Bayard—all this because of the ruthlessness and fanaticism of the besieger.

Finally, in Cologne Renaud struggles to help build the cathedral as a common laborer and dies in the odor of sainthood, slain by resentful workers. Thomas rightly, in my opinion, detects a structure of Christian imagery that pervades the chanson and orients it as a Christian epic.[4] On the other hand, it can also be maintained that the Christian analogy—Renaud, Richard, and even Bayard depicted as martyrs or Christ figures and the Aymon family three times betrayed by Charlemagne—helps create an ambiance of pathos and of melodrama for its own sake. Charles persecutes his victims again and again and again; they suffer and endure and suffer and endure, again and again and again.

The repetitiousness or, if you prefer, the multiplication of melodrama, derived from the need to compound Renaud's suffering and Charles's malice, offers one explanation for the spatial duplication and decentering: Renaud flees to Montessor and is tracked down; he flees to Montauban and is tracked down; he flees to Trémoigne and is tracked down. The spatial duplication and the temporal recurrence provide scope for exploration of the feudal dilemma in its multiple forms and for the characters' evolution in psyche over the course of years. I am also convinced that the *Renaut* poet multiplies his narrative increments for other reasons. Transgression, confrontation, flight, pursuit, confrontation, more transgression, confrontation, flight, pursuit, confrontation—the pattern is quasi-infinitely expandible. Such a patterning reveals a sophisticated author who takes pleasure in the elaboration and multiple treatment of theme and motif, a characteristic perhaps endemic to the Gothic age as opposed to the more Romanesque structure of the earlier gestes of Roland and Guillaume. It also points to a born storyteller who revels in episode and adventure for the sake of the story. It is this reveling in the story for its own sake that is one of the prime characteristics of thirteenth-century narrative, in verse and in prose, in geste and in romance.

Adventure, episode, the story—these can also help account for the presence, in "serious" chanson de geste, of a hero from another world or at least from another literary mode.[5] Cousin Maugis the sorcerer, the "good thief," on some occasions extricates the Aymon brothers from inextricable situations; on other occasions, he enters the narrative for the sheer fun of it. In addition to the "normal" feats of a warrior, a counselor, and a physician, Maugis puts Charlemagne and his army to sleep, he changes Renaud's, Bayard's, and his own appearance, he plays the role of pilgrim or fool under Charles's very nose, and he makes off with Charlemagne's crown or sword or treasure or (with Richard) the eagle from his pavilion or his son or his own imperial person. He is a one-man superarmy ever capable of snatching victory from the jaws of defeat and of turning Charlemagne's best-laid plans to naught. Beuves's son, a noble warrior who also studied in Toledo, Maugis is, far more than Renaud, a stranger to Charles's court and to the traditional chanson de geste. On the one hand, he stands as the supernatural adjuvant, the wise man in nature, who comes to the hero's assistance and contributes to his glory. He is also Renaud's alter ego, a trickster hero who does what the epic protagonist cannot do, yet by so doing it, he avenges the hero on the feudal-epic world that dooms him to disinheritance and exile. Therefore, as trickster hero, this son of Beuves d'Aigremont undermines the old chanson de geste as a genre and as a way of life: What is the point of heroism, what is the point of feudal law, when one man can put you to sleep or kidnap you at will? He mocks the code, mocks the law, and mocks the tradition. He and the Aymon brothers, whatever their chronological age, act as rebellious young sons defying and outwitting their powerful but inept surrogate *durus pater,* the *senex iratus* Charlemagne. These are acts of transgression against the convention of epic as well as against the feudal norms of society.

One means of transgression is humor. In the case of Maugis we find a quasi-Bakhtinian carnivalesque mockery of Charlemagne in his very seat of majesty. Maugis's tricks are much the same—that is, like the melodrama, they are repetitive: to change his (and Renaud's) appearance, to put his adversaries to sleep, and, above all, to steal/abduct/kidnap the adversaries or their most cherished possessions. On one level, to abscond with Charles's crown or eagle or sword is an act of symbolic castration. Yet the repetitive, cumulative effect of these deeds negates portentous symbolism, contributing instead to a Bergsonian effect: laughter created by the mechanical frequency of repetition and by the snowball effect of powerful causes leading to trivial effects (Charles is kidnapped yet won't budge an inch) or trivial causes leading to powerful effects (Maugis's little tricks bring Charles to the edge of a breakdown). Indeed, comedy almost gives way to pathos when the deranged emperor remains obsessed with Maugis even when surrounded by his entire army and enjoying the full fruits of victory. Yet the peers roar with laughter; so, presumably, should the implied audience.

A second element—supernatural and archetypal, though with less comic weight than in the case of Maugis—is provided by the great horse Bayard. Beginning with *La Chanson de Roland,* the epic hero is furnished with unique accoutrements to distinguish him from other warriors: these include, in order of decreasing importance, his sword, horse, and fiancée. It has been proposed that the four Aymon brothers, working as a team, constituting an *ensemble,* function, in part, as an emanation of Renaud, that they embody distinctive features of his being that he embodies in totality, and that they contribute to his glory.[6] The same may be true for the fifth member of the team, Maugis, and for the sixth, Bayard. Bayard, a *cheval faé,* displays a number of superequine features, including unbelievable speed, power, intelligence, and loyalty. The power is evidenced by the animal's capacity to bear two or three brothers (in later manuscripts all four) and still do all that is expected of a steed, in war or in flight. His intelligence and loyalty are evidenced when Bayard wakes Renaud and the others in time to rescue Richard, who is about to be hanged, or when, during the siege of Montauban, Bayard kneels in pity when Renaud would have slain him to feed the others. One of the great moments in the narrative occurs when Charlemagne seeks to drown Bayard in the Rhine but the animal breaks the millstone attached to his body, swims to the opposite shore, escapes into the woods, and rejoins Maugis in his hermitage. Like Maugis, Bayard comes and goes, disappearing from the story only to reappear; like Maugis, Bayard stands for beneficent forces in nature who assist the hero and contribute to his glory. The magician and the *faé* horse contribute an aura of poetry and myth to the Renaud story that helps to constitute its total literary reality. It was this poetry and myth that appealed most strongly to the thirteenth- and fourteenth-century public. In later versions of the story Bayard plays a greater role; he increases in importance, and his *sortie* is reenacted on three distinct occasions instead of the one.[7] Furthermore, the three principal continuations of the geste elaborate Maugis's story, not that of the protagonist and his brothers; and one strand of narrative attributed to Maugis recounts how he heard of, quested for, and won Bayard.[8] With all the poetry and myth, however, we pay a price: Bayard and Maugis contribute to the displacement of the feudal and political element, taken in full seriousness; they even contribute to a weakening of the element of pathos and melodrama. After all, they are quasi-omnipotent. Because of them, the pain endured by Renaud and the others is only provisional; eventually, they will intervene and the good people will be spirited out of harm's way.[9]

In the preceding pages I have sought to evoke a new kind of chanson de geste, which comes into being during the reign of Philip Augustus and, at first marginal and on the outside, comes to occupy the generic center, in the process displacing and marginalizing the older generic model derived from *La Chanson de Roland* and the first epics of the Guillaume Cycle. *Renaut de Montauban* was to be more popular and to have a greater impact on French and foreign literatures in the late Middle Ages than *La Chanson de Roland.*[10] The new chanson de geste probes the vital social reality of feudalism and the dilemmas raised by conflict between the baronry and the throne. It also probes the psychological reality of men living in the real world and forced, in strictly human terms, to work their way through these dilemmas. In addition, the genre creates an environment of pathos and melodrama, indulges in broad comedy and humor, incorporates elements of universal folklore that grant overtones of poetry and myth, and relishes storytelling and the proliferation of adventure for its own sake. All this takes place in and because of a much longer, structurally more complex narrative that in size as well as scope dwarfs *Le Couronnement de Louis* and *Le Charroi de Nîmes.*

The literary public and its taste evolved in the course of the twelfth century; the horizon of expectations was expanded due to any number of factors, including the impact of courtly romance, the first saints' lives, and the first branches of *Le Roman de Renart.* The new psychological and social realism will also be found in the *Prose Lancelot* (including *La Mort Artu*); the comedy and humor, in fabliaux and Jean de Meun; the melodrama, in romance and later hagiography; adventure and myth, in much of the narrative of the age. In this period, vernacular literature was adopting a broader panorama of life than a century earlier and already was mastering a mixture of styles (in Auerbach's sense of the term) prior to Dante and Villon. We can also say that literature was exploring aspects of dialogism (in Bakhtin's sense of the term) prior to Dostoyevsky. At the same time, the old center (*Saint Alexis, Roland, Jeu d'Adam,* for that matter Beroul and Thomas) had become marginalized and indeed forgotten, for with every gain comes a comparable loss. The early Romanesque spirituality and intensity are and were a terrible price to pay for the new Gothic expanded consciousness.[11]

In time, of course, new strangers occupied the center and displaced the Gothic chanson de geste to the margins and to oblivion: romance in prose, the allegory of love, and, finally, a new post-Gothic epic in which a certain Rinaldo occupied the seat of honor, tempted by a heretofore unknown Armida. The Italian romance epic was to be displaced in turn; meanwhile Renaud, Bayard, and Maugis lived on in the popular imagination.

With the advent of historism and nineteenth-century philology, for the first time the process of reception and loss was altered. For the first time, vernacular classics from the national past were rediscovered and readmitted into the canon. However, Roland was the only chanson de geste hero to benefit from the rehabilitation of the Middle Ages. Renaud, Raoul, Girard, Guillaume, and the others remained in the wings, hidden in a museum-margin reserved for scholars. Why was *La Chanson de Roland* alone restored to the national consciousness? Among other reasons (and I simplify), because of its ancientness (German romantic preference for the purity of the medieval urtext), its tight structure (French romantic preference for things in French being classical), and its high Christian idealism (general agreement that epics should be national, and the Middle Ages should be Christian); also, let us not forget general agreement that a nation is endowed with one great epic, not a dozen. Mass public education and the school manuals have done nothing to alter the nineteenth-century paradigm on chanson de geste any more than they have concerning Ronsard, proclaimed by Sainte-Beuve to have been a gifted singer of roses and fountains and a charming precursor of the Splendid Century.

Today some question humanism and the academic literary canon in order to demystify high culture in its totality, this in the name of multiculturalism or for other reasons. I, on the contrary, along with others, praise humanism but also seek to enlarge the canon, to create a new, scholarly canon that will treasure all the great works of the past—*Roland* and *Renaut,* the Romanesque and the Gothic, the Middle Ages, the century of Louis XIV—and our present as inspiration for us in the present and for our descendants in the future. Only then will we be worthy to renew with the old warriors and clerks, with the heroes of geste and the poets who gave them life.

Notes

1. *"Renaut de Montauban": Edition critique du manuscrit Douce,* ed. Jacques Thomas, Textes Littéraires Français 371 (Geneva: Droz, 1989). All quotations in text are from this edition; translations are by Ron Akehurst and me. The Thomas edition replaces the old

"Chanson des Quatre fils Aymon," d'après le manuscrit La Vallière, ed. Ferdinand Castets, Publications de la Société pour l'Étude des Langues Romanes 22 (Montpellier: Coulet, 1909). The reader should also consult the valuable *L'Episode ardennais de "Renaut de Montauban": Edition synoptique des versions rimées,* ed. Jacques Thomas, 3 vols., Rijksuniversiteit te Gent, Werken uitgegeven door de Faculteit van de Letteren en Wijsbegeerte nos. 129–31 (Bruges: De Tempel, 1962). For later versions of the chanson, see *"Renaut de Montauban": Edition critique du ms. de Paris, B.N., fr. 764 ("R"),* ed. Philippe Verelst, Rijksuniversiteit te Gent, Werken uitgegeven door de Faculteit van de Letteren en Wijsbegeerte no. 175 (Gent: Rijksuniversiteit te Gent, 1988); and "*Renaut de Montauban:* Deuxième fragment rimé du manuscrit de Londres, British Library, Royal 16 G II ('B')," ed. Philippe Verelst, *Romanica Gandensia* 21 (1988).

2. William Calin, *The Old French Epic of Revolt: "Raoul de Cambrai," "Renaud de Montauban," and "Gormond et Isembard"* (Geneva: Droz, 1962), chap. 3; Karl-Heinz Bender, *König und Vasall: Untersuchungen zur Chanson de Geste des XII. Jahrhunderts,* Studia Romanica no. 13 (Heidelberg: Carl Winter, 1967), 145–75.

3. Bender, *König und Vasall.*

4. See Jacques Thomas's important article, "Signifiance des lieux, destinée de Renaud et unité de l'oeuvre," *Romanica Gandensia* 18 (1981): 7–45; see also Calin, *The Old French Epic of Revolt,* chap. 2, and Micheline de Combarieu du Gres, "De l'étrange au merveilleux ou le recours aux forêts dans *Renaut de Montauban* (version du Ms. La Vallière)," in *De l'étranger à l'étrange ou la "conjointure" de la merveille (En hommage à Marguerite Rossi et Paul Bancourt*), Senefiance 25 (Aix-en-Provence: CUERMA, 1988), 127–55. Against a Christian reading, see Mario Pagano, "Rinaldo in Paradiso: proposte di rimozione," *Medioevo Romanzo* 10 (1985): 61–76.

5. On the origins of the *larron enchanteur,* see Gustav Adolf Beckmann, "Maugis d'Aigremont: Zur Genesis einer literarischen Gestalt," *Zeitschrift für romanische Philologie* 89 (1973): 148–66; Pierre Jonin, "Les Galopins épiques," in *Société Rencesvals: VIe Congrès International, Actes* (Aix-en-Provence: Université de Provence, 1974), 731–45; Philippe Verelst, "L'enchanteur d'épopée: Prolégomènes à une étude sur Maugis," *Romanica Gandensia* 16 (1976): 119–62. For criticism, I recommend the important study by Verelst, "Le personnage de Maugis dans *Renaut de Montauban* (versions rimées traditionnelles)," *Romanica Gandensia* 18 (1981): 73–152.

6. Alfred Adler, *Rückzug in epischer Parade: Studien zu "Les Quatre Fils Aymon," "La Chevalerie Ogier," "Garin le Lorrain," "Raoul de Cambrai," "Aliscans," "Huon de Bordeaux,"* Analecta Romanica no. 11 (Frankfurt am Main: Vittorio Klostermann, 1963), chap. 1; Jacques Thomas, "Les quatre fils Aymon: Structure du groupe et origine du thème," *Romanica Gandensia* 18 (1981): 47–72; François Suard, "Ogier le Danois et Renaud de Montauban," in *Essor et fortune de la Chanson de geste dans l'Europe et l'Orient latin: Actes du IXe Congrès International de la Société Rencesvals* (Modena: Mucchi, 1984), 185–202; and Combarieu du Gres, "De l'étrange au merveilleux."

7. Jacques Thomas, "La sortie de Bayard selon les différents manuscrits en vers et en prose," *Romanica Gandensia* 18 (1981): 171–98.

8. Maurice Piron, "Le cheval Bayard, monture des Quatre Fils Aymon, et son origine dans la tradition manuscrite," *Romanica Gandensia* 18 (1981): 153–70.

9. On the other hand, Maugis's quasi-omnipotence also helps extend the action. Charles demands his head in exchange for peace, a condition Renaud can never accept.

10. On the popularity of *Renaut de Montauban* and its foreign versions, sequels, and *rifacimenti,* see François Suard, "Le développement de la *Geste de Montauban* en France jusqu'à la fin du moyen âge," in *Romance Epic: Essays on a Medieval Literary Genre,* ed. Hans-Erich Keller (Kalamazoo, Mich.: Medieval Institute Publications, 1987), 141–61; and the superb bibliography by Philippe Verelst, "*Renaut de Montauban,* textes apparentés et versions étrangères: essai de bibliographie," *Romanica Gandensia* 18 (1981): 199–234, updated in *Olifant* 12 (1987): 125–44.

11. On the evolution of epic and romance in the thirteenth century, see William Calin, "Rapports entre chanson de geste et roman au XIIIe siècle: Rapport introductif," in *Essor et fortune de la Chanson de geste dans l'Europe et l'Orient latin: Actes du IXe Congrès international de la Société Rencesvals* (Modena: Mucchi: 1984), 407–24.

CHAPTER 9

"Who Was That Masked Man?": Disguise and Deception in Medieval and Renaissance Comic Literature

Janet L. Solberg

Although experience had surely shown that the villains who threatened the imagined peace of their lives were often their own friends, family members, and neighbors, the medieval and Renaissance imagination often represented such villains in art and literature as sinister strangers—spies, highwaymen or pirates, itinerant merchants or clerics, those espousing "alien" religions, or invading armies. These strangers are to be feared not only because of the crimes against property that they might perpetrate, but also because of the potential they represent for disrupting the social status quo upon which lives are founded.

The status quo is particularly important in the domain of family structure and patrilineal succession. Strangers who have a potentially disturbing effect on such long-established social structures are (1) the man who manages to gain access to another man's wife, thus threatening the certainty regarding paternity that should accompany the transmission from father to son of the paternal name and property, and (2) he who violates the ecclesiastically mandated chastity of female religious. Indeed, a common medieval and Renaissance topos is that of the stranger who invades socially sanctioned closed spaces for the purpose of obtaining illicit sex; many stories involve a male protagonist who disguises himself in women's clothing in order to gain access to otherwise unattainable women. These trickster tales, in which lusty sexual activity takes place under the noses of various authority figures, are highly amusing. Although listeners and readers no doubt enjoyed them immensely, tales about "masked" strangers with sinister sexual intentions may also mask anxiety about the inability even of powerful authority figures to control female sexual behavior and ensure full compliance with patriarchal law. These stories also inspire reflection about personal identity, verbal authority, and the adequacy of language in the medieval and early modern periods.

"La Saineresse": A Fabliau of Disguise and Revenge

"La Saineresse" (The woman healer) is a fabliau in which a foolish "borgois" boasts that no woman will ever deceive him.[1] Apparently provoked by this boastful remark (and, we may infer, by a lifetime of equally foolish behavior on his part), his wife plans a bold act of deception. Feigning illness, she summons a doctor to their home straightaway. After greeting the husband, this stranger—in reality a man disguised as a woman—takes the woman upstairs for a lengthy treatment session. After the doctor's departure, the woman describes the treatment to her husband in great detail, using an extended double entendre that is understood in one way by the unsuspecting husband and in quite another by the tale's audience.

A close reading of the story suggests that lust is not the only motivating force in this tale. In fact, summoning the doctor appears to be the wife's direct response to her husband's boasting:

Sa fame en a oi parler,
Si en parla priveement
Et en iura .i. serement
Qu'ele le fera mencongier,
Ja tant ne s'i saura guetier. (4–8)

[His wife heard talk of this
And considered it privately
And swore an oath
That she would make a liar of him
No matter how much he tried to watch her.][2]

Not long after the husband's boast and the wife's calculated response, the "rascal" (*pautonier*) arrives at the door. The narrator tells us that he "seemed more like a woman than a man ("sambloit plus / Fame que homme la moitié"). His disguise is partly sartorial; he is wearing a loose shirt/tunic and a saffron-colored wimple. No doubt the trappings of the medical profession (she/he carries suction cups for bleeding the patient) also lend credibility to the disguise. The combined effect makes the authority of the doctor hard to question.[3] The doctor's words make it clear that "she" has been summoned by the wife:

Dame, vous m'auez ci mandee
Et m'auez ci fete venir
Or me dites vostre plesir. (28–30)

[Lady, you sent for me
And had me come here.
Now tell me your pleasure (i.e., Tell me what you want).]

The wife explains that she is suffering from gout, and needs to be bled. Doctor and patient lock themselves in an upstairs room; the husband later remarks that they were gone for a long time, although the narrator describes their sexual activities in seven short lines:

Le pautonier la prent esrant
En .i. lit l'auoit estendue
Tant que il l'a .iij. foiz foutue
Quant il orent assez ioué,
Foutu besié et acolé
Si se descendent del perrin
Contre val les degrez. (42–48)

[The rascal took her right away.
He stretched her out on a bed
And he screwed her three times.
When they had had enough fun
Screwing, kissing, and embracing
They came back down from the room,
Down the stairs.]

Having fulfilled "her" function in the tale, the doctor departs, but not before a brief conversation between the husband and wife confirms what the tale's audience might already have inferred—the motivating force in this tale is not primarily sexual, but is, rather, economic. Debts incurred, whether monetary or psychological, must be paid—and by those who owe them.

Dame se dieus vous beneie [says the husband]
Paiez cele fame mout bien
Ne retenez de son droit rien
De ce que vous sert en manaie
Sire que vous chaut de ma paie
Dist la borgoise a son seignor
Je vous oi parler de folor
Quar nous .ij. bien en couuendra. (54–61)

["Lady, as God may bless you,
Pay this woman very well.
Don't hold anything that is rightfully hers
That you might use as payment."
"Sir, what does it matter to you what I pay?"
Said the wife to her husband.
"I hear you speaking foolishness,
Because the two of us can easily reach an agreement."]

The husband's "speaking like a fool" has clearly been the reason for the wife's calculated retaliatory action. He owes her satisfaction, which she will extract. Earlier, the "woman medic" had urged her to "tell her pleasure," and it now becomes clear that the real pleasure lies not in the sexual act itself, but in the telling of it. In deliciously graphic terms, which the husband does not understand, the wife describes the treatment she has just received from the accommodating stranger. In contrast to the seven lines the narrator has devoted to their coupling, the wife's description takes twenty-nine lines—approximately one quarter of the tale:

Sire merci por amor dé
Ja ai.ie esté trop traueillie
Si ne pooie estre sainie
Et m'a plus de .c. cops ferue
Tant que ie sui toute molue
N'onques tant cop n'i sot ferir
C'onques sans en peust issir
Par .iij. rebinees me prist
Et a chascune foiz m'assist
Sor mes rains .ij. de ses pecons
Et me feroit vns cops si lons
Toute me sui fet martirier
Et si ne poi onques sainier
Granz cops me feroit et souent
Morte fusse mon escient
S'un trop bon oingnement ne fust
Qui de tel oingnement eust
Ja ne fust mes de mal greuee
Et quant m'ot tant demartelee
Si m'a aprés ointes mes plaies
Qui mout par erent granz et laies
Tant que ie fui toute guerie
Tel oingnement ne haz ie mie
Et il ne fet pas a hair
Et si ne vous en quier mentir
L'oingnement issoit d'un tuiel
et si descendoit d'un forel
d'une pel mout noire et hideuse
mes mout par estoit sauoreuse. (68–96)

[Thank you, sir, for the love of God
I've just been thoroughly worked over
And I couldn't be bled.
I was struck more than one hundred times,
So much so that I'm completely softened.
Still, not enough blows were struck
That they were able to make blood come out.

I was taken three times,
And each time, two of (the healer's) lancettes
Were placed upon my loins,
And I was struck with so long a blow.
I was completely battered (martyred)
But I still couldn't bleed.
I was struck with many hard blows.
I think I might have died
If it hadn't been for a very good ointment.
Anyone who had such an ointment
Would never again be grieved by pain.
And after I had been hammered so much,
Then my wounds were anointed,
(Wounds) that were large and wide,
Until I was completely cured.
I certainly don't hate an ointment like that,
And there's nothing hateful about it,
And I don't want to lie to you about it.
This ointment came out of a pipe
That came down out of a forest (hole?)
With a very black and hideous skin,
But it was very sweet.]

The wife's earnest assurance to her husband, "Et si ne vous en quier mentir [I don't want to lie to you about it]," points to an important feature of this story: the wife's true pleasure comes in speaking openly to her husband. Given that he completely misses the point of her story, she ultimately fools him not by lying, but by telling the truth.

Cil ne s'est pas aperceu
De la borde qu'ele conta
Et cele nule honte n'a
De la lecherie essaucier
Por tant le veut bien essaier
Ja n'en fust paie a garant
Se ne li contast maintenant. (100–106)

[He didn't notice
The joke she was telling.
And she had no shame
For reveling in the lechery.
However much she wanted to try him
She never would have been paid in full
If she hadn't told him about it right away.]

"La Saineresse": Layers of Meaning and Figures of Authority

To his audience, the storyteller's moral is that a man is a fool to claim that no woman can deceive him, and part of the story's humor resides in the fact that the wife says she does not wish to lie to her husband. In fact, she has *not* lied; she has deceived him with rhetorical cleverness, with a paradoxical use of "truth" dressed in metaphor. Her disguised boasting of her sexual escapade stands as a quid pro quo for her husband's boasting about the control he thought he enjoyed over his wife. The husband's pretensions lead to the medic's being summoned, and subsequently to the wife's description of her treatment—all grist for the storyteller's mill.

In the balanced economy of the tale, each character is appropriately compensated: the healer is paid for his services, the husband is paid back for his foolish boast, and the woman revels in the payoff that comes from the pleasure of spinning her extended metaphor. All of this might serve to remind audiences (medieval or otherwise) that a certain contractual obligation exists between storyteller and audience, and that literary pleasure given calls for appropriate compensation as well.

In the story's last lines, the author evokes a tension between men and women that has existed

> Quant cele qui ot mal es rains
> Boula son seignor premerains. (115–16)
>
> [Since she who had the loin-ache
> Deceived her husband first.]

This biblical allusion suggests to what extent this tale is grounded in age-old male sexual fantasies and anxieties relating to women. The tale creates a tension between the fantasy of woman as an insatiable, always willing and available sex object, and the fear that women (having the same sexual desires as men) will cuckold their husbands. The fact that this narrative privileges to some extent the woman's point of view partially explains the richness of this tale, and invites speculation on the ways in which various audience constituencies might react to the tale.

Women in the audience may have exulted in the belief that the husband got what he deserved, in recognition of the ways in which women can act subversively—and can even be victorious—within patriarchal social structures in which they have little power. They were probably also delighted by the virtuosity of the wife's clever use of extended sexual metaphor.

The men in the audience no doubt also took a prurient pleasure in the wife's use of language, and in their own ability to decode her veiled meanings. Male rivalry may also have shaped audience reaction; after all, the men in the audience were clever enough to understand what the gullible husband could not, perhaps thinking smugly that this could never happen to them. In addition, male audience members might identify with the disguised trickster, the "woman" healer, who has his way with the willing and available wife, who receives money in addition to his sexual satisfaction—and who exits unscathed. Identification with this character gives males in the audience yet another chance to feel superior to lesser rivals.

Modern readers may want to take into account the larger historical context in which this story was created, one marked by social structures that subjugate women. Considered chattel, perhaps forced into an unhappy marriage, a woman might indeed be happy to find a venue for expressing her contempt for her husband. From a contemporary perspective, one might say that, although this woman is viewed as a whore by her culture, she is forced by her culture to become a whore. Although she initially seems to be the aggressor (or the initiator) in the sex-for-money transaction, it is she who subsequently submits to the doctor's "treatment" (a treatment couched in medical terms with an undertone of sexual violence). Her victory could indeed be seen as hollow, because her act of subversion reinforces the medieval view of woman as licentious and requiring strict control.

Although the storyteller (who we assume is male) himself has a certain kinship with the wife, whose verbal virtuosity is his own creation, he must ultimately identify with the male trickster, the "woman doctor." The storyteller, a professional himself, performs a service for his willing clients, pockets his fee, and goes on his way. Like the trickster, he ultimately profits from the precarious and flawed nature of postlapsarian human society.

Tale 45 of the *Cent nouvelles nouvelles*: The Story of "Margarite" the Washerwoman

The *Cent nouvelles nouvelles,* produced circa 1462 in the Burgundian court of Philippe le Bon, contain another version of the cross-dressing topos; this time, the cadre for the story is not a single household, but the thriving city of Rome.[4] The forty-fifth *nouvelle* portrays an enterprising young entrepreneur who disguises himself as a woman in order to corner the market in illicit sexual relations with all of the women in town. In addition to the interest generated by the transposition of the topos to a more bourgeois, mercantile setting, the story is noteworthy for the ways in which it invites reflection on the adequacy of language. The story stages the havoc that is wrought when members of a society who assume themselves to be in authority discover a counterfeiter in their midst and find themselves forever after unable to take coins (i.e., signs and words) at face value.

In this story, the protagonist, a calculating young Scotsman, begins wearing girl's clothing at the age of six or eight, and succeeds in making himself known and accepted in all of the best "hostels" in Rome; he even learns a woman's trade, that of washerwoman. It appears to be the anticipation of establishing and controlling a market that motivates the young "Escossois" to invest so much time and effort in hopes of future profit (profit of a sexual nature, of course, as "faire la lessive [do the washing]" carries strong sexual connotations).

The Scotsman next launches a sophisticated campaign aimed at two different audiences. For the first, the men in the community, he represents himself as a woman, establishing a signifying system that represents him as "woman." His clothing and traditionally feminine profession immediately cause men to perceive him as female. The word designating his profession and the name he calls himself overdetermine his apparent femininity, with their feminine endings, inscribed feminine definite articles, and possessive adjectives ("*la la*vendiere," "*Ma*rgarite"). All is calculated to suggest to the husbands that the washerwoman's identity is unproblematic and poses no threat to household stability.

The second audience for the "washerwoman's" publicity campaign consists of the women of the community. In this case, the Scotsman does not disseminate his message—that he is a man—by means of words, clothing, or behavior associated primarily with one gender or the other. Reliance upon such codes invites misunderstanding, because their interpretations are based on conventions about meaning. Instead of relying on ambiguous sign systems, he *shows* them that he is a man ("il... monstroit qu'il estoit homme"; 303), using a nonverbal and unambiguous signifier, the phallus.

The husbands do not hesitate to leave the "washerwoman" alone with their wives to "garder le mesnage" (303) in their absence. The Scot's enterprise is a success with women on all social levels; the lowliest maidservants vie with the mistress of the house for the privilege of sharing their beds with this paragon. It may be that, for the women, the sex act is Margarite's real trade; nevertheless, the washerwoman's skills prove useful as well. Margarite soils the sheets, and then washes them to erase the traces of his/her passage. The text seems to express an amused admiration for such efficiency and "industrie" (302).

The continuation of this state of affairs—and of the story—depends on the maintenance of these two different perceptions of Margarite and of what she/he does. The truth must be hidden from the men, for once the double interpretation of Margarite's identity is reduced to a univocal meaning, the tale is over. Margarite must retain control over the men's perception of his identification as a woman. When a young girl tells her father "qu'*elle* estoit homme" (303; emphasis added), the men's perception of Margarite as unambiguously female is called into question, and the end of the story is near.

In a medieval context, the punishment for the seduction of a man's wife might well have been castration. Here, in the mercantile setting of the story, the Scotsman is dealt a symbolic equivalent.[5] He is paraded through the streets with his genitals exposed.[6] The Scotsman's economic and sexual success depended on the concealment of his true identity from the men in the story; exposed, he is rendered impotent. Although a few victims admit they have been defrauded, the others remain silent, ashamed at having been deceived by false appearances and not wishing to air their dirty linen in public. Margarite loses a profitable monopoly and is expelled from the city. The narrator gently mocks both the "washerwoman" and her/his cuckolded victims, but expresses no moral outrage at Margarite's activities, remarking only that the women regretted losing his/her services.

The cross-dressing topos functions in this tale to show how social and economic stability depend upon the ability to interpret conventional sign systems accurately. Here, for instance, judgments of the propriety or impropriety of social behavior are based on the ability to distinguish accurately between men and women; the "self-made woman" is thus a truly disruptive force. The functioning of social commerce is undermined by Margarite, "qui la femme contrefist" (304). Margarite's identity as a "bad penny" is underscored by the diminutive of her name, Margot, which has been identified as "a certaine engine used by false coyners."[7] *Blanchir,* one of the washerwoman's primary tasks, is also a term used in coin making (meaning "to silver over brass or copper coins").[8] Its use here reinforces the idea of disguise and mistaken identities, but it is particularly fitting in that "coining" is a common medieval metaphor for the sex act.

The Use of Ambiguity in the Forty-fifth Nouvelle

In the forty-fifth *nouvelle,* repetitions and interconnected networks of meaning on the level of the signifier reveal some of its major textual preoccupations: tension between words designating male and female, including ambiguous expressions designating both at the same time; and oscillation between the notions of hiding and unveiling, lying and discovering truth, false interpretations enabling the story to continue, and unambiguous and univocal interpretations leading inevitably to narrative closure.

Such ambiguities are an essential feature of this story, because the dramatic tension of the forty-fifth *nouvelle* hinges on the inability of the "bons bourgeois" to distinguish between a man and a woman. Until the great unveiling near the end of the tale, most signs—on the surface, at least—point to the femininity of the young Scotsman; the name "donne Margarite," the "estat et habillement de femme" in which he conducts himself in Roman society, and the profession he pursues identify him as unambiguously female to the unenlightened bourgeois. To the reader, who is in complicity with the narrator, the frequently repeated words *Romme* and *Rommain,* phonically resembling *homme,* seem a constant reminder of Margarite's real identity. Similarly, although Margarite and its diminutive Margot are both women's names, discerning readers will distinguish a masculine signification inscribed within the feminine proper names. A *margout* or *margauts* is a tomcat or, by extension, a debaucher, and the verb *margauder* means (again apropos of cats) "to cover the female."[9] In this way, the text offers the reader another interpretation of the situation that is masked by the more accessible surface reading.

The textual preoccupation with the opposition between things covert and overt is discernible throughout the text. The young Scotsman, disguised as a woman, penetrates the homes of the "bons bourgois," "sans ce que dedans le dit terme il fust venu a la cognoissance publicque qu'il fust homme" (302). This "cognoissance," when it finally comes, is indeed "publicque," for it results in his being paraded half nude through the streets. Until then, he had "counterfeited" a woman, using women's clothing and a woman's name; what more appropriate "cover-up" could have been chosen than an occupation literally involving "covers"—the sheets and blankets handled daily by "la lavendiere"? *Blanchisseur* is also used to refer to "one who gives a good appearance to that which is bad."[10] The notion of things hidden is also underscored by Margarite's name, as a *garite* is a refuge or a hiding place.[11]

No attempt is made to conceal the Scotsman's masculinity from the reader, of course. Instead, the narrator's manipulations of masculine and feminine pronouns sustain interest by making the reader constantly aware of the difficulty of representing something perceived as now masculine, now feminine; this technique exploits for maximum effect the ambiguity inherent in the narrative situation. Conversations in other tales of the *Cent nouvelles nouvelles* are generally couched in *direct* discourse, an approach that would have made for a less confusing use of gender pronouns in this particular story; the fact that the forty-fifth *nouvelle* contains considerable *indirect* discourse suggests that this mode of discourse is being exploited multifariously. At the beginning of the tale, when "Margarite" is seen from the reader's point of view, or from the point of view of those women who know him as a man, "Margarite" is consistently referred to as "il." However, when the point of view shifts to that of the "bons bourgois," after an initial masculine pronoun, the adjectives and pronouns referring to Margarite shift to the feminine:

> Les bourgois mesmes ... *le* v[e]oient tres voluntiers en leurs maisons ... et qui plus est *la* faisoient coucher avec leurs femmes, tant *la* sentoient *bonne* et honneste. (303; emphasis added)
>
> [The bourgeois themselves ... were happy to see him in their houses ... and, what's more, they had her sleep with their wives, they were that convinced that she was good and honest.]

When Margarite's fraud is exposed, the two-gender system, designating objects and people as *either* masculine *or* feminine, proves inadequate to describe this situation, and the referential instability yields numerous comic turns of phrase:

> Une jeune fille... dist a son pere qu'*elle* avoit couché avec *elle,* et lui dist qu'*elle l'*avoit *assaillie,* et luy dist veritablement qu'*elle* estoit *homme.* (303; emphasis added)
>
> [A young girl... told her father that she had slept with her, and told him that she had assaulted her, and told him truly that she was a man.]

> *Elle* fut *regardée* par ceulx de la justice, qui trouverent qu'*elle* avoit tous telz membres et oustilz que les *hommes* portent, et que vrayement *elle estoit homme,* et *non pas femme.* (303–4; emphasis added)
>
> [She was examined by the authorities, who found that she had all of those members and tools that men carry, and that truly she was a man, and not a woman.]

Even when the men in the story learn the truth, the text vacillates between the masculine and the feminine when describing Margarite, the man in woman's clothing:

> Si ordonnerent qu'on *le* mectroit sur ung chariot et qu'on *le* mainroit par la ville... et *la* monstreroit on, voyant chacun, ses genitoires.
> ...Et Dieu scet que *la* pouvre donne Margarite estoit *honteuse* et *soupprinse*! (304; emphasis added)
>
> [And they ordered that he be put on a cart, and that he be taken around the city... and that she be shown, so that everyone could see his/her genitals.
> ...And God knows that the poor lady Margarite was ashamed and surprised!]

Indeed, the final sentences of the tale serve to remind readers of the importance of ambiguous language in the creation of fiction and fictional characters; perhaps with a wink to his audience, the narrator has the women admit that "oncques si bonne lavendiere ne fut" (404), that is, "there *never was* such a good washer*woman,*" and that they deeply regretted having lost "him":

> Il fut banny de Romme, dont les femmes furent bien desplaisantes. Car oncques si bonne lavendiere ne fut, et avoyent bien grand regret que si meschantement l'avoient perdu. (304)

> [He was banished from Rome, which upset the women very much. Because there never was such a good washerwoman, and they were very sorry to have lost her so unpleasantly.]

In the above sentence, there is no feminine agreement of the past participle, despite the fact that the antecedent of the ambiguous pronoun "l' " should be "lavendiere." Does it, perhaps, refer *not* to the "lavandiere," but to some other masculine object whose loss looms so large for the townswomen that it is simply understood to be the pronoun's antecedent?

This difficulty in identifying the antecedent of an ambiguous pronoun is also encountered in the first sentence of the tale:

> Combien que nulle des histoires precedentes n'ayent touché ou racompté aucun cas advenu es marches d'Ytalie, mais seullement face mencion des advenues en France, Alemaigne, Angleterre, Flandres et Brabant, si s'estendra *elle* toutesfoiz, a cause de la fresche advenue, a ung cas a Romme nagueres advenu et connus, qui fut tel. (302; emphasis added)

> [Even though none of the previous stories told of any event that happened in Italy, but only mentioned events in France, Germany, England, Flanders and Brabant, now, it will extend, because it's so recent, to an occurrence in Rome, that recently happened and became known, which went like this.]

The pronoun "elle" has no clear antecedent in this sentence; the text seems to be announcing, as one of its principal concerns, the playful ambiguities and confusion that result from the attempt to assign pronouns to the sometimes male, sometimes female, protagonist of the tale. The concluding wordplay of this first sentence suggests a question that could refer to the ambiguous pronoun, but that will eventually be asked about Margarite by all of the characters in the story: "qui fut tel" (302), or, rather, "Qui fut-elle?" Indeed, the most economical means of expressing the Scotsman's dual sexuality may be a pun that occurs in the words "s'estendra" (302), if those words are read as "cet andre."[12] This pun serves as yet another comment on the inherent ambiguities of sign systems, underscoring their power to amuse, frustrate, and deceive.

The good burghers in the forty-fifth *nouvelle* finally lose their faith in these sign systems, preferring instead to rely on the principle that "seeing is believing." They bring Margarite before the justices, where "elle fut *regardée*" (303; emphasis added). Desiring to warn other good citizens, they order that Margarite's genitals be *shown* so that all may *see* them ("et qu'on . . . le *monstreroit* on, *voyant* chacun, ses genitoires"; 304; emphasis added). While this procession is "*showing* Margarite's wares" ("qu'on *faisoit ostension* des denrées de donne Margarite"; 304; emphasis added), one Roman who "*saw* him" exclaimed, "*Regardez* quel galiofle:

il a couché plus de vingt nuiz avecques ma femme" (304; emphasis added). It is this impulse to strip away social conventions and to privilege the "natural language" of the genitalia that may finally explain the reason for giving the young washerwoman a Scottish nationality, aside from the possible association of Scotsmen with thriftiness and kilts. When other semiotic systems prove inadequate or ambiguous, the young man must be "escossé," that is, "unhusked," "hulled," or "shelled."[13] The Scotsman is ultimately "banny de Romme" (304), and the social order is reestablished. The guardians of the established order, "les bourgois," have surely been changed by this experience. They can no longer sustain a complacent faith in languages and social codes; despite their social and economic authority, they are now well aware of the power of counterfeit signs to disrupt and deceive.

Bonaventure des Périers's Sixty-second Nouvelle (the story of the "Jeune Garçon qui se nomma Thoinette, pour estre receu à une religion de nonnains; et comment il fit sauter les lunettes de l'abbesse qui le visitoit")

Exploiting its own version of the cross-dressing topos, the sixty-second *nouvelle* of the *Nouvelles recreations et joyeux devis* (493–95) invites further consideration of the literary uses of misreading, and of the ways in which language exerts its own authority over those who use it—or, indeed, who are used by it.[14] Interestingly, proverbs abound in the sixty-second *nouvelle*; these fixed expressions seem to function not as a means of preserving and transmitting bits of conventional wisdom, as in the oral tradition, but rather to generate the story and language of a new *written* (literary) text.

As the story unfolds, its young protagonist, an itinerant handyman, visits a convent on a religious holiday and sees several nuns so beautiful that he could have "rompu son jeusne [broken his fast]" with any one of them (493). A friend, sympathizing with his companion's lusty appetites, makes a suggestion: as he is attractive and a relative stranger, he has only to dress himself in women's clothes and the abbess will welcome him into the convent. Full of confidence, the young man takes his friend's advice. He claims to be an orphan, and is sympathetically received by the myopic abbess, who, fortuitously, is in need of a chambermaid. "Thoinette" pleases the abbess by demonstrating humble comportment and skill with a needle, and is allowed to join the order and don the habit.[15]

Thoinette wastes no time in showing certain of the most beautiful nuns "qu'elle avoit le ventre cornu, [leur] faisant entendre que c'estoit par miracle et vouloir de Dieu [that she had a horned belly, explaining that it was by a miracle and God's will]" (494). Sleeping with one or another of them each night, Thoinette continues to put "sa cheville au pertuys de sa compagne [her peg into her companion's hole]" (494), until the other nuns learn what is happening and complain to the abbess that one among them is bringing dishonor on their religion and ruining them. Having been warned that the abbess plans to call them together and make them undress in her presence, Thoinette "attacha sa cheville par le bout avec un fillet qu'elle tira par derrière, et accoustre si bien son petit cas qu'elle sembloit avoir le ventre fendu comme les aultres" [tied the end of his/her peg with a string that she attached behind, and hid its little condition so well that she seemed to have a slotted belly like the others]" (494). The abbess perches her glasses on her nose, and, as she prepares to examine "soeur Thoinette," the sight of so many nuns "toutes nues, fraisches, blanches, refaictes, rebondies" (495) makes Thoinette lose control:

> Car, sus le poinct que l'abbesse avoit les yeux le plus près, la corde vint rompre, et, en desbandant tout à un coup, la cheville vint repousser contre les lunettes de l'abbesse et les fit saulter à deux grandz pas loing. Dont la povre abbesse fut si surprinse qu'elle s'ecria; "*Jesu Maria!* Ah! sans faulte, dit-elle, et est-ce vous! Mais qui l'eust jamais cuidé estre ainsi! Que vous m'avez abusée!" (495)
>
> [For, at the point when the abbess had her eyes the very closest, the string broke, and being unstrung all of a sudden, the peg knocked the abbess's glasses, and made them jump two huge paces away. About which fact the abbess was so surprised that she cried out, "Jesus Maria! Ah, there's no doubt, she said, so it's you! Whoever would have believed it! How you have abused me!"]

Fearing that scandal would be brought upon the order, the abbess does not punish Thoinette. The text concludes with the mildly ironic comment that Thoinette was allowed to leave "avec promesse de sauver l'honneur des filles religieuses [on promising to preserve the honor of the virgin nuns]" (495).

Proverbs: Institutionalized Language as Textual Generator

As Lionello Sozzi has pointed out, the sixty-second *nouvelle* has perhaps the bawdiest plot of any of the *Nouvelles recreations et joyeux devis.*[16] Indeed, the scabrous nature of this tale suggests another possible interpretation of a remark made within it; given its plot, it is not surprising that the abbess was "esbahie de ceste nouvelle [flabbergasted by this news/story]" (494). However, the fact that the *plot* of this particular tale is still linked to the earthy topoi of the oral tradition makes the broadening literary vision of the fifteenth- and sixteenth-century *conteurs* all the more apparent. The *Cent nouvelles nouvelles* version had reworked the old familiar cross-dressing topos of earlier comic tales by situating the story within an economic cadre; the *Nouvelles recreations* version situates itself within a framework more explicitly *literary.* In addition to acknowledging its interrelations with other literary texts, it makes use of fixed expressions or traditional language, such as proverbs, as textual generator, in ways that destabilize institutions and institutionalized language.

The *Nouvelles recreations* incorporate the picturesque speech of everyday life in this literary setting. As the detailed inventories provided by Hassell show, numerous proverbial expressions are found in des Périers's works; in the ninety tales of the *Nouvelles recreations et joyeux devis* that are generally attributed to des Périers, Hassell found approximately 150 unambiguous references to proverbial expressions.[17] For example, in the sixty-second *nouvelle* itself, Hassell has found three expressions that also appear in medieval and early Renaissance French proverb collections or in historical dictionaries of the French language: (1) when the young man visits the convent, he sees several beautiful nuns, for any one of whom he would gladly have "rompu son jeusne" (493); (2) having gone to bed with one of the sisters, Thoinette "mit sa cheville au pertuys de sa compagne" (494); and (3) when summoned with the other nuns for the comic denouement, Thoinette is confident about being able to outwit the abbess, "qui ne voyoit pas la longueur de son nez [who could not see the length of her own nose]" (494). It is clear that contemporary colloquial phrases have found their way into the narrative, as these three common expressions are quoted verbatim.[18] Hassell allows that the list of proverbs he has compiled may well be incomplete; he finds that allusions to proverbial expressions in the *Nouvelles recreations* are often quite oblique.[19]

It might be argued, however, that proverbial expressions in the *Nouvelles recreations* do not function merely as allusions that illustrate the narrative, but that they may actually determine certain aspects of the narrative.[20] Indeed, the entire story of Thoinette—his disguising himself as a nun to gain entry to the convent and his unmasking as a result of the jealous nuns' admonitions to the abbess "qu'elle ne se fiast pas en l'habit [not to put her trust in the habit]" (494)—can be read as a fleshing-out of the French proverbial expression "L'habit ne fait pas le moine [The habit does not make the monk]" or, in this case, "la nonne."[21]

The text stresses the young handyman's confident attitude when his friend suggests that he disguise himself as a girl and present himself to the abbess: "Il creut assez facillement ce conseil, se pensant qu'en cela n'avoit aulcun danger qu'il n'evitast bien quant il voudroit [He believed this advice fairly readily, thinking there was no danger he could not avoid if he wanted to]" (493). Cotgrave lists a French proverbial expression, to be "fourni de fil & d'aiguille," which means both "readie for any imployment" and "never to seeke for an answer."[22] This picturesque expression of self-confidence may have influenced both the description of the young man as a jack-of-all-trades and his subsequent learning to work with a needle once in the convent; the textual aside referring to Thoinette's speedy mastery of the art of needlework—"car peut-estre qu'elle en sçavoit desjà quelque chose [for perhaps she already knew something about it]" (493)—evokes the figurative expression. It may also be a comment on Thoinette's sexual prowess (knowing how to "thread the needle") and talent as a storyteller, given that embroidering a good tale is what gains Thoinette admittance to the convent.

Yet another word in the text connotes self-confidence and *débrouillardise.* "A chaque trou une cheville," means, Cotgrave notes, "For everie fault an excuse, for each objection an answer; for any mischiefe a remedie, helpe, evasion."[23] Although this expression is not used in the text to describe the protagonist's self-confidence, it may have generated the figurative expression later used for the sex act, "mettre [sa] cheville au pertuys de sa compagne" (494).

In certain cases, associations could have been made on the level of both the signifier and the signified, and it is difficult to determine what might have been the "source" and what might have been subsequent links in an associative chain of words and ideas. Readers begin the story of the sixty-second *nouvelle* with the almost certain knowledge that "Thoinette" will amuse himself for a while, but that his masquerade will eventually be discovered; the suspense lies in speculating on what form the final dénouement will take. In the presence of so many beautiful nude women at the end of the story, Thoinette "ne peut estre maistresse de ceste cheville qu'il ne se fist mauvais jeu [She could not control this peg so that there was no bad move]" (495). From "mauvais jeu" to "beau jeu" is but a short associative step; an expression containing these words—"Il y aura beau jeu si la corde ne rompt"—may well have influenced the story's outcome. Cotgrave translates this expression as "Wee shall have good sport if the line breake not,"[24] and the bogus nun's undoing is described in terms that echo the unspoken proverbial expression: "Car, sus le poinct que l'abbesse avoit les yeux le plus près, *la corde vint rompre* [For when the abbess had her eyes closest, the cord broke]" (495; emphasis added).

The abbess protested the young man's abuse of her trust, but did nothing save ask him to go his way "avec promesse de sauver l'honneur des filles religieuses" (495). The narrator comments: "Toutesfois, qu'i eust-elle faict? [Indeed, what could she have done?]"—recognizing that there was little that could be done to remedy the situation after the fact (495). The *nouvelle*'s description of what happened when Thoinette's restraining string broke—"et, en *desbandant* tout à un coup, la cheville vint repousser contre les lunettes de l'abbesse [coming unstrung all at once, the peg struck the abbess's spectacles]" (495; emphasis added)—contains a proverbial expression anticipating this attitude of resignation. Cotgrave explains that "Desbander l'arc ne guerist pas la playe" means "The bowes unbending heales no wound it made."[25] That the word *plaie* (wound) is a euphemism for the female sex organ underscores the realization that the nuns' lost virginity can never be regained.

Hassell comments that no tale of cross-dressing before this one involves a pair of eyeglasses.[26] This detail may have been generated by a proverbial expression, one that aptly describes the shortsighted lady's gullibility: "[Elle] n'y a pas bien assis ses lunettes," or, as Cotgrave translates it, "[She] hath not observed the matter so neerely, [she] hath not looked into it so narrowly, as [she] might, or should, have done."[27]

The Scandal of Language

In *The Scandal of the Fabliaux,* R. Howard Bloch suggests that jokes, fabliaux, bawdy tales—indeed, perhaps all works of literature—thematize our unsuccessful attempts to view language as the unproblematic representation of an unproblematic reality: "In its displacements, condensations, and substitutions, the joke disrupts the assumption of a 'natural' relation between language and meaning and, at the same time, serves as a screen for the fact that such a relation never existed in the first place."[28]

Fictions are sometimes created to help cover the cracks in the facade, but such attempts to "cover up" usually expose the very gaps they seek to hide. Thus the butt of the joke, the victim of the trickery—who in literary works may be a figure for the inscribed reader—is constantly thwarted in his or her expectations that the world, and especially language, will behave in a logical and sensible manner.

Bloch notes that the relationship between poetry (or literary language) and the world it represents is often portrayed in literature as the clothing that covers a body, or by other metaphors that involve displacement, disguise, trickery, or perversion:

> Beginning with the "riotous fable," we arrived at the "textile text" only to discover, however, that the comic tale often seems to cover-up more than to cover. The robe of fiction is to some degree always inadequate to the body. It carries the odor of scandal. This scandal is thematized in a variety of ways—as theft, . . . as perversion, . . . as transvestism, adultery, trickery, prostitution. . . . Moral dereliction expressed at the thematic level is, moreover, only the most visible sign of the underlying scandal of the fabliaux, which is that of poetry itself.[29]

Language is fragmented, always polyvalent and ambiguous, and readers, be they implied or inscribed, will thus always be guilty of "deforming" or "dismembering" the texts they read.[30] The animating force of the comic tale lies in the tension between readers' initial expectations of absolute logic or sense and the thwarting of these expectations. If there is a resolution, it is to be recuperated in the "'logic of the joke' based upon the intrinsically irreconcilable copresence of conception and perception."[31]

The hearers of the joke, or the inscribed audience in the literary work, often ascribe a univocal meaning to that which is ambiguous. They are duped by the storyteller, a master manipulator of words. And yet the clues pointing to another possible interpretation are always there, if only enigmatically. The moment when the "reader" moves from blindness (often used as a theme within the tale) to insight is often marked by the feeling that one "could have known" or "should have seen" what was there all along.[32]

Authors and readers alike have a stake in textual ambiguity. Literature both illustrates and depends on the ability of language to create and to obscure "meaning." Readers (inscribed or otherwise) thus have good reason to misread. Literary language has the power to deceive; and, indeed, once the cover-up has been exposed, the tale is ended. "Properly named, the transvestite's donning of an appropriate dress is tantamount to a reduction of fiction's infinite possibilities to univocal meaning—a univocity that precludes further narrative progression."[33]

Linguistic Ambiguity: The Power of Strangers

In the three tales discussed above, the protagonists, who can be seen as thematized or inscribed narrators, trade on other characters' proclivities to misread the language of behavior and clothing, or to assume that a proper name is an adequate substitute or representation for its referent. Once the "Saineresse," "Margarite," and "Thoinette" insert themselves into particular social contexts, they derive much of their power from their "identity" as "strangers"—unanchored, floating signifiers that are invested with meaning by their interpreters. All are unencumbered by a past (the "Saineresse" appears out of nowhere, the young Scotsman's early years are cloaked in the beginnings of his deception, and "Thoinette" transforms himself from itinerant handyman to "orphan"); in attempting to sustain their deceptions over time, Margarite and Thoinette become "authors" who write their own stories, beginning with a tabula rasa. They name themselves ("[Il] se faisoit appeler donne Margarite" [302]; "[Il] s'avisa de se nommer 'Thoinette' " [493]), and proceed to mislead their readers with language that seems transparent but conceals, as surely as does their women's garb.

These stories' narrators make sure that the audience is in on the joke from the very beginning; audience members are thus able to enjoy a feeling of superiority over the hapless characters in the story, victims of linguistic and sartorial deception. They may easily choose to ignore the fact that they, too, may ultimately be victimized or manipulated by masterful narrators and ambiguous language.

In the case of the "Saineresse," we may recall, it is easy for audience members to share in the wife's verbal triumph over her boastful husband. They may be less likely to recognize the ways in which the elusive "Saineresse" profits from the wife's desire for revenge; still less are they inclined to acknowledge the degree to which they themselves eagerly submit to the manipulations of a master narrator.

Similarly, the narrator of the forty-fifth *nouvelle* of the *Cent nouvelles nouvelles* quickly establishes an understanding with his readers. Addressing them directly with such phrases as "comme vous oyez [as you hear]" and "vous devez savoir [you should know]," he exposes Margarite's ruse at the very beginning of the tale. This allows the readers to take pleasure in the blindness of the good burghers' surface reading of Margarite. In the end, however, even the readers are surprised. When Margarite is stripped and exposed—"escossé"—readers may realize that they, too, had misread the significance of his nationality—or, at the least, missed a signpost pointing to the end of the tale that was visible to them from its beginning.

The *Nouvelles recreations et joyeux devis* conveys a strong awareness of the power of poets and storytellers to deceive and shape readers' perceptions of the "real." The abbess in the sixty-second tale is accustomed to her position of power. She assumes that she is in control of her world, and that she knows how to "read" it, although the text warns "[qu'elle] ne voyait pas la longueur de son nez" (494). Thoinette, the storyteller within the story, tells the abbess the story the abbess expects to hear. With his false name, his female disguise, and his ability to "embroider" a good tale, he covers up not only his sex, but his role as master in his relationship with the abbess. Little by little, however, the abbess finds that she cannot sustain her unproblematic "reading" of "Thoinette." She puts on her glasses in order to see what should have been obvious from the first. But the glasses prove unnecessary; in that sudden movement from blindness to insight, they are knocked several feet away by the phallus, which, as one is tempted to say in French, "saute aux yeux." The abbess is literally "assaulted" by the truth. Thoinette, who had restrained himself, now springs up, and it is the abbess "abusée" (495) who is "abaissée." If readers are also surprised by the tale's outcome, it is perhaps because their point of view has shifted from amused distance to voyeuristic involvement. Titillated by the erotic description of the nude sisters, they now figuratively draw closer to the abbess in an attempt to get a closer look at the phallus; thus they too are slapped in the face with their prurient desire to see, to know.

In its treatment of the idea of "mastery" or "authority," the story of "soeur Thoinette" exhibits a keen awareness—as does the fabliau of "La Saineresse" and the forty-fifth tale of the *Cent nouvelles nouvelles*—of the slipperiness of language and of the faulty nature of human perceptions. Although the abbess believes herself to be in control throughout most of the story, she is really Thoinette's puppet; it is Thoinette who is pulling the strings. Although the abbess is determined to find the truth, the clever Thoinette *seems* to have the situation under control. This, however, is not the case, for Thoinette is "undone" when his unrestrainable sexual desire breaks the string. Thoinette does not write the ending of the story; it writes him, demonstrating perhaps that even the most confident readers and authoritative authors are ultimately mastered by the very language they seek to control.

In the end of each story, the mysterious stranger is again free to seek out new interpretive communities who do not see through his disguise. The woman healer and the washerwoman are again free to take on new clients, and Thoinette leaves the convent "avec promesse de sauver l'honneur des filles religieuses" (495). The inscription of this promise, impossible to keep, given that the nuns' honor is already lost, is a final nod to the potential falseness of language, to the gap between language and reality. Thoinette, too, is now back in circulation, an old tale looking for a new place to happen, as it were—yet another floating signifier emblematic of the gap between the signifier and its multiple interpretive possibilities—that gap, in fact, in which fictions are made.

Notes

1. *Nouveau receuil complet des fabliaux (NRCF),* ed. Willem Noomen and Nico van den Boogaard, 7 vols. to date (Assen, Netherlands: van Gorcum, 1983-), 4:303–12.

2. All translations are my own. When Old French passages are requoted, they are not retranslated. Old French quotations consisting of a word or two are generally not translated.

3. The husband's gullibility seems particularly amusing, given the fact that—according to Peggy McCracken—women healers were rare or nonexistent in medieval France. Peggy McCracken, University of Illinois, Chicago, personal communication.

4. *Les Cent nouvelles nouvelles,* ed. Franklin P. Sweetser (Geneva: Droz, 1966).

5. That the Scotsman's punishment is indeed a symbolic castration is suggested by the graphic similarity between the word *ostension* (showing) and the verb *oster* (to remove).

6. This forced march may be seen as a parody of the Christian *ecce homo* motif, a rewriting of the Christological scene in economic terms.

7. Randle Cotgrave, *A Dictionarie of the French and English Tongues* (Amsterdam: Da Capo, 1971[1611]).

8. E. Huguet, *Dictionnaire de la langue française du seizième siècle,* 7 vols. (Paris: Champion, 1925, 1932; Didier, 1946–67).

9. Ibid.

10. Ibid.

11. Yet another possible reference to hiding and to disguises may be seen in the phrase "Et soubs cest umbre, hantoit... par tout es bonnes maisons de Romme..." (302–3)—a possible allusion to the proverb "Sous ombre d'asne entre le chien au Moulin," translated by Cotgrave as "So many a knave sneaks into good places in companie, or under the pretext, of honest men." *A Dictionarie,* entry for *ombre.*

12. The word *andre,* though deriving from the Greek *andros,* was used in the sixteenth century as a vulgar way of designating a woman, rather like the modern connotations of the word *garce. Dictionnaire de la langue française.*

13. Cotgrave, *A Dictionarie.*

14. Bonaventure Des Périers, *Les nouvelles récréations et joyeux devis,* ed. Pierre Jourda, *Conteurs français du XVIe siècle* (Paris: Gallimard/Pléiade, 1965).

15. Given the relative scarcity of proper names in the *nouvelle* in general, one is tempted to attach great significance to those one does find. François Rigolot points out that, because "Thoinette" is "Anthoinette" deprived of its prefix, and because it is marked with the "ette" suffix of the diminutive, "Thoinette" is an apt alias for someone attempting to pass himself off as both poor and humble. Probably associating it with the word *nette* or *honnête,* Rigolot sees this proper name as connoting a certain disarming candor as well, one that encourages "Thoinette's" dupes to accept him as a woman. François Rigolot, "L'Émergence du nom propre dans la nouvelle: Des Périers onomaturge," *Modern Language Notes* 92 (1977): 678–80.

16. Lionello Sozzi, *Les contes de Bonaventure Des Périers: Contribution à l'étude de la nouvelle française de la renaissance* (Turin: Giappichelli, 1965), 353 n. 75.

17. James Woodrow Hassell, "The Proverb in Bonaventure des Périers' Short Stories," *Journal of American Folklore* 75 (1962): 35–42. See also the following three articles by Hassell: "The Proverbs and Proverbial Expressions in the *Nouvelles Récréations et Joyeux Devis* of Bonaventure des Périers," *Journal of American Folklore* 75 (1962): 43–57; "The Proverbs and Proverbial Expressions in the Works of Bonaventure des Périers," *Journal of American Folklore* 77 (1964): 58–68; "Proverbs in the Writings of Bonaventure des Périers," *Journal of American Folklore* 77 (1964): 53–57.

18. Hassell, "Proverbs and Proverbial Expressions in the *Nouvelles Récréations,*" 43–55.

19. Hassell, "The Proverb," 36.

20. See also Krystyna Kaspryzk's interesting article on proverbs, which concludes with the suggestion that "en abordant avec une telle désinvolture et une telle liberté créatrice le lieu commun, Des Périers ne veut-il pas lancer un défi aux stéréotypes de la pensée aussi bien que ceux de la langue? [By approaching the commonplace with such airiness and liberty, is not des Périers trying to throw down a challenge to the stereotypes of thought as well as of language?] Une telle attitude me paraît d'autant plus vraisemblable qu'elle se trouve confirmée par le niveau narratif du recueil." Krystyna Kasprzyk, "Un example de comique subversif: l'emploi du proverbe dans les *Nouvelles récréations* de B. Des Périers," in *Le comique verbal en France au XVIe siècle* (Warsaw: Éditions de l'Université de Varsovie, 1981), 226.

21. Rigolot also evokes this proverb in relation to the story of "Thoinette." "L'Émergence du nom propre," 680.

22. Cotgrave, *A Dictionarie,* entry for *fil.*

23. Ibid. Huguet supplies an additional variant, "Avoir les chevilles toutes prestes," which he defines as "Etre toujours prêt à riposter, avoir réponse à tout." *Dictionnaire de la langue française.*

24. Cotgrave, *A Dictionarie,* entry for *corde.*

25. Ibid., entry for *arc.*

26. James Woodrow Hassell, *Sources and Analogues of the* Nouvelles Récréations et jouyeus devis *of Bonaventures des Périers,* 2 vols. (Chapel Hill/Athens: University of North Carolina Press/University of Georgia Press/1957–69), 2:66.

27. Ibid., entry for *lunettes.* Just as a closer reading of the rows of naked nuns "en chapitre" finally enabled the abbess to discover the identity of the culprit, a closer inspection of the text will allow readers to make a similar discovery: the perpetrator of the text can be identified as well. The "authorial signature" is inscribed within the text in the description of the abbess, who "*de bonne aventure* n'avoit point de chambriere" (493; emphasis added).

28. Howard R. Bloch, *The Scandal of the Fabliaux* (Chicago: University of Chicago Press, 1986), 127–28.

29. Ibid., 60

30. Commenting on the medieval comic tale, Bloch remarks: "The ubiquitous theme of bodily dismemberment thus stands as the most manifest sign of a constant questioning of the sufficiency of poetic representation, which is also evident formally in the multiple modes of linguistic disruption to be found throughout . . . [whether it be] in word play;

phonological, onomastic, and semantic misunderstanding; use of proverbs and extended metaphors; bilingualism." Ibid., 101.

31. Ibid., 117

32. Ibid., 115–17.

33. Ibid., 46.

Contributors

F. R. P. Akehurst is a professor in the Department of French and Italian at the University of Minnesota. His publications include translations of medieval law texts and *A Handbook of the Troubadours.*

William Calin is a research professor in the Department of Romance Languages and Literatures at the University of Florida.

Susan Crane is a professor of English at Rutgers University. She is currently working on a book on self-presentation in late medieval courts.

Maria Dobozy is an associate professor in the Department of Romance Languages and Literatures at the University of Utah.

Edward R. Haymes is a professor of German and comparative literature in the Department of Modern Languages and director of the Classical and Medieval Studies Program at Cleveland State University.

William Chester Jordan is a professor in the Department of History and director of the Shelby Cullom Davis Center for Historical Studies at Princeton University.

Derek Pearsall is Gurney Professor of English Language and Literature at Harvard University. His recent publications include a biography of Geoffrey Chaucer (1992).

William D. Phillips Jr. is a professor of history at the University of Minnesota. Among his various publications are *Slavery from Roman Times to the Early Transatlantic Trade* (1985, University of Minnesota Press) and *Before 1492: Christopher Columbus's Formative Years* (1992).

Kathryn L. Reyerson is a professor of history at the University of Minnesota. Her many publications include *City and Spectacle in Medieval Europe* (1994, University of Minnesota Press).

Janet L. Solberg is an associate professor in the Department of Foreign Languages at Kalamazoo College. Her field of interest is early modern French literature.

Stephanie Cain Van D'Elden is director of graduate studies for the Program in Germanic Philology at the University of Minnesota. She is currently working on illustrations of the verse *Tristan*.

Index

MEDIEVAL CULTURES

VOLUME 4
Edited by Barbara A. Hanawalt
Chaucer's England: Literature in Historical Context

VOLUME 3
Edited by Marilyn J. Chiat and Kathryn L. Reyerson
The Medieval Mediterranean: Cross-Cultural Contacts

VOLUME 2
Edited by Andrew MacLeish
The Medieval Monastery

VOLUME 1
Edited by Kathryn Reyerson and Faye Powe
The Medieval Castle